STUDYING EDUCATION

STUDYING EDUCATION

AN INTRODUCTION TO THE STUDY AND EXPLORATION OF EDUCATION

EDITED BY JANET LORD

Learning Matters
A SAGE Publishing Company

A SAGE Publishing Company
1 Oliver's Yard
55 City Road
London EC1Y 1SP

SAGE Publications Inc.
2455 Teller Road
Thousand Oaks, California 91320

SAGE Publications India Pvt Ltd
B 1/I 1 Mohan Cooperative Industrial Area
Mathura Road
New Delhi 110 044

SAGE Publications Asia-Pacific Pte Ltd
3 Church Street
#10-04 Samsung Hub
Singapore 049483

Editor: Amy Thornton
Senior project editor: Chris Marke
Project management: Swales & Willis Ltd, Devon, UK
Marketing manager: Lorna Patkai
Cover design: Wendy Scott
Typeset by: C&M Digitals (P) Ltd, Chennai, India
Printed in the UK

Library of Congress Control Number: 2019954900

British Library Cataloguing in Publication data

A catalogue record for this book is available from the British Library

ISBN 978-1-5264-9048-3
ISBN 978-1-5264-9047-6 (pbk)

At SAGE we take sustainability seriously. Most of our products are printed in the UK using responsibly sourced papers and boards. When we print overseas we ensure sustainable papers are used as measured by the PREPS grading system. We undertake an annual audit to monitor our sustainability.

CONTENTS

ABOUT THE EDITOR AND CONTRIBUTORS

THE EDITOR

Janet Lord is Head of Education for the faculty of education at Manchester Metropolitan University. She has worked as a social sciences teacher and a lecturer in higher education for many years, specialising in education studies, teacher education and social sciences. She has a professional doctorate in education from the University of Manchester; her thesis concerned the development of identity in teachers. She has experience in school governance and educational consultancy. Janet's research and writing concerns pedagogy, student experience, assessment, the nature of critical spaces in higher education (HE), and in initial teacher education.

THE CONTRIBUTORS

Pete Atherton is a highly experienced teacher and now a senior lecturer in Teacher Education at Liverpool John Moores University. He has published a book, academic papers and many blogs on edtech and also has a podcast called 'Edtech Innovators'. His research interests are edtech and pedagogy and also autoethnography.

Kate Bacon has taught and researched in HE for over 20 years. She has designed and developed sociology and childhood studies degree programmes and worked with programme teams to generate creative and engaging teaching and learning strategies. She studied for her sociology degree and PhD at Hull University. Karen is currently Reader in Teaching and Learning at Manchester Metropolitan University.

Andrew Brogan has a background in politics and international relations. His PhD examined the role of critical and anarchist pedagogies in HE, prominent themes in his continuing research and writing. He is a lecturer in education studies at Birmingham City University where he teaches on a variety of modules connected to his background and interests, including philosophy of education, international and comparative education, and research methods in the social sciences.

Clare Campbell is a primary school head teacher who has worked in schools for 20 years; she specialises in SEND. She has a master's in SEND and a professional doctorate of education from the University of Manchester. She has written six books for teachers and a children's book. Her research and writing concerns pedagogy, mindfulness, art therapy, environmental education and Catholic education.

Marta da Costa has worked with children and young people in different formal and non-formal education settings, and she has been a tutor in education studies for the last three years. She currently teaches at Manchester Metropolitan University, where she is also completing her PhD studies. Her research focuses on post/decolonial approaches to development education and global citizenship education.

Vicky Duckworth lectures in post-compulsory education and training at Edge Hill University. Vicky teaches on a wide range of modules, which include strong theoretical and practically based specifications, from level 5 to level 7 MA delivery. Vicky is also a supervisor for PhD study. She is passionate about feeding research into her teaching.

Jonathan Glazzard is a professor of teacher education at Leeds Beckett University. He is the professor attached to the Carnegie Centre of Excellence for Mental Health in Schools. Jonathan teaches across a range of qualified teacher status (QTS) and non-QTS programmes and is an experienced teacher educator, having previously been head of academic development at Leeds Trinity University and head of primary initial teacher training courses at the University of Huddersfield.

Liz Gregory worked in the further education (FE) sector for many years, first as a teacher of GCSE and A-Level English and then as a lecturer and programme lead in the HE centre of an FE college. Here she led and taught on a number of courses, including early years and primary education, teacher education, and working with children, young people and families. She has a professional doctorate in education from the University of Manchester. Liz is currently a senior tutor at the University of Manchester.

Stephen Henry has worked as a social science teacher, senior leader and lecturer for many years. His experience in secondary schools has included senior leadership positions in five schools across the north west of England. His last post before entering higher education was head teacher of a secondary school. Stephen is currently a lecturer in the School of Teacher Education and Professional Development at Manchester Metropolitan University.

Eleanor Hoskins is a senior lecturer in early years (EY) and primary education at Manchester Metropolitan University where she teaches and supervises many EY trainees working towards their QTS qualification. Prior to this, Elly worked for many years as a teacher and deputy head teacher within EY and primary settings where she led initiatives that focused upon bridging the transitional gap between Early Years Foundation Stage (EYFS) and Key Stage 1.

Kate Hoskins is a reader in education at Brunel University and has worked in higher education for many years. She has a PhD from Kings College London. Her research focuses on education policy, identity and inequalities in relation to early years, further education and higher education. Her current research project draws on life history interviewing to explore early years educators' construction and enactment of their professional identities, with a particular focus on their higher education pathways.

Steve Ingle is an experienced teacher educator, inspector and consultant. He has worked on a number of national training and development programmes, as well as carrying out inspection and quality assurance work across the UK and internationally. Steve has a master's in education and postgraduate qualifications in coaching and mentoring and professional learning. For more information, please visit: www.steveingle.com.

David Menendez Alvarez-Hevia is senior lecturer in education studies at Manchester Metropolitan University, core member of the Education and Social Research Institute and executive member of the British Education Studies Association. He has been involved in teaching, leading, and developing undergraduate and master's programmes in education. David's research covers a variety of topics related to emotional education, higher education and alternative education.

Yvonne Moogan is associate professor of online business education and director of apprenticeship programmes at the University of Leeds. Before entering Leeds University Business School in 2017, she was Director of MBA and Executive programmes at Salford Business School, Associate Dean for Research in the private sector of Kaplan Financial and Director of postgraduate programmes at Liverpool John Moores University. Yvonne's voluntary work with disadvantaged pupils takes her into local schools and colleges.

Zoe O'Riordan has taught on childhood-related courses for a number of years. Before moving into higher education she worked with young people with a range of social, emotional and behavioural difficulties. Zoe studied for a PhD in educational inclusion at the University of Manchester, and has published research relating to resilience, inclusion and transition. She is currently working on studies relating to children's understandings of childhood.

Elizabeth Parr is a senior professional tutor in initial teacher education and head of the master's of education with QTS at Liverpool Hope University. Prior to this, she led the School Direct programme which aims to deliver a dynamic school-led model of initial teacher education in partnership with school alliances. Elizabeth also has experience as a primary school teacher and governor in schools across the north west of England. She recently completed her doctorate of education at the University of Manchester.

Karen Pashby is reader of education studies at Manchester Metropolitan University. She teaches undergraduates and postgraduates and is co-lead of the Education and Global Futures Research Group. She is adjunct professor in the Department of Educational Policy Studies at the University of Alberta and docent in the Faculty of Educational Sciences at the University of Helsinki. Karen is a former secondary educator (in Canada and Brazil) and an experienced teacher educator.

Jayshree Patel is a senior lecturer in education at Manchester Metropolitan University. Jayshree worked in secondary education for 17 years, with eight in senior management. She has extensive experience of child protection and pastoral support, a sociology degree from the University of Liverpool and a master's from Manchester Metropolitan University. Jayshree has delivered training to a wide variety of audiences and is Vice-Chair of governors for a local primary school.

Stephen M. Rayner has worked in and with secondary schools in England for more than 30 years as a teacher, senior leader, governor and education adviser. After graduating with a professional doctorate in education in 2017, Stephen began a new career as a lecturer at the University of Manchester. He currently teaches on programmes in educational leadership and research methods, including master's programmes for teacher training through Teach First.

Edda Sant is a senior lecturer at Manchester Metropolitan University where she teaches on the BA Education Studies. She completed her PhD in the Universitat Autònoma de Barcelona after having worked as a social studies and citizenship teacher and year and Key Stage coordinator in different schools in Spain. In 2016, she was co-awarded the Children's Identity and Citizenship European Association Best Publication Award.

Rachel Stenhouse has worked in education for 15 years, specialising in mathematics education. She has taught in primary and secondary schools. She has a professional doctorate in education from the University of Manchester. Her research concerns teachers' capital and how it might advantage students and doctoral student identity. She is a governor of a primary school. Rachel is currently a senior lecturer in secondary mathematics education at Manchester Metropolitan University.

Gemma Stephens is an experienced social sciences teacher with a specialism in A-level psychology. She has considerable experience in leadership, and has a master's degree in teaching and learning. She also has expertise in mentoring trainee teachers. Gemma is currently an A-level psychology teacher at a large sixth form college with an active role in pastoral care; she has an interest in mental health for young people.

Samuel Stones is an associate researcher in the Carnegie School of Education at Leeds Beckett University. His research outputs are linked with the Centre for LGBTQ+ Inclusion in Education and the Carnegie Centre of Excellence for Mental Health in Schools. Samuel's research explores the experiences of teachers who identify as Lesbian, Gay, Bisexual and Transgender, with specific emphasis on the impact of sexual orientation on teacher identity and mental health.

Helen Underhill is a lecturer at Manchester Metropolitan University specialising in education, learning and teacher education. She has a PhD from the University of Manchester. Helen has experience of leading English teaching in secondary schools, educational consultancy, school governance and teacher education. Her research is particularly concerned with reimagining education in ways that can enable communities to tackle inequality and exclusion.

EDUCATION IS THE MOST POWERFUL WEAPON WHICH YOU CAN USE TO CHANGE THE WORLD.

NELSON MANDELA,
SPEECH,
MADISON PARK HIGH SCHOOL,
BOSTON, 23 JUNE 1990

INTRODUCTION

JANET LORD

Education is the most powerful weapon which you can use to change the world.

Nelson Mandela, speech at Madison Park High School, Boston, 23 June 1990

The idea expressed in this quote from Nelson Mandela is the main reason why I work in education – and why I am passionate about it. I believe that working in education is one of the most important things that people can do. I'm really pleased that you are also interested in education and that you have picked up this introductory book.

As you think about education and read the chapters in this book, you will start to see how education, and in particular the state system of education, involves thinking about all kinds of factors. Some of these include:

- *Social factors* (e.g. the background, class, gender, race and sexuality of the people – both educators and pupils – who are involved in education). How do these factors affect learners' access to education? How do these factors affect educators' interactions with the education system and learners?

- *Cultural factors*. These can be to do with the culture of the country or society, the culture of an educational establishment (e.g. the norms and values of a school), as well as of a particular local area or subcultural group. For example, some cultural groups might prioritise the education of males over females.

- *Economic factors*. For example, what funding is available for education? Is early years education given less priority than that for other years, and hence underfunded? Is there a need for a particular employment skill in an area or country that means that a particular approach to education is taken (e.g. in a country or area where the economy relies on engineering, is there more funding for engineering apprenticeships than for media courses)?

- *Political factors*. All kinds of political questions have an effect on education. For example, should education be in the hands of the state, and should private schools be allowed? How much should we pay teachers? Should we test children at particular ages and publish school league tables?

These factors interact in complex ways, as you will see throughout the book.

HOW THE BOOK IS STRUCTURED

In the first part of the book, we look at the background and context of education, as well as its historical, sociological, philosophical and psychological roots. We also introduce some of the current themes in education policy and practice in the UK and western hemisphere, such as the marketisation of education, the performativity culture and evidence-based practice.

The second part of the book is about teaching, learning and the curriculum. Each chapter introduces an issue for discussion, and you will find activities and questions to help you develop your critical thinking skills, your reading skills and your academic writing.

The final part of the book concerns contemporary themes and issues. In this section, you will find a number of opinion pieces, written by different authors, each with their own view on a particular topic. Again, there will be questions and ideas linking the opinion pieces together, which will stimulate you to develop your own views about these ideas.

You might want to read the book straight through, but I think that's unlikely. Usually, with books like this, people dip in and out. All the chapters will have questions in them that you can use to help you start thinking about some of the ideas that are introduced; please don't just skip the questions – use them to help you think and reflect.

So, this book is an introductory book, and it looks at some key ideas in the study of education. It will be useful for you whether you are thinking about teaching, another career in education or are just interested in education. Studying education can help you develop transferable skills, and of course there will always be jobs for educators.

We hope that this book will be the start of a lifelong love of education for you – as Mandela said, using the power of education, we really can change the world!

PART 1

BACKGROUND AND CONTEXT

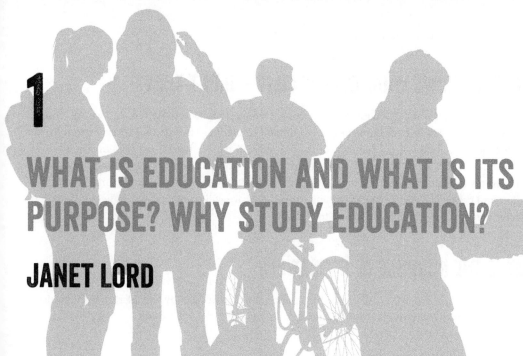

1

WHAT IS EDUCATION AND WHAT IS ITS PURPOSE? WHY STUDY EDUCATION?

JANET LORD

KEY WORDS

- **INTERDISCIPLINARY**
- **DYNAMIC**
- **SOCIALISATION**
- **QUALIFICATION**
- **SUBJECTIFICATION**

KEY NOTES

- Education is a worthwhile and powerful subject to study.
- There is no one 'correct' definition of education or view as to what the purposes of education are.
- According to one view, education has particular functions, including getting qualifications, assimilating the values and ideas of society, and developing your own agency as an independent thinker and actor in the world.
- A number of subjects or disciplines have something to say about education; these include sociology, psychology, philosophy, history, economics and politics.

EVERYONE KNOWS WHAT EDUCATION IS – DON'T THEY?

Everyone thinks they know what education is; after all, we have all been to school, and we are all educated. But trying to define education formally is quite a challenge. There is no real agreement about what education is or about what 'education studies' is. And really, there is no agreement either on what education is for. Some books try to define these terms; in this book, we are going to do it differently. In this first chapter, I'm going to introduce some thinking about the nature and function of education and pose some questions. At the end of the book, we will come back to those questions and see what the material we have read leads us to think.

WHAT IS THE PURPOSE OF EDUCATION?

First of all, what is the purpose of education? It's important that we start by considering this question, and to have it in mind as we work through the book.

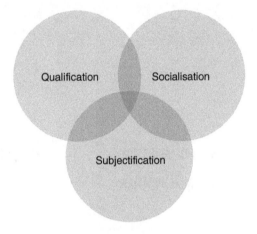

Figure 1.1 Biesta's three domains of education

Gert Biesta, a well-known, well-respected educationalist, has done some thinking about the purpose of education. He suggests that education tends to function in relation to three domains (see Figure 1.1). By this, he means that education always *functions* in relation to these three domains, or that education always *impacts* on these three domains. He calls these domains qualification, socialisation and subjectification (Biesta, 2010).

Qualification

Qualification has to do with the transmission and acquisition of knowledge, skills and dispositions. This is important because it allows children and young people to 'do' something – it qualifies them. This might be something such as becoming qualified to perform a certain task or job. Or we can think about qualification more generally, as the idea that education qualifies people to live successfully and purposefully in today's complex society.

Socialisation

As you will have seen through your experiences in the education system so far, education is not just about knowledge and skills. Through education, children and young people can also learn about and assimilate different cultural, professional, political and religious traditions and ways of being and doing (Biesta, 2010). Partly, this is a stated aim of education, but socialisation also works through what we call the 'hidden curriculum', or the '[lessons] which are learned but not openly intended' (Martin, 1976, p136). The hidden curriculum might be about the ways in which existing social structures, divisions and inequalities are transmitted, for example.

Subjectification

According to Biesta (2010), education also impacts on individuals as people, or 'subjects'. This might be to do with how learners may become empowered as people, perhaps because of the knowledge and ways of thinking that they acquire, and it might also be about how people can become disempowered as they adopt particular ideas and ways of being and doing. So, subjectification is about how education contributes to how we exist as human beings, or as human 'subjects'. It's about how we have agency (i.e. the capacity to act independently and to make your own decisions and choices).

KEY INFORMATION

Biesta, G.J.J. (2010) *Good Education in an Age of Measurement*. Boulder, CO: Paradigm Publishers.

In this book, Biesta considers the different purposes and dimensions of education. He also emphasises the importance of teacher judgements, considering the different judgements that are made in education and what it means to judge.

It's interesting to think about how these ideas of Gert Biesta's might link to our thinking about our study of education, whether that is as a trainee teacher or as a student of education studies. It's perhaps easiest to see how 'qualification' might be key to our studies, as we get a degree, Access qualification or qualified teaching status.

Our own socialisation, whether that is as a teacher, education professional or student of education, is something that we rarely think about explicitly. We also rarely think about ourselves as someone with agency and as an individual who is empowered and/or disempowered in various ways.

THINKING ABOUT SOCIALISATION AND SUBJECTIFICATION

Below, you will find some questions to help you start thinking about socialisation and subjectification. If you haven't yet been introduced to thinking about your own position in relation to education, as well as how education has affected you, then reading this case study might be a useful way for you to start that thinking.

CASE STUDY

Sarah

Sarah is training to be a teacher. She studied community and informal education at university and is now completing a postgraduate teacher training course. On her teaching course, she's just been introduced to Biesta's ideas. Sarah can see that education has given her some qualifications, but more than that she sees that she has learned a lot about the world through her schooling and university education, and through the way that she was educated (more informally) at home by her family, through her friendships, and so on. She comes from a household where her mum and many other members of her family are teachers, and she has been brought up to believe it is important to do a job that is in some way useful to society. Professional behaviour and thinking are also part of her socialisation.

In terms of Sarah's thinking about herself as an agent or a subject, she thinks that she is perhaps both empowered and disempowered by her education. She has been taught how to think and she has been exposed to the world views of others. She is now a committed feminist and is passionate about social justice. Her educational experiences have involved her being taken seriously, her values have been talked about and discussed both at home and at school, and she has been taught that her values matter, even if they are not the same as those she has been exposed to at home or at school, and even if she has been challenged in them. But she is wondering whether she is also disempowered as a person – are the choices that she has made about ways of being, thinking and doing really 'free' choices?

KEY QUESTIONS

Of the three domains that Biesta talks about, would you say that any one is more important than the others?

Are the three domains dependent on each other, as Biesta's diagram seems to imply, or are they quite separate?

Think about your own experience so far of education. How have you been socialised into ways of thinking and behaving professionally? For instance, what cultural ideas and ways of being and doing have you assimilated or responded to because of your educational experiences?

Can you identify ways in which the hidden curriculum might have affected you? This is quite tricky to think about!

How have your educational experiences affected you as a person? Has education empowered you and given you agency?

Are these choices really free choices, or has education somehow taken away your ability to think or act as an agent? If so, how?

Has education both empowered and disempowered you?

Are your ways of thinking, being and doing affected by your educational experiences?

STUDY SKILLS

How can I start to think critically about this material about qualification, socialisation and subjectification?

If you search the internet, you will find that there are many people who have written about Biesta and his ideas. Some of these people are bloggers whose work is quite accessible, so you could start by reading around the topic in a bit more depth. As you read Biesta's work, as well as the work of other authors who have something to say about Biesta, you might want to have a few questions and prompts on hand to help you think critically - to help you explore and challenge complex ideas. For example:

Clarity questions

Why are you saying that?

What exactly does this mean?

Can you give me an example?

Questions to help you think about 'taken-for-granted' assumptions

What else could we assume?

How were those assumptions chosen?

How might the assumptions be verified or disproved?

Questions to help you think about other people's reasoning

How do you know that?

Can you give an example?

Are the reasons you have given good enough?

Questions to help you challenge certain viewpoints ('Another way of looking at this is ...')

Does this seem reasonable?

What alternative ways of looking at this are there?

What are the strengths and weaknesses of ...?

How are ... and ... similar?

Education studies is an interesting area of study – there has always been some discussion about whether or not it is a 'discipline' in its own right or whether it is a multidisciplinary or interdisciplinary field. We'll look at this later in the chapter. Certainly, the study of education has its roots in subjects with which you will be familiar, or at least have heard of – subjects such as psychology, sociology, philosophy and politics.

THE ROOTS OF EDUCATION STUDIES AS A DISCIPLINE

In the last half of the twentieth century in the UK, teaching became a graduate profession, and more and more theory was brought into teaching degrees to reflect that. Increasingly, it became necessary to connect the theory to trainee teachers' classroom experiences and their practice. A further move in teacher education came quite quickly (i.e. to make teaching and teacher education government-regulated). As a result of this regulation, some people working in education decided that they would like to be free of such regulation, and so this was really the start of education studies. Some people also wanted to study education as a subject that was interesting in its own right, and others wanted to work using ideas relevant to education, but not in schools or as teachers.

THE MANY DEFINITIONS OF EDUCATION

You will be starting to see now that education can't be – and isn't – defined as any one thing. At first, it can be quite unsettling to think that there is no 'right' answer to such a fundamental question as 'What is education?' As you read this book, you will see that there are a number of voices, each of which reflects a particular viewpoint or sees education through a particular lens. You will see that questions about the nature and purpose of education are complex and multilayered, and so one of the things that you will start to get used to is that the multiplicity of voices, ideas and opinions is a reflection of education. We will be encouraging you to think about these different voices, their strengths and limitations, and start to develop your own view as to what education is and what its functions might be. One of the lovely things about doing this kind of thinking is that you will start to find your own voice and be able to express your own ideas about education.

Some famous definitions of education

The function of education is to teach one to think intensively and to think critically. Intelligence plus character - that is the goal of true education.

Martin Luther King, civil rights activist

The principal goal of education in the schools should be creating men and women who are capable of doing new things, not simply repeating what other generations have done; men and women who are creative, inventive and discoverers, who can be critical and verify, and not accept, everything they are offered.

Jean Piaget, Swiss developmental psychologist

Knowledge is power. Information is liberating. Education is the premise of progress, in every society, in every family.

Kofi Annan, Secretary-General of the United Nations, 1997-2006

SOME FAMOUS DEFINITIONS OF EDUCATION

" The function of education is to teach one to think intensively and to think critically. Intelligence plus character - that is the goal of true education.

MARTIN LUTHER KING,
Civil Rights Activist

The principal goal of education in the schools should be creating men and women who are capable of doing new things, not simply repeating what other generations have done; men and women who are creative, inventive and discoverers, who can be critical and verify, and not accept, everything they are offered.

JEAN PIAGET,
Swiss Developmental Psychologist

Knowledge is power. Information is liberating. Education is the premise of progress, in every society, in every family.

KOFI ANNAN,
Secretary-General of the United Nations
1997-2006

KEY QUESTIONS

Which one of these quotes 'speaks to you' the most?

What is it about your favourite quote that is meaningful for you? Or does the Nelson Mandela quote at the start of the chapter resonate best with you?

THE DISCIPLINES RELATED TO EDUCATION

Education is sometimes referred to as having a multidisciplinary nature. This means that there are a number of different disciplines that have something to say about education. Each of the different disciplines has a different perspective on a particular topic, theme or issue.

Typically, some of the disciplines that are considered to be related to education are the following.

Philosophy

Philosophy can be related to education in different ways. It's very much concerned with the functions, goals, methods and results of the process of educating and of being educated. It's also concerned with the beliefs, values and understandings of an individual person or group of people with respect to education, as well as concerning its function and purpose.

Psychology

Psychology is the scientific study of mind and behaviour. In relation to education, psychology concerns how people learn, including topics such as the nature of intelligence, student outcomes, the teaching and learning process, and learners of different abilities.

History

The history of education discusses how the nature, function, structures and processes of education have evolved over time – from ancient times to now.

Politics

Politics is about actions or activities that are concerned with achieving and using power. In relation to education, politics considers how individuals and groups of people who are concerned with education use formal and informal power, as well as how decision-making is conducted in local, national and international contexts.

Economics

Economics is about how societies, governments, businesses, households and individuals use their limited resources. In relation to education, economists consider issues such as the demand for education, how education is financed and resourced, and how efficient various education systems and policies might be.

Sociology

Sociology is concerned with the study of the development, structure and functioning of human society. Sociologists consider education to be a social institution and think about how it is related to other social institutions, such as the family, government and the media. Sociology is also concerned with how social forces (ways of doing things that influence or force people to behave in particular ways) can affect and shape the practices and policies of education.

These disciplines can help us to understand how education systems, both formal and informal, might work. They can also help us to understand and broaden our knowledge about how people of all ages learn, as well as the factors that can impact positively and negatively on this.

As you have read about these disciplines or subject areas, you will have seen that they are all linked to each other. In fact, we might consider that any boundaries between these disciplines are maybe fuzzy at best, and maybe they are artificial and do not exist at all.

CASE STUDY

Firas

Firas is a Muslim student who lives in a large city in an area that is disadvantaged. He is the first student from his family to go to university. This is a massive achievement for him, especially as he's also struggling with dyslexia and has never been able to get any extra support to help him with this. His family is very proud of him – they see his education as a route to success and a professional career. As the family doesn't have much money, Firas has to work a 30-hour week at a local fast-food restaurant to help out with the family budget. He also takes his two young sisters to school every day. He does this because his mum is disabled and his dad works shifts. Firas tries to get to university for classes on the days when he has timetabled lectures and seminars, but he is quite often too tired to study and can't concentrate.

KEY QUESTIONS

Look again at the subjects and disciplines that are listed above. How do they relate to Firas and his situation? Try to answer these questions for yourself.

(Continued)

(Continued)

Philosophy: What are Firas' family's beliefs about the functions and goals of education?

Psychology: How does Firas' dyslexia affect his educational experiences? How might his learning be affected? Might other factors also affect his ability to achieve?

History: How has society changed so that Firas is able to access a university education? What might it be about the historical context that might explain why his parents did not go to university?

Politics: What political forces might be impacting on Firas and his family? Does Firas have any power himself?

Economics: Why do you think Firas' family is struggling for money? How might this affect Firas and his siblings' ability to access education?

Sociology: In what ways does education interact with other institutions of society, such as the family, government and the healthcare system?

As you have thought about Firas in relation to these different disciplines, one of the things you will see is how they all interact. For example, Firas' family's lack of money (economics and politics), as well as the fact that he is the first in his family to go to university (history and sociology), affect his ability to engage with his studies, but so does his dyslexia (psychology) and the fact that he has caring responsibilities (sociology). It is important to his family that he gets a good education so he can get a good job (philosophy and economics), and this maybe puts pressure on him to attend and try to learn even when he is tired and busy (psychology and economics).

MULTIDISCIPLINARY OR INTERDISCIPLINARY?

As we think about how these disciplines all have something to say about Firas' situation, it might be helpful to consider two different terms:

- If we take a *multidisciplinary* approach to education, this means that different disciplines work together, each drawing on their disciplinary knowledge, but staying within their own boundaries.

- *Interdisciplinarity* is different; it means that two or more disciplines might be combined. It is about combining knowledge and methods from different disciplines, synthesising and integrating approaches.

It therefore seems that education does have its own subject matter, but that other disciplines work together and are combined to make education into what we call an *interdisciplinary field*.

EDUCATION IS DYNAMIC

As well as being interdisciplinary, the other feature of education as an area of study is that it is *dynamic*. This means that the field is characterised by constant change. For example, the English national curriculum changes frequently, as does the Ofsted framework for inspecting schools in England. On a wider scale, attitudes and opinions change as to whether children with special educational needs and/or disabilities (SEND) should be educated with other children in mainstream provision, or whether there should be separate schools aimed at providing specialised support and education for SEND children. Educators need to be responsive and flexible to adapt to policy changes, to changes in the way that thinking about teaching methods evolve, and to societal changes that change the context of education over time, because it is such an ever-changing, dynamic field.

KEY INFORMATION

www.open.edu/openlearn/education/what-are-the-benefits-interdisciplinary-study

If you follow this link, you can read an introduction to some ideas about interdisciplinarity. This will help you start to think more about what 'interdisciplinary' study really means. Why is it so desirable? Do you think interdisciplinarity might have its disadvantages?

TEACHER'S VOICE

As well as actually teaching the children in my classroom, I spend a lot of time looking at the latest policy documents, guidance from the local authority, and reading articles in teaching journals and newspapers. It really helps to do this, so I know that I am keeping up with the many changes that happen every year, every term, in fact every day!

Claire, who has been a primary school teacher for a number of years

ASSIGNMENT

How might I use the material in this chapter in an assignment?

Sometimes assignments ask the question 'What is education?' If you are asked a question such as this, you might want to review the material in this chapter and then think about what you think and believe. You could try to break down the material in this chapter, perhaps like the following.

Analysing a topic

Try to think about how different aspects of the topic or subject are related to one another. One simple way to do this is by using bullet points. For example:

(Continued)

(Continued)

- Key point 1
- Sub-point 1
- Further point 1a
- Further point 1b
- Another point 1c
- Sub-point 2
- Further point 2a
- Another point 2b

If you were to analyse the argument that I am trying to make in this section, it might look as follows.

Education is a complex area of study and of practice

- There are different views as to the functions of education.
- Here, you could talk about Biesta's ideas.
- And here, you could do some further reading or research and get another point of view.
- There are different disciplines that impact on education.
- Here, you could mention some of them (e.g. philosophy, sociology, etc.).
- Then you could talk about whether education is a multidisciplinary or interdisciplinary field.
- To finish, you might talk about the dynamic nature of education, both as an area of practice and an area of study.

TO CONCLUDE

In this chapter, we have seen that education is a complex area or field of study. We have started to think about the dynamic, interdisciplinary nature of education as a field of study, and we have seen how critical education is to people's lives. Throughout this chapter, the idea that education is a worthwhile and powerful subject to study comes through strongly.

Look back at the quote from Kofi Annan:

> *Knowledge is power. Information is liberating. Education is the premise of progress, in every society, in every family.*

We have seen that education is a complex and challenging subject, but understanding the nature of education enables educators and others who work in the field to empower others and to facilitate individuals' development and progress, as well as that of society.

RESOURCES FOR FURTHER LEARNING

http://infed.org

A wide variety of web pages exploring education, learning and community. The site focuses on theory and practice of informal education, social pedagogy, lifelong learning, social action, and community learning and development, but you can usually find an introduction to almost any topic in education you might want here.

Massive open online courses (MOOCs) are a great way of finding information you need. If you're interested in teaching, then there are some good MOOCs on the FutureLearn platform. Go to **www.futurelearn.com** and then search for courses using terms such as 'education' and 'teaching'. You can do the same on Coursera (**www.coursera.org**). There are other MOOCs too – it's worth having a look around.

www.ted.com/talks/michelle_obama/discussion

If you would like to see an introductory video about education, watch this TED Talk by Michelle Obama, the wife of former US President Barack Obama. Listening to her will help you think about what education is, what influences there are on it, and what it is for.

REFERENCES

Biesta, G.J.J. (2010) *Good Education in an Age of Measurement.* Boulder, CO: Paradigm Publishers.

Martin, J. (1976) What should we do with a hidden curriculum when we find one? *Curriculum Inquiry,* 6(2): 135–51.

2

HOW DOES THE STUDY OF OTHER SUBJECTS EXPAND OUR UNDERSTANDING OF EDUCATION?

DAVID MENENDEZ ALVAREZ-HEVIA

KEY WORDS

- **FOUNDATION DISCIPLINES**
- **SOCIOLOGY**
- **PHILOSOPHY**

- **HISTORY**
- **PSYCHOLOGY**
- **PURPOSE OF EDUCATION**

- **PROGRESSIVE EDUCATION**
- **TRADITIONAL EDUCATION**
- **LEARNING THEORIES**

KEY NOTES

- Philosophy, history, sociology and psychology have contributed significantly to the academic study of education.
- The philosophy of education focuses on some important questions that help us to consider the nature of education.
- Historians argue that if we understand education in the past, we can apply that understanding to the present and to our thinking about the future of education.
- Sociology is the study of society and social life at the macro and micro level. Sociology helps us to explore the function and position of education in society.

(Continued)

(Continued)

- Psychology is the study of the human mind and behaviour, including how people learn.
- Many disciplines or areas of knowledge must be considered when trying to understand education as a complex human and social phenomenon.

INTRODUCTION

When you hear the word 'education', you usually think of schools and teachers. However, the academic study of education requires a wider approach. Education as a discipline (an area of study) is multidisciplinary (meaning that the study of education also relates to the study of other subjects). Although education is influenced by a wide range of other areas of study, the main 'foundation disciplines' (the disciplines that are considered to be the 'roots' of education as an area of study) are:

- philosophy;

- history;

- sociology; and

- psychology.

This chapter introduces and explores the way that these foundation disciplines contribute to expand our understanding of education as a rich and exciting area of study.

We begin by examining the relationship between education and philosophy, focusing on two fundamental questions that frame all the debates about education. We go on to explore history, sociology and psychology. This chapter will help you to develop a critical awareness of the contribution of the foundation disciplines. It will also support you to understand the multidisciplinary nature of education itself.

HOW DOES PHILOSOPHY CONTRIBUTE TO THE STUDY OF EDUCATION?

Philosophy as an academic discipline is concerned with essential questions about knowledge, concepts, meaning, reality and existence. When we try to understand how it relates to education, it may sound abstract. However, we should bear in mind that the work of many of the most renowned philosophers (such as Plato, Confucius, Rousseau and Kant) touches on educational issues through a philosophical lens.

KEY INFORMATION

Gaarder, J. (1996) *Sophie's World*. London: Phoenix.

This fiction novel introduces philosophical thinking and the history of philosophy through the story of a teenager (Sophie Amundsen) who receives some mysterious letters. It is a useful tool to help you really start to think about and develop an understanding of philosophy.

The philosophy of education focuses on some important questions and 'illuminates the ideas which explore action and thought in education' (Bartlett and Burton, 2016, p8).

Fundamental questions

Two fundamental questions underpin and run through any discussion about education:

1. What is the nature of education? (*nature*)

2. What is the purpose of education? (*purpose*)

The main challenge here is to understand that these two questions are related and have multiple answers; there is no 'right' answer. The various different responses that different people give show us how they understand and practise education. Understanding this idea is at the heart of the philosophy of education.

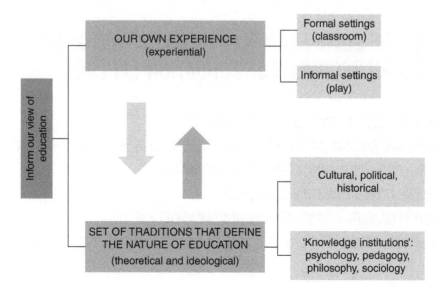

Figure 2.1 Influences on our views of education

QUESTIONING IS A PHILOSOPHICAL TOOL AND ESSENTIAL ACADEMIC SKILL.

HERE ARE SOME EXAMPLES OF THE KINDS OF QUESTIONS THAT PHILOSOPHERS OF EDUCATION EXPLORE.

- WHO DECIDES WHAT WE LEARN IN SCHOOLS?
- WHAT ARE THE QUALITIES OF A GOOD EDUCATOR? WHAT IS THE MOST IMPORTANT SUBJECT?
- WHEN DOES (OR SHOULD) EDUCATION START AND END?
- WHERE SHOULD EDUCATION TAKE PLACE?
- WHY IS EDUCATION EMPHASISED BY SO MANY SOCIETIES?
- HOW DOES EDUCATION FIT IN WITH OTHER PARTS OF SOCIETY?

What is the nature of education?

Gallagher (1992) explains that our responses to this question are formed in reference to our personal experiences of education, such as our experiences of school or informal settings like the playground. At the same time, our understanding of education is also influenced by how we interact with and think about more abstract ideas. For example, how education is presented to us by our parents, teachers, the media and politicians is important and helps to define our own understanding of education. The way that knowledge is organised is also important. Figure 2.1 helps to summarise and illustrate this complex process.

KEY QUESTIONS

What experiences and ideas do you think influence your understanding of the nature of education?

What is the purpose of education?

This question is central to the work of Gert Biesta (2013, 2015), who is a philosopher of education. Biesta explains that responses to this question are multidimensional as they are defined in relation to at least three interconnected dimensions: *qualification, socialisation* and *subjectification* (see Figure 2.2). We looked briefly at Biesta's work in the last chapter; here is a reminder.

QUALIFICATION

Refers to the transmission of knowledge, skills and dispositions to learn

SOCIALISATION

Reflects on the capacity of education to introduce us into particular social, cultural and political orders

SUBJECTIFICATION

Considers the development of freedom and individuality

Figure 2.2 Dimensions of education

As you study education, you will learn that there are many different and conflicting responses to the question of the purpose of education. It is important that you begin to understand the complex nature of this question, the many things that influence people's responses, and that education is constantly changing and evolving.

KEY INFORMATION

On YouTube, you can find some useful videos, podcasts and interviews where Biesta explains his ideas about education and the question of purpose (e.g. **https://youtu. be/CLcphZTGejc**).

How are questions about the nature and purpose of education linked?

There are two conflicting sets of ideas or traditions of education emerging from analysing different responses to questions about education. Although they go under many names, they are usually called 'progressive' and 'traditional' (Thomas, 2013):

- From a *progressive* perspective, education is an active act or process of discovering, experimenting and experiencing. The main purpose of education is to nurture freedom and participation in the transformation of the individual's life and their social context.

- From a *traditional* perspective, education is a process of transmitting and receiving information (such as facts and established ideas). The main purpose of education is to prepare students to live in and contribute to a world that is already organised for them.

KEY QUESTIONS

To study is not to consume ideas, but to create and re-create them.

(Freire, 1985, p4)

Think about whether this statement is more in line with the traditional perspective or the progressive perspective. Do you agree with the statement?

HOW DOES HISTORY CONTRIBUTE TO THE STUDY OF EDUCATION?

History is mainly concerned with the past, but is also interested in the present, as well as future projections. Cultures, people and events have an impact on social, political, economic and cultural changes. Historians argue that if we understand the past, we can apply that understanding to the present and to our thinking about the future.

Some of the themes that the history of education brings into focus are:

- trends in education (e.g. testing);

- influential ideas and innovative educational experiences (e.g. the development of ideas such as 'authentic assessment' and the use of educational technology);

- changes in educational priorities and concerns;

- development of the schooling system; and

- key educational events, policies and structural reforms.

KEY QUESTIONS

How are your school experiences different to those of someone quite a bit older than you?

What elements are different?

Why do you think that might be? Think about the different historical contexts.

A chunk of the history of education in England

The history of education before the eighteenth century in England is characterised by a lack of organisation and a lack of equal access to education as there was no national education system. Formal education was a luxury only available to a small group of people. It was not until the end of the nineteenth century that the idea of mass education was really considered. In 1870, the Elementary Education Act, commonly known as Forster's Education Act, was the first piece of legislation that demonstrated a national commitment to education. Following this piece of legislation, there were others, such as the Education Act 1902 (Balfour Act), the Education Act 1918 (Fisher Act) and the Education Act 1944 (Butler Act). These Acts initiated a series of significant structural and organisational reforms that led to the implementation of compulsory primary education and then universal secondary education.

The 1960s and 1970s were considered relatively 'good times' for education in England. Education was perceived key to the promotion of economic wealth and social justice. In the 1980s, a major change came with the Education Reform Act 1988, which introduced a 'national curriculum' for the first time in England and Wales.

KEY INFORMATION

www.educationengland.org.uk/history

This is a useful overview of the history of education in England, from the Roman occupation to recent events.

Looking to the future

Something that we have learned from studying the history of education in modern Western societies is that despite the many organisational changes, reforms and innovative practices, what goes on in the classroom has not changed much over time.

These days, schooling practices are arguably much the same as they have always been. However, it is worrying to see that inequality is still present in the education system and that teacher dissatisfaction is increasing (Hargreaves, 1994). However, in recent times, there has been a huge increase in the use of new information and communications technology (e.g. electronic devices, virtual learning spaces, lecture capture).

KEY QUESTIONS

Do our previous experiences of working in and thinking about education prepare us for twenty-first-century educational challenges?

Are we approaching a time of radical change for schooling and education?

HOW DOES SOCIOLOGY CONTRIBUTE TO THE STUDY OF EDUCATION?

Sociology studies society and social life. It explores the elements of society and social life and studies at the macro level (with a focus on large-scale issues such as the contribution of compulsory education to society), the micro level (with a focus on small-scale individual and small group interactions) or the interconnection of both. Sociology also encourages people to be critical and to change the way they engage with the social world by linking individual problems with public issues (Wright Mills, 1959). It involves thinking about issues to do with identity, such as gender, social class and ethnicity, as well as considering particular experiences (e.g. poverty and unemployment) and activities (e.g. governing and teaching).

Waller (2011) summarises the main areas of focus of the sociology of education:

- What is the purpose of schooling?

- How does education affect the life chances of different groups in society?

- Why do some social groups generally 'win' in terms of educational outcomes and others 'lose'?

- What causes individual members of such groups to vary from these norms?

- How can educational processes be understood?

- What do pupils learn at school along with the official curriculum?

- Does education liberate people or control them?

- How are educational outcomes and economic success related for individuals and the wider society?

- How do people's educational experiences affect their sense of identity?

- What role does post-compulsory education play in society?

(p107)

KEY QUESTIONS

Using your sociological lenses (i.e. trying to think like a sociologist), try to respond to some of the questions in the list above.

Different sociologists emphasise some questions rather than others, and different people come up with different answers to these questions. These differences can be linked to the three main sociological approaches that guide sociological thinking:

1.   the functionalist approach;

2.   conflict theory; and

3.   symbolic interactionism.

The functionalist (or consensus) approach

Functionalists conceptualise society as a system made of interconnected parts that work together in relation to an integrated whole. From this perspective, each element of society plays a particular role, necessary for the existence and correct balanced functioning of society. The main intention of functionalists is to understand what the contribution of each element is and how they work together for the good of society.

The father of functionalism and modern sociology, Emile Durkheim (1956), suggests that education is a fundamental part of society, and one which serves to integrate the social organisation of society by transmitting shared values, knowledge, rules and specialised skills for work.

From this perspective, schools are social institutions that have two main functions:

1. to prepare individuals for social life and perform certain social roles (i.e. to maintain social order); and

2. to prepare individuals for work (i.e. to contribute to the economy).

Conflict theory

Conflict theory emerged as a response to functionalist ideas about social consensus and natural order. It is influenced by the work of Karl Marx (1818–1883) and ideas developed from theorists such as John Dewey (1859–1952) and Jürgen Habermas (1929–). From this perspective, society comprises all kinds of tensions and complex power dynamics that create divisions between people.

Conflict theorists believe that schools and other educational organisations work to serve the interests of the wealthy elite (the ruling class). They do this by:

• supporting the world view of the elite ruling classes;

• reproducing differences and inequalities between social groups; and

• keeping some people in submissive roles and some in powerful roles (e.g. a teacher and head teacher).

Sociologists who take this approach challenge the idea that inequality is natural and unavoidable. They suggest that education should contribute to social change by:

• practising and encouraging democratic practices and attitudes;

• encouraging students to question the idea that education is neutral and unbiased;

• stimulating freedom and independence;

• promoting ideas of social justice; and

• developing students' critical skills.

Symbolic interactionism

Symbolic interactionists are concerned with the actions of different members of society and their relationships to help us to understand the social world. In contrast to the two previous approaches, they are not interested in understanding social or educational phenomena through studying the 'big picture'. They are more interested in the activities and interactions that take place between different people. Symbolic interactionists believe it is through these interactions that we give meaning to the social world.

This idea was initially developed by George H. Mead (1863–1931) and Charles H. Cooley (1864–1929) and was further extended by Erving Goffman (1922–1982).

According to this approach, education is seen as a social activity where meaningful interactions take place (e.g. between students and teachers in schools or between parents and children at home). Through those interactions, we learn what it means to be a child, a student, a mother, a father, and so on, and so we learn how to behave in different roles and social contexts. In other words, from a symbolic interactionist perspective, education provides us with opportunities to participate in social interactions that help us to know how to perform, identify with and understand social roles.

Exploring and studying education through these different approaches can help us to deepen and develop our understanding of what education is. If you understand how these approaches have developed, it can help you think about the approaches more critically.

HOW DOES PSYCHOLOGY CONTRIBUTE TO THE STUDY OF EDUCATION?

Psychology is primarily concerned with the study of human behaviour through the examination of cognitive processes, personality, social behaviour, human development, emotions and mental disorders.

There are usually thought to be five main traditions or approaches in psychology. Each one has a different focus. These traditions are *biological, psychodynamic, behaviourist, humanistic* and *cognitive*.

Table 2.1 Traditions in psychology

Approach	Focus	Key thinkers	Suggested introductory readings
Biological	Internal biological processes situated in the physical system and the genetic make-up. Biological psychologists are especially interested in understanding how the brain works.	Charles Darwin, Hans Eysenck, Wilhelm Wundt	Sapolsky (2017)
Psychodynamic	The role of internal mental processes, explained through the analysis of the unconscious that focuses on an individual's past experiences.	Sigmund Freud, Carl Jung, Alfred K. Horney, Erik Erikson	Ward and Zarate (2011)

(Continued)

Table 2.1 (Continued)

Approach	Focus	Key thinkers	Suggested introductory readings
Behaviourist	Observable responses (behaviours) learned through classical conditioning (pairing of two stimuli) or operant conditioning (changing behaviour using punishment or reinforcements).	Ivan Pavlov, John B. Watson, Edward Thorndike, Burrhus F. Skinner	Watson (1919)
Humanism	The whole individual as human being, emphasising individual subjective experiences and personal choices.	Carl Rogers, Abraham Maslow, Martin Seligman	Rogers and Freiberg (1994)
Cognitive	Focusing on mental processes such as attention, perception, memory, language, learning and higher reasoning.	Jean Piaget, Lev Vygotsky, Wolfgang Köhler, Howard Gardner, Jerome Bruner	Gardner (1985)

Source: Developed and expanded from ideas presented in Glassman and Hadad (2009)

The discipline of psychology has a strong influence over how we understand and organise modern education (e.g. the psychological construct – idea – of intelligence).

Child development theories in psychology inform curriculum design and the organisation of education systems into levels or stages. Nowadays, it is quite normal to see an educational psychologist working in schools, colleges and other educational institutions, supporting teaching practices, working on behaviour management, and providing advice to teachers and other education professionals. To a large extent, psychology owes its success in the field of education to the fact that it is rooted in science, and because it contributes to the understanding of learning processes, learning difficulties and socio-emotional factors that impact on learning.

Behaviourist and cognitive approaches provide the most influential explanations of these issues.

Behaviourism

Behaviourism emphasises external stimuli and observable responses. From this perspective, the mind and internal processes are not considered to be relevant. Given that it is impossible for us to have direct knowledge of what is going on in people's minds, behaviourists focus on the behaviours and environmental factors – these can easily be perceived and modified.

Learning (or what behaviourists call *conditioning*) is seen by behaviourists as happening in one of two ways: *classical conditioning* (the association of two stimuli) and *operant conditioning* (the association of behaviour and response).

Cognitive learning theory

In contrast to behaviourists, cognitive theorists explain learning by focusing on individuals' mental processes. Educators and psychologists who take this approach are interested in understanding how information is perceived, interpreted and integrated during the learning process. They are also interested in other mental processes such as memory, attention and reasoning. Cognitive theorists aim to optimise cognitive processes with the aim of improving the quality of learning (e.g. they might develop study methods or memory techniques that can be taught in an educational context).

Contributions to education from developmental cognitive psychology can also provide information about how children might think at a particular age or stage of development. This kind of information can be useful in diagnosing learning difficulties and disabilities, as well as helping teachers to provide appropriate support.

TO CONCLUDE

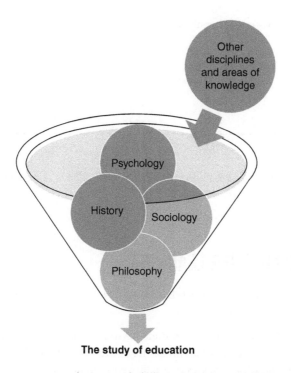

The study of education

Figure 2.3 Disciplines associated with the academic study of education

First philosophy, then history, and more recently sociology and psychology have contributed significantly to the academic study of education, and this is why they are known as foundational subjects (see Figure 2.3). However, their contributions are also questioned:

- The philosophy of education, and to some extent also the sociology of education, have been criticised for being very abstract and for not proposing solutions for the day-to-day problems associated with educational practices.

- Lessons learned from the history of education have sometimes been deliberately ignored or misconstrued.

- The psychology of education has been accused of providing oversimplified solutions to complex educational problems (e.g. by reducing questions and ideas about the education debate to a discussion about learning).

There are also other disciplines or areas of knowledge that must be considered when trying to understand education as a complex human and social phenomenon. For instance, contributions from economics, politics, anthropology, geography and neuroscience impact on education.

KEY QUESTIONS

How do you think other disciplines might contribute to education?

Educational studies should be regarded principally as the application of a range of approaches borrowed from the disciplines, rather than as a single discipline.

(McCulloch, 2002, p101)

RESOURCES FOR FURTHER LEARNING

Dufour, B. and Curtis, W. (eds) (2011) *Studying Education: An Introduction to the Key Disciplines in Education Studies*. Maidenhead: Open University Press.

This textbook is written for education studies students and enables you to explore more in depth the different contributions of the foundational disciplines of education. Each chapter can be read independently and is organised around key themes that help you to understand how debates about education look within the different disciplines.

Thomas, G. (2013) *Education: A Very Short Introduction*. Oxford: Oxford University Press.

This pocket-sized book provides an accessible but rigorous introduction to the subject of education. It is a useful reading to understand the contributions over time of the different disciplines associated with education.

REFERENCES

Bartlett, S. and Burton, D. (2016) *Introduction to Education Studies*, 4th edn. London: SAGE.

Biesta, G.J.J. (2013) *The Beautiful Risk of Education*. Boulder, CO: Paradigm Publishers.

Biesta, G.J.J. (2015) What is education for? On good education, teacher judgment, and educational professionalism. *European Journal of Education*, 50(1): 75–87.

Dufour, B. and Curtis, W. (eds) (2011) *Studying Education: An Introduction to the Key Disciplines in Education Studies*. Maidenhead: Open University Press.

Durkheim, E. (1956) *Education and Sociology*. London: Free Press.

Freire, P. (1985) *The Politics of Education: Culture, Power, and Liberation*. Westport, CT: Greenwood Publishing Group.

Gaarder, J. (1996) *Sophie's World*. London: Phoenix.

Gallagher, S. (1992) *Hermeneutics and Education*. New York: SUNY Press.

Gardner, H. (1985) *The Mind's New Science: A History of the Cognitive Revolution*. New York: Basic Books.

Glassman, W. and Hadad, M. (2009) *Approaches to Psychology*, 5th edn. London: McGraw-Hill.

Hargreaves, A. (1994) *Changing Teachers, Changing Times: Teachers' Work and Culture in the Postmodern Age*. London: Continuum.

McCulloch, G. (2002) Disciplines contributing to education? Education studies and the disciplines. *British Journal of Educational Studies*, 50(1): 100–19.

Rogers, C.R. and Freiberg, H.J. (1994) *Freedom to Learn*, 3rd edn. Upper Saddle River, NJ: Merrill.

Sapolsky, R.M. (2017) *Behave: The Biology of Humans at Our Best and Worst*. New York: Penguin Press.

Thomas, G. (2013) *Education: A Very Short Introduction*. Oxford: Oxford University Press.

Waller, R. (2011) The sociology of education. In B. Dufour and W. Curtis (eds), *Studying Education: An Introduction to the Key Disciplines in Education Studies*. Maidenhead: Open University Press, pp106–31.

Ward, I. and Zarate, O. (2011) *Introducing Psychoanalysis: A Graphic Guide*. London: Icon Books.

Watson, J.B. (1919) *Psychology from the Standpoint of a Behaviourist*. Philadelphia, PA: Lippincott's College Text.

Wright Mills, C. (1959) *The Sociological Imagination*. New York: Oxford University Press.

3

WHAT ARE THE MAIN FACTORS AFFECTING SCHOOL ORGANISATION AND THE CURRICULUM IN ENGLAND TODAY?

STEPHEN M. RAYNER

KEY WORDS

- ACADEMY
- AUTONOMY
- COMPETITION
- CURRICULUM
- MARKETISATION
- OFSTED
- PERFORMANCE TABLES
- PUBLIC EDUCATION

KEY NOTES

- Daily life in schools is shaped and influenced by the decisions of policymakers in national government.
- School staff are affected by changes to the whole system in which they work, as well as changes in how individual schools are managed.
- As education has increasingly become a market, new pressures have developed, including competition between schools, teachers being judged according to their pupils' results, and moves to a more 'traditional' curriculum.

THINKING ABOUT EDUCATION POLICY AND SCHOOLS

In this chapter, I am asking you to think critically about education policy and how it affects practice in schools in England. I begin by looking at the landscape of school education in England today. That is 'England', rather than 'the UK', because Scotland, Wales and Northern Ireland have their own education departments and policies that are different from those in England.

ACADEMIES AND ACADEMISATION

Since 1990, a series of government policies has fundamentally changed the way in which schools are governed and managed. Through the academies programme, around 70 per cent of secondary schools and 30 per cent of primary schools have moved from local authority control to being part of a charitable trust, often referred to as a multi-academy trust (MAT) (NAO, 2018). An academy is an independent school funded by the government. It is part of the public education system in England, where all children are entitled to free education funded by the state. For families in many parts of England, the neighbourhood schools are now all academies. Between 1990 and 2010, about 200 academies were opened. They were either new schools or replacements for 'failing' local authority schools (NAO, 2018). In 2010, however, the Conservative-led coalition government changed the nature of the academies programme, with the aim that all publicly funded schools in England should be academies. The term 'academisation' is often used to refer to the process whereby a school moves from the local authority to 'private' control and governance as part of a charitable trust.

Some critics refer to this as the privatisation of education, because it involves the transfer of a public asset – the land, buildings and human resources of the school, along with its history, reputation and status within the community – into private hands. Local authority schools have some democratic accountability, because local councils have an Education Committee or Cabinet Member for Education who are elected by public vote. MATs, on the other hand, are accountable directly and only to national government. They appoint the governors or may decide to have no local governing bodies at all.

Supporters of academisation say that a MAT is not a private enterprise; it is a charitable trust whose purpose is to provide education for the public benefit. However, privatisation is not just about how schools are governed. Governments in the last 30 years have claimed that competition in a diverse market will raise standards. In other words, schools get better results when they are in competition with other schools to attract children to apply to them. That means providing different types of school and creating a market where consumers (mainly parents) can choose between schools. This is a different form of privatisation: which school a child attends becomes a private matter (it is the parents' responsibility to choose) rather than a public one (it is the state's responsibility to provide).

Is it all about autonomy?

One of the main arguments for academisation is that it gives schools and their head teachers autonomy: they are free to make their own decisions without being controlled by a local authority.

That was the claim of the then UK Prime Minister David Cameron when he announced in 2015 that every school should have the opportunity to become an academy, 'and benefit from the freedoms this brings' (Cameron, 2015). But the claim about autonomy is contradicted by some of the realities of working in a MAT. Some MATs have developed corporate styles and branding across all their schools. This may be more than superficial: they may prescribe schemes of work, revision programmes, behaviour strategies and human resources policies that go beyond anything that a local authority can impose. A head teacher in a MAT may therefore have less autonomy than a head teacher in a local authority school and may feel more like the branch manager of a large company.

KEY INFORMATION

Some key definitions:

Academisation refers to the process whereby a school moves from the local authority to 'private' control and governance as part of a charitable trust.

A *multi-academy trust (MAT)*, sometimes called an academy chain, is a charitable trust that runs one or more academy schools. It is directly funded by the government through a funding agreement. It operates as a limited company and is independent of the local authority in which it operates. It has a long-term lease on the land and employs the staff of its academy schools.

Local authorities (called local education authorities until 2010) are responsible for distributing and monitoring funding to maintained schools (i.e. those that are not academies). They own the land and employ the staff of those schools. They are responsible for ensuring that every child in their area has a school place.

KEY QUESTIONS

Think about the schools that you attended.

Were they comprehensive or selective?

Were they mixed or single-sex?

Were they state-funded or fee-paying?

When you reached the age of 11, how was it decided which secondary school you would attend? When you reached the age of 16, how was it decided where you would continue to study?

Do you think that education is a 'public' or 'private' matter?

Should it be the state's responsibility to provide school places and allocate children to schools, or the parents' right to choose from a range of possible schools for their child?

Is either of these systems completely fair? Why or why not?

What happens when it goes wrong?

The local authority provides a safety net, but at a time of budget cuts there are no local area agreements about managing difficulties – these are the responsibility of the MAT. There have been some high-profile cases where MATs have ceased to trade because of financial difficulties or mismanagement. An academy cannot legally be returned to local authority control, so it can only be 're-brokered' to another MAT. However, in a competitive market, a failing academy with a budget deficit is not a good business proposition. As a result, there are some schools – sometimes referred to as 'orphan schools' – that are not part of a trust. In these cases, the government has to take direct responsibility; it may have to pay off the MAT debt, and the staff and pupils are left in an uncertain and often distressing position.

What difference might it make to life in school if the school is an academy?

Pupils may well notice very little difference if their school becomes an academy. The changes may be no more surprising or radical than others that they experience during their years in school. Maybe the school has new signage and they have to wear a new uniform. For staff, the changes can be more significant. Their contracts are now held by the MAT, which may make changes to their pay and conditions of service, even if they have previously been negotiated nationally by unions. If funds are limited, MAT finance directors may require cuts to be made in all the MAT schools. Teachers and subject teams may find it easier or more difficult to access support, depending on the MAT structure and resources.

CHANGES TO THE CURRICULUM

In 1988, the first national curriculum was introduced in England. For the first time, schools were required by law to teach a specific range of subjects to all pupils. Compulsory schooling was divided into four Key Stages (KSs): KS1 for children aged 5–7, KS2 for ages 7–11, KS3 for ages 11–14 and KS4 for ages 14–16. Programmes of study were specified for each subject in each Key Stage. Since then some of the details of the national curriculum have changed, but the principle of a curriculum for all children and young people has remained. The thinking behind the national curriculum is that all children should be introduced to the essential knowledge that they need to be educated citizens. Schools should offer a broad and balanced curriculum, which should support children's spiritual, moral, cultural, mental and physical development, as well as preparing them for the opportunities and responsibilities of later life.

What is considered to be 'essential' knowledge depends on the government of the day and the personal interests of the Secretary of State for Education. Between 1997 and 2010, under Labour governments, there was a strong push for vocational education, so school subjects such as business studies expanded. Since 2010, the policies of Conservative-led governments have favoured more traditional subjects such as history, geography and modern foreign languages.

KEY INFORMATION

The most recent version of the national curriculum dates from 2014. This is the list of subjects and the stages at which they must be taught in schools:

- English, mathematics, science, computing and physical education - all Key Stages (ages 5-16).
- Art, design, technology, geography, history and music - Key Stages 1, 2 and 3 (ages 5-14).
- Foreign languages - Key Stages 2 and 3 (ages 7-14).
- Citizenship - Key Stages 3 and 4 (ages 11-16).

Note that academies are not required to follow the national curriculum. However, as I shall explain in the next section, the system of school inspection and reporting of results means that almost all academies do follow the national curriculum.

KEY QUESTIONS

Do you think that the government should require schools to teach a prescribed curriculum, or should individual schools be allowed to set their own curriculum?

Which subjects do you think should be compulsory and which should be optional? At what ages?

PERFORMANCE TABLES AND SCHOOL INSPECTION

Successive governments have advanced two main arguments for inspecting schools and publishing examination results. The first is based on the idea of parental choice. Parents should be able to choose their child's school, rather than have a place allocated by the local authority, which is what happened previously. In order to make an informed choice, they need as much information as possible about the school, including its latest results and inspection report. The second argument is that competition is an effective way of raising standards. When schools have to compete with other schools, it is claimed, they are more likely to focus on achieving the best possible results for their pupils.

Earlier in this chapter, I referred to a developing market in education, where schools compete with each other to attract pupils to apply to them. A school can make itself more attractive by publicising good examination results or a positive Ofsted inspection report. You may have seen banners outside schools advertising, 'We are an outstanding school', quoting their latest Ofsted inspection report. This is an outward sign of the local market in educational provision.

KEY INFORMATION

The Office for Standards in Education, Children's Services and Skills (Ofsted) is responsible for inspecting schools in England. A team of inspectors visits each school at intervals of between three and ten years. The inspection team looks at the test and examination results, speaks to staff and pupils, observes lessons, and checks that pupils are safe. It then provides a report under several headings. These headings change from time to time, but from 2019 they are 'Quality of Education', 'Behaviour and Attitudes', 'Personal Development' and 'Leadership and Management'. Under each heading, a grade is awarded:

- Grade 1: Outstanding.
- Grade 2: Good.
- Grade 3: Requires improvement.
- Grade 4: Inadequate.

These grades are combined into a grade for *overall effectiveness*.

'League tables' are not published as such by the government. The Department for Education lists results alphabetically by the name of the school. However, many broadcasters, local newspapers and websites draw on these lists to compare schools, either by providing a 'search and compare' function or by placing them in a list with the best results at the top and the worst at the bottom.

KEY QUESTIONS

Do you think it is right that Ofsted inspection judgements and school test and examination results should be made public? Why or why not?

If you were advising someone on which school to choose for their child – or making that decision for your own child – what factors would you think are important, apart from the inspection report and examination results?

Can you see any problems with the idea of all parents being able to choose their child's school?

What difference might the publication of results and inspection grades make to life in school?

For parents, there may be a mixture of gratitude and anxiety. In a society where people are used to making decisions as consumers, using websites such as Which? and TripAdvisor, having as much information as possible seems to be important and welcome. However, when the choice of school may be one of the most difficult decisions that a parent has to make, the fear of making a wrong decision or not getting the first-choice school can be stressful. Realistically, there can only be a limited number of schools and school places in any area. The principle of school choice allows children to travel some distance to school, but not all parents are in a position to enable that to happen.

For teachers in schools, the measurement and publication of pupils' performance has made a significant difference in the last 20 years. Performance management is now embedded in all schools, where teachers are set performance targets based on their pupils' achievement and progress. In annual reviews, those targets are scrutinised, and decisions are made about possible promotion and salary increases. If the results are below the target, this may lead to anything from 'teacher support plans' to a disciplinary process. School league tables are based on examination results in national curriculum subjects, so an academy that decided not to teach the national curriculum would be at a disadvantage when compared with other schools.

As for the pupils, there is now a wealth of evidence of the increased stress placed on the mental health of children and young people by the focus on test and examination results. I shall illustrate that with the following case study, which is a composite based on recent interviews with children in a school in England.

CASE STUDY

Meena and Jamie

Meena and Jamie are in Year 6, the final year of primary school. They are discussing the SATs tests that they will take in a few weeks' time. Meena explains how important the tests are, because in future 'you might not get the job you really want'. She says that 'in other years, we haven't been stressing, but this year we're really stressing about our progress'. Jamie also feels nervous, but goes on to say that he feels OK about sitting the tests because he goes to 'a special place outside the school where I get extra help'. This is despite the fact that both Jamie's parents work shifts and have not been able to pay for extra trips put on by the school. Meena goes on to talk of the targets that her teachers have set over the years: 'In Year 2, I had a WTS target, but now I have a GDS target, so if I push myself I can get the job I want'. Meena explains that WTS means 'working towards' and GDS means 'greater depth'. Jamie is thinking about the immediate future. He understands that SATs are important because they 'show what you can do', but also that 'it shows how good the teachers are at teaching stuff'. Jamie feels 'kind of scared', because 'the tests might be used by high school and there might be seven sets and you don't want to be in the lowest one'.

KEY QUESTIONS

Read the case study of Meena and Jamie again.

Do they understand the purpose of SATs?

(Continued)

(Continued)

What issues does the case study raise about the experience of these children in their last year of primary school?

What advice would you give to Meena and Jamie?

TO CONCLUDE

In this chapter, I have explained some of the ways in which policy decisions at government level affect the daily experience of those who learn and work in schools. As you continue to study education, you should continue to think about where the responsibility lies for making important decisions that can affect the future of both individual children and the country as a whole. For example, you might agree that government is responsible for managing and organising an education system for the benefit of the country but still wonder whether those important decisions should be made by politicians or by trained educational professionals. I have also raised questions of fairness and equality. As you continue to read this book, you will see those questions discussed in greater detail in later chapters.

RESOURCES FOR FURTHER LEARNING

https://schoolsweek.co.uk

Schools Week is an online journal, published weekly, that covers a wide range of educational issues. It is worth consulting for reports and background information on all the matters covered in this chapter.

https://cstuk.org.uk

The Confederation of School Trusts (CST) is an organisation of multi-academy trusts and other collaborative groups that advocates a system of academies and school trusts as the way forward for public schooling in England.

www.educationuncovered.co.uk

A subscription is required for Education Uncovered. It covers policy issues in education and takes a critical review of structural reform, especially the academies programme.

www.gov.uk/government/collections/education-inspection-framework

The latest Ofsted inspection documents can be found here.

www.bbc.co.uk/news/education-42310494

This BBC web page is an example of how the general public can easily find and compare the test and examination results of different schools.

REFERENCES

Cameron, D. (2015) Tory ideas can shape the next decade for all Britons. *Daily Telegraph*, 14 August. Available at: www.telegraph.co.uk/news/politics/conservative/11804367/david-cameron-tory-ideas-can-secure-britain.html

National Audit Office (NAO) (2018) *Converting Maintained Schools to Academies*. London: NAO/DfE.

4

HOW DOES IDENTITY SHAPE YOUNG PEOPLE'S EXPERIENCES OF SCHOOLING AND EDUCATION?

KATE HOSKINS

KEY WORDS

- **IDENTITY**
- **SOCIAL CLASS**
- **GENDER**
- **ETHNICITY**
- **SCHOOLING**
- **POLICY**

KEY NOTES

- Identity shapes people's experiences of education.
- Social class is not easily defined. It is understood in different ways by different groups.
- Social class remains an underlying factor in the continued inequality in the education system in England.
- Gender is a social construct. There are many factors influencing the development of children's gender identities.
- Exclusion rates for some ethnic groups demonstrate that racial stereotypes remain an influence in schools.
- The study of issues in education is more valid if the multiple contexts and influencing factors are considered.

INTRODUCTION

This chapter explores how identity (social class, gender and ethnicity) shapes young people's experiences of schooling and influences the type of schooling and education that young people can access. The chapter begins by exploring terms such as 'social class', 'gender', 'race' and 'ethnicity', and asks: What do we mean by these? It goes on to discuss key policy moments that have influenced the types of state schooling available in England, including the Education Act 1944 and the Education Reform Act 1988, and to show how different types of schooling are provided for different types of children and young people. The chapter ends with a discussion of how aspects of identity continue to influence young people's experiences of education, focusing on the types of schooling and educational trajectories available to them in twenty-first-century Britain.

SOCIAL CLASS AND EDUCATION

Conceptualisations (the ways in which ideas about a subject are formed) of social class in Britain have changed and evolved over time as the nature of education and employment has altered. Between 1911 and 1998, the Registrar-General's classification of occupations was 'the most commonly used system of classifying people' in the UK (Hill, 1999, p85). This way of classifying occupation puts people (typically men) into categories according to the status value of different occupations and provides a way of conceptualising social class as a tool for social analysis. However, social class categorisations are more complex and are not only related to economic and employment status. Reay (1998) argues:

> Limiting class debates to the purely economic sphere results both in the marginalization of women and a neglect of the myriad ways in which social class differences contribute to social inequalities.

> (p259)

Social class has been increasingly viewed as related to tastes and dispositions (Bourdieu, 1977, 1984) that are manifest in 'socially inscribed norms and values'. 'Social norms' here are the accepted behaviours that an individual needs to conform to in a particular group (the group here being the social class). For example, members of one social class may use different words or language than those in other groups. In this way, social class is also embodied in language, accent and degrees of 'respectability' (Skeggs, 1997). It can be considered that social class is indicated by the conscious and unconscious choices individuals make. When considering education, this could relate to schooling. People make choices about the educational path that they will follow based on what they consider to be possible or impossible for them.

Since the 1980s, there have been claims that class, as a concept, has outlived its usefulness (Pakulski and Waters, 1996), and it is considered to be an 'outdated category which is no longer relevant in the context of a (post-modern) society which has become classless' (Hill, 1999, p89). However, sociologists of education argue that social class remains an underlying factor in the continued inequality in education systems in England (Ball, 2008). This inequality is particularly evident in terms of access to education, career opportunities and outcomes available to particular social class groups (Ball, 2010). Reay (2005) contends that 'social class is not only etched into our culture, it is still deeply etched into our psyches despite claims of classlessness' (p912). Sociologists of education argue that social class influences daily life, even though these influences can be difficult to identify as they are different for individuals and communities.

KEY QUESTIONS

Do you consider yourself to be from a particular social class? If so, do you think this has influenced the choices about your education path made by yourself or others?

GENDER AND EDUCATION

To begin this section, it is useful to start by summarising the differences between 'sex' and 'gender'. According to the World Health Organization:

> _Sex_ refers to the biological and physiological characteristics that define men and women. _Gender_ refers to the socially constructed roles, behaviours, activities, and attributes that a given society considers appropriate for men and women.

> (WHO, 2013)

Gender is a 'cultural and social construction, not a biological given' (Cherland, 1994, p243). This means that gender is not a 'biological and physiological characteristic', but is instead something that is created by societies and cultures. It is a widespread view that gender is natural, normal and different for boys and girls. However, according to Cherland (1994), 'gender is something that people create while interacting with each other in all the practices of their daily lives, including their literacy practices' (p243).

In the text _Social Constructionism_, Burr (2015) argues that 'prevailing discourses of femininity often construct women as, say nurturant, close to nature, emotional, negatively affected by their hormones, empathic and vulnerable' (p87). Burr points out how these discourses are constructed by a capitalist society that thrives on the concept of the family as a site for reproducing the status quo. The social constructions of gender differences between males and females continue to be a powerful organising principle in people's lives, in both the personal and professional spheres (Francis, 2006).

Gender differences

Gender differences occur as a result of living in a socially constructed society. Cultures where this con-structed society is a patriarchal one (a society where men have authority over women) create 'a form of social organization in which a male acts as head of the family/household, holding power over females and children' (Jary and Jary, 1991, p445). Evidence shows that historically, in Western culture, 'power has rested with men and been handed on to men', thus creating patriarchal societies (Moon, 1990, p5). Moon (1990) goes on to point out:

> Patriarchal cultures do not admit that gender is constructed for people. Instead, they try to blur the distinction between biology and culture by making gender roles seem natural. The process of naturalising gender takes place not only through social structures but also through language and literary texts.

> (p5)

Indeed, according to Minns (1991), 'language, attitudes, expectations, the media and stories – all play their part in reinforcing gender roles' (p12). Therefore, it can be argued that the wider influences in the media and society shape children's development of a gendered identity from an early age.

Despite a number of policy initiatives in the English education system across primary and secondary education (e.g. a shared national curriculum for boys and girls), gender differences remain an important influence that limit young people's aspirations and opportunities for their future. Thus, gender can be viewed as a factor that shapes and influences girls' and boys' experiences of education, and the oppositional nature of gender is used to legitimate the multiple layers of inequality that persist between the sexes.

RACE, 'RACE' AND ETHNICITY AND EDUCATION

In the context of education studies, race can be viewed as socially defined, but on the basis of physical criteria, and refers to the embodied, physical self. The history of the word race is rooted in the oppression of minorities by white groups across the world and the associated colonialism, domination and racism that gave way to the idea of a hierarchy of racial groupings. Because of this negative, deficit association with the word race, in recent decades in England sociologists have increasingly referred to 'race'. The inverted commas are used to signify that the writer is aware of the problematic history of the word race, but that it is still a useful term to use to refer to the physical aspects of racial difference.

The term 'ethnicity' refers to a group with a shared culture, cultural traditions, language and ancestry; it does not include physical characteristics (Fitzgerald, 2017). Sociologists view ethnicity as 'socially defined but on the basis of cultural criteria' (van den Berghe, 1967, cited in Goldberg, 1993, p553). Ethnic differences are argued to be socially constructed by people and social groups.

One context where social differences such as ethnicity become reinforced and ethnic stereotypes become entrenched is schooling. According to Barth (1969), 'for social boundaries to be actively maintained, they need to be continually validated, and this requires regular interaction with members of out-groups' (pp32–33). Schooling provides a space for interaction with those from different ethnic groups. Children and young people can often stay together in ethnic groupings in their schools, actively maintaining distance from the 'other'.

An example of the impact of stereotypes in schools relates to the differential exclusion rates for different ethnic groups. It was found that 'black students in some LEAs [local education authorities] are nineteen times more likely to be excluded than their white counterparts' (CRE, 2000). Different reasons have been put forward by race and education researchers, including teachers' racism, cultural differences between the norms at home and school, and the construction of black masculinity, which can be viewed as a collective response in a racist culture. Alongside exclusion rates, other issues where minority ethnic groups experience inequality have included academic underachievement and fewer academic opportunities, such as attending an elite university.

To sum up this section, it is important to remember that ethnicity is not just defined by 'race'; it is much more than physical appearance. Ethnicity, like social class and gender, needs to be understood as a social category that is situated in a historical and political context (Gillborn, 2010). Social categories are not neutral, and students must ask themselves why these categories might be mobilised at particular moments. Whose political, social or economic interests are being served? Finally, substantial work is involved in maintaining boundaries of identity categories, and these boundaries can contribute to a view of the world that is divided according to us and them.

KEY QUESTIONS

Can you think of any ways that your social class, gender and/or ethnicity have influenced your school experiences?

UNDERSTANDING THE INTERSECTIONS BETWEEN ASPECTS OF IDENTITY

Increasingly, sociologists of education have recognised the value of carrying out research that takes account of and brings together the complexity of the analysis of social class, gender and ethnicity. This is possible through the theory of intersectionality. Brah and Phoenix (2004) describe intersectionality as:

> *signifying the complex, irreducible, varied, and variable effects which ensue when multiple axis [sic] of differentiation – economic, political, cultural, psychic, subjective and experiential – intersect in historically specific contexts. The concept emphasizes that different dimensions of social life cannot be separated out into discrete and pure strands.*

(p75)

Brah and Phoenix are here arguing that identity is intertwined and cannot be separated out into neat and simple categories. As a white woman from a working-class family background, I am simultaneously influenced by these features of my identity at all times and in all social contexts. According to Blair et al. (1995), 'the major axes around which difference coalesces into identities [are] – gender, race and class' (pxi). Through exploring the intersections (the points at which these different influences cross) between social class, gender and ethnicity in research, it is possible to gain a deeper, richer and holistic understanding of people's lived experiences. All of us are influenced by our identity in relation to the choices we make, our preferences, our aspirations and future plans. Intersectionality theory provides a way to understand the interconnectedness of identity and the far-reaching impact it has on our choices and pathways.

The next section of the chapter draws on the example of different types of secondary schooling to show how identity influences young people's education.

KEY INFORMATION

Blair, M., Holland, J. and Sheldon, S. (eds) (1995) *Identity and Diversity: Gender and the Experience of Education - A Reader*. Bristol: Multilingual Matters in association with The Open University.

A useful reader to help you understand intersectionality.

IDENTITY AND TYPES OF SCHOOLING

This section outlines the Education Act 1944 and the Education Reform Act 1988 to show how types of secondary schools and education on offer have changed over time and how pupils' identities (i.e. social class, gender and ethnicity) influence the type of schooling they can access.

KEY QUESTIONS

While reading this section, consider the type of secondary school(s) you attended. In what ways did your social class, gender and ethnicity shape the type of school your parents chose for you?

Post-war schooling in England

The Education Act 1944 introduced three types of secondary schools: secondary modern, technical and grammar schools (and, to a lesser degree, direct grant schools, which were a type of grammar school) into the state sector. Entry to school was informed by passing or failing the 11+ examination. Children that passed the 11+ attended a grammar or technical school and those that failed attended a secondary modern school. This tripartite system of education, as it was known, was premised on providing different types of education for different types of pupils.

In practice, school attendance tended to correlate with social class background in the distribution of pupils to a type of school (Jackson and Marsden, 1962). Many working-class children attended secondary modern schools, which were aimed at pupils more suited to 'a general education to prepare them for their future lives as citizens and (largely unskilled) workers' (Bartlett et al., 2001, p94). The education offered was gender-differentiated and focused on basic literacy and numeracy skills alongside gendered vocational training: the boys' curriculum included woodwork and PE, and by contrast the girls' curriculum included needlework and cookery (Miller, 1996).

The expectation of girls and boys educated in the 1950s and 1960s 'was of traditionally gendered aspirations and outcomes' (Maguire, 2006, p7). Indeed, 'girls and boys, it was argued, needed an education which related specifically to their designated roles in society' (Arnot et al., 1999, p35). This positioning continued in the post-war period because, as Martin (1999) argues, 'the victorious politicians saw the domestic role of women as crucial for the construction and rehabilitation of social harmony and cohesiveness' (p104). These gendered assumptions and beliefs underpinned the schooling provision for girls in the 1950s and 1960s. Gendered education provision was particularly pertinent to those from working-class backgrounds, who were almost exclusively educated in the state sector.

The schooling system in England moved to a comprehensive model in 1965 when 'Circular 10/65 requested LEAs to submit plans for comprehensive reorganization and the 1976 Education Act made this a legal requirement' (Ball, 2008, p70). By 1977, 80 per cent of schools in England were comprehensive schools, up from 8.5 per cent in 1965 (Ball, 2008). Bartlett and Burton (2007) argue:

> *The move towards the comprehensive school was designed to heal the divisions of the tripartite system; it was an attempt to provide a form of education that would cater for all.*

> (p69)

However, as Ball (2008) argues, the 'term "comprehensive school" remained slippery and such-named schools differed widely in their ability intakes, commitments and practices' (p70). According to Pring and Walford (1997), 'throughout British history social class and gender have been major determinants of the quality of schooling children received', but the 'move to comprehensive schools began to make a difference and to interrupt this pattern' (p57). But despite the move to more socially just comprehensive schools, the problem, according to Pring and Walford (1997), was that in reality, 'Britain has never had a truly comprehensive system' (p57), which they attribute to the existence of private schools, which educate between 7 and 20 per cent of children from middle- and upper-class backgrounds. Thus, Bartlett and Burton (2007) argue that comprehensivisation 'was not to make a dramatic break with the thinking and practice of the time' (p70). This was partly because within comprehensive schools, pupils were still streamed by ability (Bartlett and Burton, 2007). Participating in education at the time of the comprehensive system meant that children were still in a schooling system that perpetuated social class, gender and racial inequality.

Contemporary context

Following the introduction of the Education Reform Act (ERA) 1988, the contemporary education context has become even more fragmented than in the past. The ERA 1988 significantly altered the provision and delivery of compulsory state education. As Barker (2010) points out, the ERA 'shocked and awed' schools with a 'ferocious accountability regime' aimed at raising standards for all pupils and introducing school effectiveness regimes to address school failure, with the intention of increasing the UK's economic competitiveness globally (p1). The New Labour government (1997–2010) retained the focus on raising standards and pupil achievement in state-maintained schools, and they worked to 'align public institutions and services with the requirements of the global economy' (Barker, 2010, p167).

To raise standards the ERA 1988 introduced the idea of parental choice with regard to the school they could choose for their child. The secondary school system today still consists of grammar schools, comprehensive schools, religious schools, and most recently introduced are academy and free schools, and parents are advised they can 'choose' the right school for their child (Gunter, 2011). In practice, parents find they have very little choice about the school their child will attend because those schools that are Ofsted-rated as outstanding have long waiting lists and are typically located in more economically affluent neighbourhoods with more homogenous white populations (Ball, 2003). Housing close to these desirable schools tends to be expensive and in short supply, and therefore those families who are socio-economically well off tend to dominate. Thus, despite the variety of schooling that exists, it remains the case that the type of school a child can attend will be influenced by their social class, gender and ethnicity. Understanding how identity relates to inequality is important for undergraduate education students.

KEY INFORMATION

Jones, K. (2003) *Education in Britain: 1944 to the Present.* Cambridge: Polity Press.

A key reading on the different types of schools.

TO CONCLUDE

This chapter began by providing definitions of social class, gender, and race, 'race' and ethnicity, and gave some examples of how these aspects of identity can shape children and young people's engagement with the English state education system. There is a wealth of rich research in the sociology of education that shows how many aspects of the education system, such as the curriculum, examination system and teacher expectations, are shaped by discourses of identity. The chapter then included an overview of the different types of schools since the Second World War and described the policies that introduced them. This outlined how different types of schools tend to cater to different types of children and young people on the basis of their identity. To end this chapter, I argue that despite being told by successive governments that the English schooling system is meritocratic and rewards people based on individual merit, in practice the system is deeply divisive and structurally unfair for many children and young people, which is why critical studies in education are required to challenge this inequality and strive for change.

REFERENCES

Arnot, M., David, M. and Weiner, G. (1999) *Closing the Gender Gap: Postwar Education and Social Change.* Cambridge: Polity Press.

Ball, S.J. (2003) *Class Strategies and the Education Market: The Middle Classes and Social Advantage*. London: RoutledgeFalmer.

Ball, S.J. (2008) *The Education Debate*. Bristol: Policy Press.

Ball, S.J. (2010) New class inequalities in education: why education policy may be looking in the wrong place! Education policy, civil society and social class. *International Journal of Sociology and Social Policy*, 30(3/4): 155–66.

Barker, B. (2010) *The Pendulum Swings: Transforming School Reform*. Stoke-on-Trent: Trentham Books.

Barth, F. (1969) *Ethnic Groups and Boundaries: The Organization of Cultural Difference*. Boston, MA: Little, Brown & Company.

Bartlett, S. and Burton, D. (2007) *Introduction to Education Studies*, 2nd edn. London: SAGE.

Bartlett, S., Burton, D. and Peim, N. (2001) *Introduction to Education Studies*. London: Paul Chapman Publishing.

Blair, M., Holland, J. and Sheldon, S. (eds) (1995) *Identity and Diversity: Gender and the Experience of Education – A Reader*. Bristol: Multilingual Matters in association with The Open University.

Bourdieu, P. (1977) *Outline of a Theory of Practice*. Cambridge: Cambridge University Press.

Bourdieu, P. (1984) *Distinction*. London: Routledge & Kegan Paul.

Brah, A. and Phoenix, A. (2004) Ain't I a woman? Revisiting intersectionality. *Journal of International Women's Studies*, 5(3): 75–86.

Burr, V. (2015) *Social Constructionism*, 3rd edn. London. Routledge.

Cherland, M.R. (1994) *Private Practices: Girls Reading Fiction and Constructing Identity*. London: Routledge.

Commission for Racial Equality (CRE) (2000) *Learning for All: Standards for Racial Equality*. London: CRE.

Fitzgerald, K.J. (2017) *Recognising Race and Ethnicity: Power, Privilege and Inequality*, 2nd edn. Boulder, CO: Westview Press.

Francis, B. (2006) The nature of gender. In C. Skelton, B. Francis and L. Smulyan (eds), *The SAGE Handbook of Gender and Education*. London: SAGE, pp7–17.

Gillborn, D. (2010) The colour of numbers: surveys, statistics and deficit-thinking about race and class. *Journal of Education Policy*, 25(2): 253–76.

Goldberg, D.T. (1993) *Racist Culture: Psychology and the Politics of Meaning*. Oxford: Blackwell.

Gunter, H.M. (2011) Governance and education in England. *Italian Journal of Sociology of Education*, 8(2): 31–45.

Hill, D. (1999) Social class and education. In D. Matheson and I. Grosvenor (eds), *An Introduction to the Study of Education*. London: David Fulton Publishers, pp84–102.

Jackson, B. and Marsden, D. (1962) *Education and the Working Class: Some General Themes Raised by a Study of 88 Working-Class Children in a Northern Industrial City*. London: Routledge.

Jary, D. and Jary, J. (1991) *Dictionary of Sociology*, 2nd edn. Glasgow: Collins.

Jones, K. (2003) *Education in Britain: 1944 to the Present*. Cambridge: Polity Press.

Maguire, M. (2006) Gender and movement in social policy. In C. Skelton, B. Francis and L. Smulyan (eds), *The SAGE Handbook of Gender and Education*. London: SAGE, pp109–24.

Martin, J. (1999) Gender in education. In D. Matheson and I. Grosvenor (eds), *An Introduction to the Study of Education*. London: David Fulton Publishers, pp126–41.

Miller, J. (1996) *School for Women*. London: Virago.

Minns, H. (1991) Language, *Literacy and Gender*. London: Hodder & Stoughton.

Moon, B. (1990) *Reading in Terms of Gender in Studying Literature*. Perth, Australia: Chalkface Press.

Pakulski, J. and Waters, M. (1996) *The Death of Class*. London: SAGE.

Pring, R. and Walford, G. (1997) *Affirming the Comprehensive Ideal*. London: Routledge.

Reay, D. (1998) Rethinking social class: qualitative perspectives on class and gender. *Sociology*, 32(2): 259–75.

Reay, D. (2005) Beyond consciousness? The psychic landscape of social class. *Sociology: Special Issue of Class, Culture and Identity*, 39(5): 911–28.

Skeggs, B. (1997) *Formations of Class and Gender: Becoming Respectable*. London: SAGE.

World Health Organization (WHO) (2013) *What Do We Mean by Sex and Gender?* Available at: www.who. int/gender/whatisgender/en/

5
WHAT COUNTS AS SOCIAL JUSTICE IN EDUCATION?

EDDA SANT

KEY WORDS

- JUSTICE
- REDISTRIBUTION
- RECOGNITION
- PARTICIPATION
- SOCIAL MOBILITY
- EQUALITY
- EQUITY

KEY NOTES

- There are many different understandings of what is meant by 'social justice'.
- Education is often seen as a way to tackle injustices.
- Even if there is a broad agreement about what inequalities need 'fixing', there can remain disagreement as to the best way to tackle these.
- Social justice in education matters for students, teachers and the communities we live in.

INTRODUCTION

A number of us decide to study and/or work in education because we want to contribute to making a more just world. But what is a more just world, and how can education contribute towards this? This chapter explores different theoretical understandings of social justice. Drawing upon multiple examples, the chapter outlines different ways in which education can help us to fight for social justice.

WHAT IS SOCIAL JUSTICE?

The first question about social justice is: Can we define what social justice means? For a long time, Western philosophers aimed to find a way to calculate how 'just' (fair) a society was. Nowadays, most academics in education agree that there is not a single right answer to the question of justice. Instead, there are different understandings of what social justice means. In this section, we will examine three of these understandings.

> ## KEY QUESTIONS
>
> Do you think you can apply the same criteria of social justice to everybody and everywhere?

Academics in education often discuss social justice in relation to Nancy Fraser's frameworks (Gewirtz, 2006; North, 2006). Fraser is a well-recognised philosopher who outlines three different dimensions of social justice: redistribution, recognition and participation (see Figure 5.1). We will look at each of them in turn.

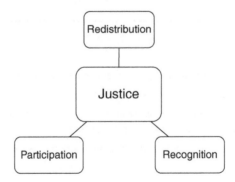

Figure 5.1 Fraser's three dimensions of social justice

The redistribution dimension

Within the *redistribution dimension*, a just society is a society where material resources (e.g. savings, properties, etc.) and non-material resources (e.g. access to rights, education, employment, etc.) are equally distributed. For instance, a society where only some students can buy textbooks is not a fair society because material resources (textbooks) are not equally distributed, and a society where only males can attend schools is not a fair society because only males can access non-material resources (formal education).

KEY QUESTIONS

What material resources might stop people from accessing or succeeding in education?

KEY INFORMATION

John Rawls is one of the most influential theorists of distributive justice. For Rawls, justice can be defined as the equal distribution of rights and resources. See: **https://plato.stanford.edu/entries/rawls/#JusFaiJusWitLibSoc**

Marion Iris Young is one of the most important theorists of recognition justice through her essay 'Five Faces of Oppression'. See: **www.sunypress.edu/pdf/62970.pdf**

The recognition dimension

The *recognition dimension* focuses on why some norms, values, identities, practices, traditions, behaviours, and so on are considered more important than others. From this perspective, a society is just when different cultures and identities are equally valued. For instance, when a teacher of English literature only selects texts from white male authors, he is not considering the contribution of females and black and other ethnic groups to English literature. This situation is not fair for those students who may feel ignored in the English curriculum.

KEY QUESTIONS

Have you ever felt that who you are (your values, identities and traditions) were not recognised by your teachers or the school curriculum? How and why did this happen?

The participation dimension

Within the *participation dimension*, a society is just when all individuals and groups can equally and effectively participate in the decisions that impact on their own lives. For example, students in schools and universities should be represented in the spaces where key decisions are made, such as school boards, academic boards, and so on. If they are not, we could think that this is a situation of injustice.

KEY QUESTIONS

Do you think students can effectively participate in decisions within schools? Why or why not?

CASE STUDY

Dimensions of justice: the case of Martin

Gewirtz (2006) discusses the case of a mother whose son, Martin, was permanently expelled from secondary school without her having a say about this. She cites the mother, who explains:

I think that people are prejudiced, and I hope this does not come across as being a real victim statement, but I believe that if I lived in a big house with more money then maybe we would have stood a better chance, and I spoke a bit better and I had a husband, and I had more support, and Martin wasn't mixed race then maybe Martin may have been helped a bit more, considered a bit more.

(p73)

WHAT IS SOCIAL JUSTICE IN EDUCATION?

Education is very often understood as a universal problem-solver. We often expect education to solve
injustices and to contribute towards a more just world. But even if we agree on how a just world
should look (we have already seen that this is very unlikely), we would probably disagree on what are
the better educational *initiatives* to pursue this world.

Education is the most powerful weapon which you can use to change the world.

Nelson Mandela

Let's look at Figure 5.2 to explain this. Very often people (politicians, teachers, managers, etc.) want to tackle a situation of injustice. They want to move from an initial situation of injustice to a better situation where this injustice has been resolved. Educational initiatives here are teaching practices, institutional policies (see Chapter 3), laws, and so on, which function as pathways, solutions or 'weapons' (in Mandela's terms) to move from the unfair present to this more desirable future. However, there are multiple routes to the same destination.

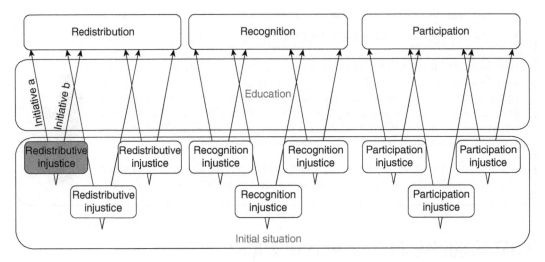

Figure 5.2 Social justice and education

KEY QUESTIONS

The famous sociologist of education, Basil Bernstein, once said, 'School cannot compensate for society'. Do you think education can 'solve' all situations of injustice? Why or why not?

For example, you and I may well both agree that the gender pay gap – with women paid less than men – is unfair (redistributive injustice in grey in the diagram). We may also agree that in a better society, we should not have a gender or any other form of wage gap (redistribution). But if I argue that for this to happen, we will introduce an educational initiative providing funding for women who want to study for an MA in leadership and management (initiative 1), you might think that this wouldn't really be fair for men or women who aren't interested in this kind of study or this kind of topic. Instead, you might suggest an awareness campaign in schools, encouraging the celebration of Equal Pay Day (initiative 2). People not only have different ideals of justice, but also different ideas of what might be the best educational route to achieve these ideals.

STUDY SKILLS

Sometimes, as you study education, you might be requested to examine the educational initiatives, policies, proposals, approaches or recommendations of a particular theory, political party or individual educator. For example, you might be encouraged to discuss what Maria Montessori (a very well-known educator) thought about education, or the education policies of a particular political party, or how a particular teacher approaches a difficult situation in her classes.

Considering what we have just discussed, think about the following questions:

- What is the initial situation of injustice this theory, party or individual aims to tackle?
- What is the ideal future situation of justice this theory, party or individual attempts to achieve?
- What is their recommended educational initiative (route)?

WHAT IS SOCIAL JUSTICE-ORIENTED EDUCATION?

When an educational initiative aims to tackle situations of injustice, we talk about social justice-oriented education. There are two key controversies around how social justice-oriented education should look (see Table 5.1). The first controversy is the *equality/equity* dilemma (e.g. see Espinoza, 2007):

- *Equality* refers to the same educational treatment by asserting the equality of all people. Social justice-oriented education, in this case, means that we need to treat all students in the same way.

- *Equity* takes the individual circumstances into consideration to provide educational treatment. In this understanding, social justice-oriented education means that we need to treat students differently. Some argue that we need to treat students differently because of their different *needs* and *abilities*. Others argue that we need to treat students differently according to their *achievements* and *merits*.

Figure 5.3 A famous cartoon about 'fairness' (or equality) in education

A very well-known comic vignette (see Figure 5.3) shows different animals, including a monkey, a penguin, an elephant and a fish, in front of a teacher, who asserts, 'For a fair selection everybody has to take the same exam: please climb that tree'. This vignette is used as an example of equality. The teacher is providing the same educational treatment (the same exam, 'climb the tree') to all students. Think about this vignette.

KEY QUESTIONS

Think about the vignette in the cartoon.

Do you think this is a fair situation?

What alternative, based on the principle of equity, could you think of?

Would this alternative consider students' needs and abilities or students' achievements and merits?

Can you think of another example in which an equality initiative would be fairer than an equity one?

The second key controversy for social justice-oriented education is the *question of when*. Think about your own educational journey in primary school, secondary school or college. You accessed an educational level (e.g. college), you had many educational experiences (you read, you interacted with others, you passed exams, etc.) and you obtained a qualification or outcome at the end of this process (you obtained your A levels and gained access to university) (see Figure 5.4). The question here is: At what point on this journey (access, experiences or outcomes) should the social justice-oriented initiative take place?

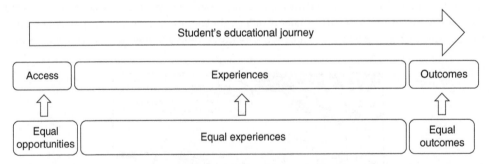

Figure 5.4 Educational journey and social justice-oriented initiatives

- *Equal opportunities for accessing education* means that we should not have political, legal, economic, social, physical or cultural barriers for students. For instance, according to the Equality Act 2010, all students, regardless of their sex, race, disability, religion or belief, sexual orientation, gender reassignment, and maternity or pregnancy, are entitled to access schools.

KEY QUESTIONS

If we aim for a just society, is it enough for educators and policymakers to remove barriers for people to access education, or should more be done? If so, what?

- *Equal experiences* means that all students should benefit from educational experiences that are enriching, empowering and relevant to their own knowledge and lives. For instance, in England, several policy-driven reports, such as the Parekh Report (Parekh, 2000), have strongly recommended the inclusion of the histories of minority ethnic and cultural groups in the national curriculum.

- *Equal outcomes* refers to the need of guaranteeing that different groups in society are equally successful. To do so, we might give some additional support/recognition to disadvantaged groups. For instance, Women into Science and Engineering (WISE) leads campaign initiatives to guarantee the gender balance in science, technology and engineering (see also Chapter 11).

Table 5.1 Perspectives on social justice-oriented education

Questions	Answer	Perspective	Example
What treatment shall we give to students?	Same treatment	*Equality*	All students need to pay the same fees.
	Different treatment according to needs	*Equity*	Students from low-income families need to pay less fees.
	Different treatment according to merits		Students with higher grades need to pay less fees.
When should we intervene?	Access	*Opportunities*	Schools are adapted so that students using wheelchairs can access all spaces.
	Process	*Experiences*	Writers from different backgrounds are included within recommended readings.
	Outcome	*Outcomes*	Teacher training programmes save some spaces for male applicants (to guarantee there are male teachers).

KEY INFORMATION

Department for Education (DfE) (2014) *The Equality Act 2010 and Schools: Departmental Advice for School Leaders, School Staff, Governing Bodies and Local Authorities*. Available at: https://assets.publishing.service.gov.uk/government/uploads/system/uploads/attachment_data/file/315587/Equality_Act_Advice_Final.pdf

This guidance provides clear recommendations on how to guarantee equal access to primary and secondary school settings.

Parekh, B. (2000) *The Future of Multicultural Britain: The Parekh Report*. London: Prolific.

The Parekh Report offers good advice on how all students, regardless of their ethnic and cultural background, can have access to relevant educational experiences.

Women in Science and Engineering (WISE) (2018) *Why WISE?* Available at: www.wisecampaign.org.uk/why-wise/

WISE is a well-recognised company that has long campaigned to guarantee equal outcomes for girls in sciences.

WHY DOES IT MATTER?

So far, we have developed a typology to examine potential situations of injustice (see Figure 5.1) and potential educational initiatives to solve these injustices (see Table 5.1). But you might be wondering: Why does it matter?

Social justice matters in education for multiple reasons and for multiple people. It matters to policymakers and others deciding how we organise our educational institutions. It is probably the case that education will not solve all injustices, but it might help. Social justice is a moral compass to analyse the present situation (is it fair?), to think of better possibilities for the future (how would a better society look?) and to consider what policies could be put in place to improve the present situation (what type of social justice-oriented initiatives?). Imagine you become a head teacher of a school. You will need to assess multiple situations of injustice (e.g. bullying practices) and think of possible solutions.

It matters to students and their communities. It is important for them so they can explain why a particular educational situation or initiative is or is not working for them (because it is unfair, because it discriminates, because it is not effective, etc.) and to think how this could be improved. As a student, knowing about social justice and education might empower you to evaluate whether you are treated fairly.

> *Great teaching is about so much more than education; it is a daily fight for social justice.*
>
> Arne Duncan, former United States Secretary of Education (2009-2015)

It is also very important for teachers and other educators. It serves as a compass to check our own pedagogical practices and how we interact with students. If you ever become a teacher, a teaching assistant, a lecturer or any other educator, you will probably constantly be thinking: Have I been fair to my students?

KEY QUESTIONS

What decisions related to social justice do teachers often have to make?

And it matters to all of us as a society. In a democracy, we all should decide how we would like our future to look and how we want education to contribute towards this future.

CASE STUDY

Dimensions of social justice and social justice-oriented education, and the case of Amber and Jamila

Amber is a college student in Wales. Her whole family once worked in the mines, but since its closure the family has suffered economic struggles. Amber is the youngest child of five. Her sister has two kids; Amber often babysits them and loves to play with them. Amber has to combine part-time jobs with full-time studies. Amber also loves cars, and her dream is to buy herself a luxury sports car. She is also a very hard-working student who excels at different subjects. She is expected to gain four A* for her A levels in mathematics, further mathematics, English and history. Amber is sure she wants to go to university, but she is uncertain about what to study and where. She was involved in a widening participation initiative at the University of Cambridge that helped her (and other students from disadvantaged backgrounds) to develop her confidence. She was advised to apply to Cambridge and consider studying maths. Maths does indeed have great career prospects for her to buy her car and help her family! But Amber loves being with her family and taking care of her nephews, and she would like to stay closer to them and perhaps become a teacher.

Jamila is Amber's history teacher at college. Amber has asked her advice on what and where to study. After a shaky start, with Amber questioning the relevance of what they study in history class, Jamila

(Continued)

(Continued)

gave Amber some extra reading on the miners' strike of 1984-1985, where her family took part, and discussed the readings with her after class. Amber was very appreciative of this, and since then they have both been good friends. Jamila is now finishing her PhD in education, and she knows statistics suggest that Amber will probably gain a higher salary if she graduates in maths than if she becomes a teacher. But she wonders whether she should still suggest to Amber that she should study what she enjoys the most. Amber could become a very inspiring teacher! Cambridge is also better for career prospects, but she knows that only 10 per cent of Oxford and Cambridge entrants are from working-class schools (Boliver, 2017) and these students are far less likely to succeed in their studies there. She is also aware that even those who successfully graduate often feel they do not fully 'fit in' (Reay et al., 2010). Jamila does not know what to suggest.

Think about how the different dimensions of social justice and social justice-oriented education can be applied to Amber's case. Try to answer the following questions by yourself or discuss it with a friend.

KEY QUESTIONS

Dimensions of justice

For the following statements, consider: (a) Is this a fair situation? (b) What dimensions of justice does this situation apply to?

- Amber needs to work part-time to be able to carry on her studies.
- Amber and her peers are not able to decide what they learn in the history curriculum.
- If Amber goes to Cambridge to study maths, she might feel she does not 'fit in' there.
- If Amber decides to become a teacher, she will probably gain a lower salary.

Social justice-oriented education

For the following statements, consider: (a) Is this an equality or equity initiative? (b) Is this initiative tackling equal opportunities, experiences or outcomes?

- Jamila decides to teach Amber about the miners' strike.
- Amber was involved in a widening participation initiative.

Why does it matter?

What initiatives could be put in place to solve these injustices?

Why do you think social justice matters on Amber's educational journey?

Do you think knowing and thinking about social justice might help Jamila to advise Amber? If yes, how so?

For our society, is it better if Amber becomes a mathematician or an inspiring teacher? Why?

KEY INFORMATION

The Labour government launched 'widening participation' initiatives in 2006. The aim of these initiatives was to widen access of under-represented and disadvantaged groups to higher education. For more on this, see: **https://dera.ioe.ac.uk/6204/1/barriers.pdf**

TO CONCLUDE

This chapter has outlined different dimensions of justice (distribution, recognition, participation) for us to examine existing situations of injustice and start to think about more desirable futures. We then discussed different perspectives on how social justice-oriented education should look. How should initiatives address these injustices (equality, equity for equal needs, equity for equal achievement) and what part of the educational process should these initiatives address (opportunities, experiences, outcomes)? We then discussed why social justice in education matters for students, teachers and the communities we live in.

RESOURCES FOR FURTHER LEARNING

https://coe.k-state.edu/walk-in-my-shoes/social-justice/

The College of Education at Kansas State University in the US created a documentary called *A Walk in My Shoes: Social Justice in Education* where they show the lives of five committed teachers who struggle every day for social justice. The documentary is a good introduction to the question of why social justice matters in education, and it is very helpful to start thinking about different dimensions of justice and social justice-oriented education.

Francis, B., Mills, M. and Lupton, R. (2017) Towards social justice in education: contradictions and dilemmas. *Journal of Education Policy*, 32(4): 414–31.

This article examines some of the contradictions and dilemmas of social justice education that we have explored in this chapter. The authors' main focus is on social justice-oriented initiatives. Illustrated with different examples from educational policies from England and Australia, the authors explore in depth the experience/outcome dilemma. The article helps us to consider ways in which discussions about social justice education are not as straightforward as they look.

REFERENCES

Boliver, V. (2017) Misplaced optimism: how higher education reproduces rather than reduces social inequality. *British Journal of Sociology of Education*, 38(3): 423–32.

Department for Education (DfE) (2014) *The Equality Act 2010 and Schools: Departmental Advice for School Leaders, School Staff, Governing Bodies and Local Authorities*. Available at: https://assets.publishing.service.gov.uk/government/uploads/system/uploads/attachment_data/file/315587/Equality_Act_Advice_Final.pdf

Espinoza, O. (2007) Solving the equity–equality conceptual dilemma: a new model for analysis of the educational process. *Educational Research*, 49(4): 343–63.

Francis, B., Mills, M. and Lupton, R. (2017) Towards social justice in education: contradictions and dilemmas. *Journal of Education Policy*, 32(4): 414–31.

Gewirtz, S. (2006) Towards a contextualized analysis of social justice in education. *Educational Philosophy and Theory*, 38(1): 69–81.

North, C.E. (2006) More than words? Delving into the substantive meaning(s) of 'social justice' in education. *Review of Educational Research*, 76(4): 507–35.

Parekh, B. (2000) *The Future of Multicultural Britain: The Parekh Report*. London: Prolific.

Reay, D., Crozier, G. and Clayton, J. (2010) 'Fitting in' or 'standing out': working-class students in UK higher education. *British Educational Research Journal*, 36(1): 107–24.

Women in Science and Engineering (WISE) (2018) *Why WISE?* Available at: www.wisecampaign.org.uk/why-wise/

PART 2

EDUCATION, LEARNING AND TEACHING

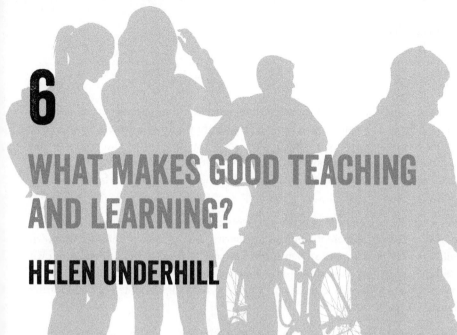

6

WHAT MAKES GOOD TEACHING AND LEARNING?

HELEN UNDERHILL

KEY WORDS

- **TEACHING**
- **LEARNING**
- **PEDAGOGY**
- **CLASSROOM**
- **KNOWLEDGE**
- **MINDSET**

KEY NOTES

- What makes good teaching and learning is a question that continues to prompt debate.
- There are many ways to define 'teaching'. Some put the emphasis on teaching as the imparting of knowledge from teacher to students. Others suggest that teaching is far more complex.
- A teacher's knowledge of their subject is not the same as their ability to teach it.
- Students can be considered as passive *receivers* of knowledge or active *participants* in learning.
- Social factors influence both teaching and learning.
- The idea of 'excellence' in teaching is subjective: we all have beliefs about the purpose of education, and we draw from our own experiences to develop these views.

INTRODUCTION

What makes good teaching and learning is a question that continues to prompt debate among academics, practitioners, parents and carers, government institutions, and policymakers. Everyone involved in schooling has an opinion on what makes good teaching; after all, everyone has engaged with the school system in some way or another. In addition to having a view on schools, teachers or the curriculum, many assumptions are also made about the connection between teaching and learning.

This chapter explores some of the connections between teaching and learning and introduces some of the key terms often used in schools. It presents some of the debates and asks you to consider your own perspectives. We will hear from teachers and students, and you will be asked to think about your own experiences of teaching and learning to consider how your views might have been shaped. Finally, the chapter explores the question of what is meant by 'excellent' teaching, using teacher and learner voices to demonstrate the range of viewpoints.

Before we explore teaching and learning, it is important to place these terms in context – to think about the relationship between education and teaching and learning. Keep this *key question* in mind as you read the chapter. We will reflect on this in the conclusion.

KEY QUESTIONS

How might my view of education shape how I define teaching and learning?

THINKING ABOUT TEACHING

Defining teaching

Before we look at different understandings and perspectives of teaching, take a moment to consider your own understanding. Consider these questions:

- What does teaching mean?

- What does teaching look like?

- What image do you have when you think of a teacher?

- What is the relationship between teaching and learning?

- How and where do people learn?

It is likely that your responses to these questions centred on what happens in schools. After all, because most of our experiences of teaching take place in the formal education system, it would make sense for our image of a teacher to be in a classroom, perhaps standing in front of a group of children or young people, sharing knowledge or giving instructions. This image would certainly fit with the essence of the Oxford English Dictionary (n.d.) definitions of the verb 'teach':

1. To show, present, have a view.

2. To show by way of information or instruction.

3. To handover or deliver.

These definitions focus on the teacher as a person with knowledge that they give to or share with a learner. However, if we approach a definition of 'teaching' by considering the relationship to learning where teaching *causes* learning or understanding, then teaching becomes more complicated. Take a moment to consider what a broader definition of teaching as *causing* learning or understanding might mean for the way in which a teacher might work with their students. How would this compare to teaching from the first definition (instruction/delivery)?

KEY QUESTIONS

How might what a teacher does in the classroom differ between the two approaches to defining teaching given above?

The two definitions paint slightly different views of teaching. Whereas the first tells us that the learner is *given* information, the second has more scope for interpretation, suggesting that there are other ways to learn – perhaps by experiencing something for ourselves or through participation.

TEACHER'S VOICE

Teaching is the most rewarding thing I have ever done. For me, it is a process of constantly learning too, and I think when a teacher stops learning or being prepared to learn she needs to stop teaching. I learn about the texts I teach constantly. I have taught Keats' 'Ode to Autumn' so many times, for example, and each time a student comes up with another way of thinking about an image or a line. I learn about the ways young people learn, about different lives, about relationships.

Sophie, English teacher

Teaching as knowledge sharing

As well as fulfilling many functions within a school, a key part of a teacher's role relates to subject knowledge – teachers need to know their stuff! But can we expect a primary teacher to be an expert in every aspect of primary schooling? Can we expect a secondary science teacher to be an expert in all aspects of biology, chemistry *and* physics, or an English teacher to have read every novel and poem? Realistically, no. However, teachers do need to have a secure understanding of the subjects they teach because this grounding provides them with a greater understanding of what different learners can be expected to know or be able to do.

KEY INFORMATION

Pedagogical content knowledge (Lee Shulman)

This theory, outlined by Lee Shulman (1986), explained how teachers transform knowledge of their subject (content) into knowledge of *how to teach* the content. Pedagogical content knowledge is therefore a particular type of knowledge: it is the understanding of how to make a subject 'teachable'.

Teachers constantly make choices about the activities and resources they use in their teaching, thinking about how to teach different topics within a subject. This requires them to draw on their pedagogical content knowledge (even if they don't call it that).

Think about a subject area you know well. Why might you choose a different approach to teach different aspects of the subject?

Shulman's argument highlights the difference between being an expert in a subject and knowing how to teach it. Despite this, some commentators and policymakers believe that the level of qualification in a subject area is an indicator of a person's ability to teach. For example, UK government policy implemented in 2011 awarded additional bursaries to teaching students with a first-class degree, going against research that showed subject knowledge in itself does not improve student achievement: it's what we *do* with the knowledge that counts (Hattie, 2008). Indeed, some critics argued that the policy suggested the higher the degree qualification, the better the teacher. This view could fit with the first definition of teaching, which emphasises knowledge sharing. In this approach, the expert teacher (with all their subject knowledge) imparts information to someone less knowledgeable. This might involve reading aloud from notes, books or slide shows, or providing long periods of teacher talk while students listen and take notes. While this remains a feature within higher education, most teachers would argue that there is very little of this kind of *lecturing* in schools today, and that – positively – there has been a significant shift away from extended teacher talk in lessons.

Consider why school leaders might be concerned if it was found that teachers were lecturing their students.

Freire (1970) argued that approaches to education that depend on the giving and receiving of knowledge force learners to be passive recipients of knowledge rather than active thinkers or creators. For many who would agree with these arguments (see hooks, 1994; Apple, 2003), Freire's insights into the dangers of passive approaches to education are essential for thinking less about what teachers do and paying more attention to how learners learn. The next section will ask you to think about your understanding of learning.

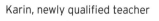

TEACHER'S VOICE

Teaching is about being able to inspire and motivate students both in their academic lives and the development of themselves and their identities.

Karin, newly qualified teacher

THINKING ABOUT LEARNING

Defining learning

Establishing a universally accepted definition of learning is a significant challenge. The previous section raised questions about whether teaching is a process of *giving* knowledge. In this section, as we turn to learning, we will question whether we can define learning simply as *acquiring* knowledge, or whether it is more complex.

Before we look at some of the complexities around defining learning, take a moment to note down your own thoughts in response to this question: How would you define learning? The list of comments below shows that teachers with different subject specialisms conceptualise learning in many ways:

- being able to do something you couldn't do before;

- having a deeper understanding of the world;

- being able to apply knowledge to new situations;

- developing skills/being able to do something;

- gaining new knowledge and information;

- a constant process of change;

- making predictions;

- making mistakes and correcting;

- experimenting and trying things out; and

- analysing and reflecting.

As we can see, learning means many things to many people. While it is about knowledge, skills and capacities, many teachers describe learning as a continuous process that involves different types of thinking. It is clear that defining learning as acquisition is problematic. The next section looks at this in more depth to consider why.

The problem of learning as 'acquisition'

Traditional definitions of teaching emphasise the *giving* of knowledge or skills. It would follow, then, that learning is about *acquisition*. However, if the relationship between teaching and learning is reduced to giving and receiving, then the relationship between teacher and learner is purely transactional: it is the job of the teacher to give the learner knowledge. If we look back to Freire's concept of 'banking education', conceptualising the teacher–student relationship on the basis of transactions is problematic because it suggests teachers have power over learners. In this way, learning is something that happens *to* you and it is a process over which you have no control.

KEY QUESTIONS

If learning is defined as the *receiving* of knowledge, what would this look like in the classroom? Think about what this means teachers and students would be doing.

What might be the problem with this approach?

WHAT IS LEARNING?

RESPONSES FROM STUDENT TEACHERS ACROSS A RANGE OF CURRICULUM SUBJECTS

Being able to do something you couldn't do before

Having a deeper understanding of the world

Being able to apply knowledge to new situations

Developing skills / being able to do something

Gaining new knowledge and information

A constant process of change

Making predictions

Experimenting and trying things out

Making mistakes and correcting

Analysing and reflecting

For many people, it might not seem problematic for students to be powerless in the learning context. However, we know that:

> students react to the learning activities teachers provide ... but they also act on them – modifying them, enriching them ... and even creating or requesting them in the first place, rather than merely reacting to them as a given.
>
> (Reeve and Tseng, 2011, p258)

Defining teaching and learning through a transactional definition where the teacher gives and the student receives fails to recognise the learner's contribution to the process and that they have *agency* in the classroom – in other words, learners react in different ways to a task, and we need a broader understanding of learning to understand how and why.

STUDY SKILLS

Your understanding of the different approaches to teaching will develop as you spend time in schools. To get the most out of any chances you get to engage in observations of teaching, think about how you could best use these opportunities to observe what goes on in educational settings.

What could you look for when you observe teachers in lessons?

What should you pay attention to throughout the school day?

The social dimensions of learning

Moving away from defining learning as the acquisition of knowledge encourages us to take into account other factors that might shape learning. Illeris (2007) offers a broader approach within his definition of learning to acknowledge that there are social factors at play. In his words, learning can refer to 'any process that in living organisms leads to permanent capacity change and which is not solely due to biological maturation or ageing' (p3). He went on to develop a framework of learning (Illeris, 2009, pp10–12) which challenged the idea that learning is a purely cognitive process. Instead, Illeris showed that there are important aspects of learning that relate to how we feel and the environment in which learning takes place. For instance, if you think about your own experience of learning in school, it is likely you particularly enjoyed some subjects and disliked others, perhaps thinking some were more relevant, easier or more interesting. Although the relationship between enjoyment or interest and learning outcomes has been debated for decades (e.g. see Clifford, 1972), more research has suggested that 'the more enjoyable an educational experience, the more students perceive it as increasing their learning' (Blunsdon et al., 2003, p51).

The question of enjoyment illustrates the continued relevance of reflecting on the different social dimensions of learning. An important framework for theorising learning that many teachers draw on today is Bloom's taxonomy of educational objectives (Bloom, 1956), which outlined three areas of learning: cognitive, affective and psychomotor. More recently, Illeris (2009, pp10–12) established three key areas of learning: *content* (what is learned, including both knowledge and skills), *incentive* (the feelings, emotions and motivation that it takes to learn) and *interaction* (the processes, experiences and activities that prompt learning). Although there are differences between them, Bloom and Illeris both remind us that learning is about more than acquiring new content; there are social and emotional factors we need to consider to really understand our students, how they learn, and what we can do to help them achieve their potential.

KEY QUESTIONS

Bloom and Illeris both include emotion and feeling within their theories of learning.

Why and in what ways do you think emotions might be important to understanding how young people learn?

The psychological approach: the growth mindset

American psychologist Carol Dweck offered a theory of learning that has been widely adopted in schools across the world and recognises the role of emotions in how we learn: *growth mindset*. Her research in schools showed that students' perception of their abilities 'played a key role in their motivation and achievement' (Dweck, 2015). This approach highlights the difference between a fixed mindset (when an individual believes their capacities cannot be changed, even with feedback) and a growth mindset (when an individual believes that, whether through effort or experience, they can improve, and is willing to fail along the way). In a growth mindset, students are encouraged to see failure as part of the process of learning, 'to try new strategies and seek the input from others if they are stuck' (Dweck, 2015).

While Dweck has been pleased to see the growth mindset approach adopted in schools, her 2015 reflection highlights some of the traps that teachers fall into, particularly in relation to the difference between feedback and praise (Boyd et al., 2015). Consider how these different comments from a teacher might impact a student's mindset. Teacher A says, 'Great effort! You tried your best'. Teacher B says, 'The point isn't to get it all right away. The point is to grow your understanding step by step. What can you try next?' (see Dweck, 2015). Hopefully, you can see that while Teacher A is being encouraging, it is Teacher B that encourages *and* challenges the student to keep learning by *trying something new*.

Paying attention to how we feel about our learning experience reminds us that learning is a constant process. Teachers have a key role in preparing students to learn and guiding them, a process that requires us to grow ourselves.

STUDY SKILLS

What and how we learn extends beyond the content of that learning or the cognitive process. We also need to think about how feelings, emotions, experiences and activities shape learning.

(Continued)

(Continued)

What does this mean for classroom practice?

Write some notes reflecting on your own experience of classroom-based learning. What questions are raised by paying attention to emotion and experience in the classroom?

Also, go back to the previous study skills task. Now that we know emotions are also a factor in learning, what can you add to your list to look for when you might get the chance to be in a school or to observe a lesson?

THE INTERPLAY OF TEACHING AND LEARNING

Connecting teaching and learning

Although many theoretical perspectives treat teaching and learning as separate, this section looks at their intersections. Before we go further, take a moment to consider your own view.

KEY QUESTIONS

Can we separate teaching and learning? If not, why not? If yes, is it helpful? Why or why not?

Looking at the interplay of teaching and learning allows us to engage with the *act* of teaching in relation to the *experience* of learning. Instead of seeing teaching as what teachers do, we pay attention to what the teacher and student are doing *at the same time*. For example, a teacher plans to 'explain that *Macbeth* is an example of a tragedy'. What does this tell us about what the students will experience during this activity? By thinking about teaching and learning *together*, we are more likely to consider activities that would involve the students being more actively involved. Essentially, looking at teaching and learning together helps us to answer a critical question: Why did that work or not work?

TEACHER'S VOICE

I don't think you can separate teaching and learning at all. When I was training, I was often told I was talking for too long. After reflecting on my planning, I realised it was because I wasn't thinking about what the students were actually doing when I planned to explain things or give information.

I started to plan with teaching and learning side by side, which made it much clearer to see when the students would be passive and active. My lessons have been much more enjoyable to teach too!

Sunny, recently qualified science teacher

KEY INFORMATION

Engaged pedagogy: values in education practice

'Pedagogy' is a key educational term used to explore teaching practice and beliefs about education. However, it is important to think about pedagogy in relation to the values and philosophies that shape what and how we teach, our understanding of how people learn, and our beliefs in education more broadly. Our world views therefore shape our pedagogy.

Let's take feminism as an example of a philosophy that has been significant for pedagogical theory. Feminist anti-racist educator bell hooks (1994) wrote her first book about education while still a student. For her, education is about freedom and liberation, and engaged pedagogy challenges oppression based on social identities such as race, gender and class. Thinking in an *engaged* way about power and dominance should make us aware of how our practice might reinforce bias, stereotypes and, subsequently, oppression. For example: How do we approach diversity in our classroom practice? How do we speak to and include different identities, both in our language but also the texts and resources we use?

These are complex questions but are important to consider, whether new to teaching or an experienced practitioner. Make some notes about your philosophy of teaching and learning: What is the purpose of education? What values and philosophies are important to you? How might they shape the kind of teacher you hope to be?

Student-centred approaches

Theories of education and learning continue to shape practice in schools, whether they are broader philosophical theories that make us think about the purpose of education or they theorise how we learn.

There is a large body of research that explores how and why teaching practices have changed in schools in recent years. A significant change is down to student-centred approaches that place much more emphasis on the way a student learns. Student-centred learning emerged from *constructivist* theories of learning developed by scholars such as Dewey and Piaget (see Chapter 8). Constructivism explains that learners are active in the learning process because they bring together new and old knowledge and experiences within the process of learning. Building on this insight,

Kember (1997) highlighted the contrast between two central themes within teachers' perspectives on teaching: teacher and teaching versus student and learning. This distinction is key to student-centred learning because it shifted many teachers' thinking towards the active inclusion of students in their teaching.

The rise of student-centred approaches to teaching and learning shifted the balance of activity in classrooms, changing the relationship between teacher and student from transactional and instructional to one of partnership (Trigwell and Shale, 2004) and collaboration. Building on this vision, Boyd et al. (2015) argue that teaching and learning should be understood as a process of *co-construction*, explaining how the teacher becomes 'a guide or mentor, providing expert guidance and suitable inquiry-based activities to challenge the learner and help her to become a member of the subject discipline community' (p16). While that might sound simple, it's worth taking a moment to think about what student-centred approaches look like in the classroom. Here are some comments from teachers about 'student-centred' lessons:

- I have to include group work. Without it, it feels like the lesson is about me!

- Students need time to work things out and build the knowledge themselves and through peer learning.

- To me, student-centred means reducing teacher talk and ensuring they are working harder than I am for the whole lesson.

- I have to pay attention to what each of the students is doing and learning, rather than the lesson being about them having to pay attention to what information I'm giving them.

- It's about student talk, giving them opportunities to create the learning together.

- Since we started to talk about student-centred learning, I have focused on making my students more active thinkers, collaborators and questioners. This way, they are more than participants in the room. It's almost like we are co-creating learning together.

Teaching and learning are interconnected. By thinking in much more depth about how teaching relates to learning, the learner becomes key to all aspects of classroom practice. Indeed, many would argue that student-centred approaches are the foundation of excellent teaching and learning.

KEY INFORMATION

Coe, R., Aloisi, C., Higgins, S. and Major, L.E. (2014) *What Makes Great Teaching? Review of the Underpinning Research*. Available at: www.suttontrust.com/wp-content/uploads/2014/10/What-Makes-Great-Teaching-REPORT.pdf

This report summarises research on teacher effectiveness. It explores 'good pedagogy' and the importance of pedagogical content knowledge and introduces the different ways teacher effectiveness is judged.

'STUDENT-CENTRED' LESSONS: THE TEACHER'S PERSPECTIVE

I have to include group-work. Without it, it feels like the lesson is about me!

Students need time to work things out and build the knowledge themselves and through peer learning

To me, student-centred means reducing teacher-talk and ensuring they are working harder than I am for the whole lesson

I have to pay attention to what each of the students are doing and learning rather than the lesson being about them having to pay attention to what information I'm giving them

Since we started to talk about student-centred learning, I have focused on making my students more active thinkers, collaborators, questioners. They are more than participants in the room, this way. It's almost like we are co-creating learning together.

it's about student talk, giving them opportunities to create the learning together

WHAT DOES 'EXCELLENT' TEACHING MEAN?

Schools are under increasing pressure to show that standards of teaching are improving, and they continue to be judged on the basis of student outcomes. Gert Biesta (2015) argues that with the focus on outcomes, school systems have entered the 'age of measurement': students are measured by being assessed and reports are written about their progress; teachers create data and are measured by the progress of their students; schools are measured through league tables to compare performance and inspections that require evidence they meet required standards; and so on. In an important discussion of how the wider social and political context impacts education, Steven Ball (2003) argues that the emphasis on results has resulted in a culture of 'performativity' where teaching focuses on ensuring that students meet their target grades. A related concern is that the emphasis on data (e.g. exam results) has resulted in the suggestion that teachers resort to 'teaching to the test'.

The idea of 'excellence' in teaching is clearly subjective: we all have beliefs about the purpose of education, and we draw from our own experiences to develop these views. For example, if you attended a school that actively promoted creative arts and learning other languages within a culturally rich curriculum, you might have a different outlook from someone who attended a school where the range of subjects available to study was limited due to policy directives and assessment targets (see Maguire et al., 2019). The wider educational context and our personal experiences and values will undoubtedly shape the kind of teaching and learning we would want to experience ourselves, and therefore must have some impact on how we perceive excellence. Indeed, sociocultural issues such as gender, class and the presence of migrant children in a class have been shown to impact how teachers perceive 'good' classroom practice (Devine et al., 2013). In short, judgements are made about students, teachers and schools all the time, despite the boundaries between good, excellent and outstanding being very fuzzy.

Although reaching agreement as to what defines excellent or outstanding is difficult, the interplay between teaching and learning highlights the significance of students' *thinking* to their learning. As such, many would agree with Boyd et al. (2015), who argue that outstanding teaching depends on challenge:

> *Challenge, doubt and complexity are to be valued and pursued as fertile territory for the construction of both deep and surface meanings, for the asking of new questions and for the exploration of new lines of inquiry.*

> (p18)

If we look back to earlier in this chapter and Carol Dweck's *growth mindset*, we can see some clear connections: both perspectives promote exploration and questioning, as well as arguing that excellent teaching allows for risk-taking and failure of both learner and teacher.

KEY QUESTIONS

Think of an example of teaching or a teacher from your own experience that you would say was 'excellent'. Why was that lesson or teacher excellent?

When you think about the idea of 'excellent teaching' or an 'outstanding school', to what extent do you think these judgements should be based on summative (final) data such as exam results?

Some perspectives on excellent teaching

John Hattie (2012) argued that student achievement improves when teaching and learning are 'visible': the teacher and students are all clear about what is being taught and learned, and the teacher focuses on how their practice impacts the learning. By adapting teaching strategies according to the needs of the students, every learner is involved in the learning process. However, to teach in this way requires being open, honest and reflective, a process that can bring its own challenges.

This area of teaching and learning that emerged alongside the drive for excellence is most commonly referred to as *reflective practice*, and there is an expectation that all teachers will engage with the process of reflection, no matter what stage they are at in their career. This means thinking about everything we do and how it impacts our students' learning (e.g. the content and design of resources and whether they were printed or displayed, the type of questions you used with particular students, why one group struggled to complete a task but others managed it easily, etc.). Reflection might take place during or after a lesson, at the end of a unit of work or assessment, or the times in between. The key to reflective practice is not just to think about what has been done, but to consider the impact of the different choices made.

KEY QUESTIONS

When you think about learning, to what extent do you think we should be concerned with being able to measure or demonstrate an outcome?

Although he acknowledged many of the problems with the 'excellence' agenda and the link to measurement and performativity, Skelton (2009) outlined his perspective on excellent teaching. A critical question is: Do teachers have a personal philosophy of teaching based on an understanding of their own values and beliefs? In addition, Skelton (2009, p109) questions whether teachers accept that there will be challenges but engage fully with the 'struggle' to live out their values in their teaching practice. This perspective requires teachers to see excellence as a 'dynamic concept – something which drives us forward, a force that makes us want to get better and keeps us curious about what we do', even when the going gets tough.

An excellent teacher, in teachers' words:

- is intelligent;

- isn't afraid to try new things (in fact, they embrace new ideas);

- is very knowledgeable about their subject and understands the common mistakes people make in this subject;

- is able to translate knowledge of a subject into classroom-ready content;

- prepares lessons that reflect a deep knowledge of their students and their capacities and prior learning;

AN EXCELLENT TEACHER – IN A TEACHER'S WORDS

- Is intelligent
- Isn't afraid to try new things. In fact, they embrace new ideas
- Is very knowledgeable about their subject and understands the common mistakes people make in this subject
- Is able to translate knowledge of a subject into classroom-ready content
- Prepares lessons which reflect a deep knowledge of their students and their capacities and prior learning
- Believes all their students can succeed and imbues the students with the confidence to do so, even if they have to fail along the way
- Is supportive, approachable and inclusive
- Is creative enough to design interesting and engaging lessons
- Is deeply reflective and acts on successes and failures to keep improving

- believes all their students can succeed and imbues the students with the confidence to do so, even if they have to fail along the way;

- is supportive, approachable and inclusive;

- is creative enough to design interesting and engaging lessons; and

- is deeply reflective and acts on successes and failures to keep improving.

TO CONCLUDE

This chapter has introduced the concepts of teaching and learning, considering them individually and as interconnected. We have established that broader socially oriented definitions of learning and teaching are useful for showing that the relationship between teacher and student is more complex than the giving and receiving of knowledge. Drawing on more expansive definitions of teaching and learning has established that student *participation* is critical to ongoing processes of learning. This insight has clear implications for how we teach.

Exploring the interplay of teaching and learning, introducing the term 'pedagogy' and reflecting on ideas of excellence has highlighted the importance of *values* within theories and practices of education. We need to locate ourselves in relation to the beliefs and values we hold, in particular about the purpose and value of education and our subjects. Reflecting on our values is crucial for us to become more aware of how wider contextual factors and our own experiences can shape all aspects of our classroom practice and our perceptions of educational policies (e.g. approaches to assessment and data, league tables or curriculum design).

Before moving on to explore other issues related to education and teaching, take some time now to return to the question posed at the start of the chapter: How might my view of education shape how I define teaching and learning? While your views will inevitably change throughout your career, it is important to take time now to consider the beliefs and values you hold, including related to the purpose of education. These will undoubtedly shape the kind of teacher you will be, and subsequently your students' experiences of teaching and learning and all its complexities.

RESOURCES FOR FURTHER LEARNING

Dweck, C.S. (2006) *Mindset: The Psychology of Success*. New York: Ballantine Books.

Carol Dweck's theory of *fixed and growth mindset* is still widely referred to in schools and is very useful for challenging many of the ideas about learning that determine how teachers perceive students. As well as telling us a lot about different ways of thinking in relation to the classroom, the framework Dweck developed is important for exploring the connection between learning and behaviour.

Illeris, K. (ed.) (2009) *Contemporary Theories of Learning: Learning Theorists … in Their Own Words*. London: Routledge.

This is an interesting collection of academic articles written by scholars who have theorised learning in different ways and in many contexts. You will gain an understanding of how complex it is to reach one agreed definition of learning and will be introduced to some of the developments in its theorisation from beyond schools. This is a more challenging text for beginning educators but introduces you to a range of ideas.

REFERENCES

Apple, M.W. (2003) *The State and the Politics of Knowledge*. London: Routledge.

Ball, S.J. (2003) The teacher's soul and the terrors of performativity. *Journal of Education Policy*, 18(2): 215–28.

Biesta, G.J.J. (2015) *Good Education in an Age of Measurement: Ethics, Politics, Democracy*. London: Routledge.

Bloom, B.S. (1956) *Taxonomy of Educational Objectives: The Classification of Educational Goals*. London: Longman, Green & Co.

Blunsdon, B., Reed, K., McNeil, N. and McEachern, S. (2003) Experiential learning in social science theory: an investigation of the relationship between student enjoyment and learning. *Higher Education Research & Development*, 22(1): 43–56.

Boyd, P., Hymer, B. and Lockney, K. (2015) *Learning Teaching: Becoming an Inspirational Teacher*. Northwich: Critical Publishing.

Clifford, M. (1972) Effects of competition on motivational technique in the classroom. *American Educational Research Journal*, 9(1): 123–37.

Coe, R., Aloisi, C., Higgins, S. and Major, L.E. (2014) *What Makes Great Teaching? Review of the Underpinning Research*. Available at: www.suttontrust.com/wp-content/uploads/2014/10/What-Makes-Great-Teaching-REPORT.pdf

Devine, D., Fahie, D. and MacGillicuddy, D. (2013) What is 'good' teaching? Teacher practices and beliefs about their teaching. *Irish Educational Studies*, 32(2): 83–108.

Dweck, C.S. (2006) *Mindset: The Psychology of Success*. New York: Ballantine Books.

Dweck, C.S. (2015) *Carol Dweck Revisits the 'Growth Mindset'*. Available at: www.stem.org.uk/system/files/community-resources/2016/06/DweckEducationWeek.pdf

Freire, P. (1970) *Pedagogy of the Oppressed*. New York: Continuum.

Hattie, J. (2008) *Visible Learning: A Synthesis of Over 800 Meta-Analyses Relating to Achievement*. London: Routledge.

Hattie, J. (2012) *Visible Learning for Teachers: Maximizing Impact on Learning*. London: Routledge.

hooks, bell (1994) *Teaching to Transgress: Education as the Practice of Freedom*. New York: Routledge.

Illeris, K. (2007) *How We Learn: Learning and Non-learning in Schools and Beyond*. London: Routledge.

Illeris, K. (ed.) (2009) *Contemporary Theories of Learning: Learning Theorists … in Their Own Words*. London: Routledge.

Kember, D. (1997) A reconceptualisation of the research into university academics' conceptions of teaching. *Learning and Instruction*, 7(3): 255–75.

Maguire, M., Gewirtz, S., Towers, E. and Neumann, E. (2019) Policy, contextual matters and unintended outcomes: the English Baccalaureate (EBacc) and its impact on physical education in English secondary schools. *Sport, Education and Society*, 24(6): 558–69.

Oxford English Dictionary (n.d.) *Teacher*. Available at: www.oed.com/view/Entry/198350?result=2&rsk ey=qVTdA5&

Reeve, J. and Tseng, C.M. (2011) Agency as a fourth aspect of students' engagement during learning activities. *Contemporary Educational Psychology*, 36(4): 257–67.

Shulman, L.S. (1986) Those who understand: knowledge growth in teaching. *Educational Researcher*, 15(2): 4–14.

Skelton, A. (2009) A 'teaching excellence' for the times we live in? *Teaching in Higher Education*, 14(1): 107–12.

Trigwell, K. and Shale, S. (2004) Student learning and the scholarship of university teaching. *Studies in Higher Education*, 29(4): 523–36.

7

WHAT'S SO GREAT ABOUT FINLAND? AN INTRODUCTION TO COMPARATIVE AND INTERNATIONAL EDUCATION

ANDREW BROGAN

KEY WORDS

- **COMPARATIVE**
- **PISA**
- **INTERNATIONAL**
- **GENDER**

KEY NOTES

- Comparative and international education are different but overlapping fields of study.

- Comparative education is the study of two or more education systems that aims to better understand their differences and similarities.

- Comparative and international education aim to explore what can be learned from different countries, rather than deciding if one education system is better than the other.

- There are two main types of research data in comparative and international education: qualitative and quantitative.

- It is important to make the right comparisons to help us better understand what is happening, why it is happening and what we can learn from it.

INTRODUCTION

This chapter introduces you to the study of comparative and international education. It asks what comparative and international education are and the impact they can have on our understanding of education. It also asks how we can compare different education systems. The case study compares Finland's education system to the education system in the UK and gives you a practical example of comparative education.

WHAT ARE COMPARATIVE AND INTERNATIONAL EDUCATION?

Comparative and international education have been described as 'twin fields' (Bray, 2010, p720) because they look at overlapping areas. As Phillips and Schweisfurth (2014) point out, many comparative studies of education are international, and many international studies are – by their very nature – comparative. In order to understand the difference between the two fields, we can use Halls' typology of comparative education (see Figure 7.1), which illustrates the main areas within comparative education and their connections to each other. The typology is not designed to be exact and rigid, and studies will stretch across and between these areas, but it is a useful visual tool to start with.

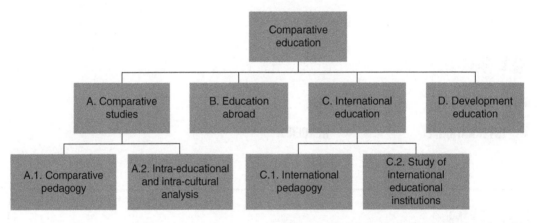

Figure 7.1 Halls' typology of comparative education

Source: Adapted from Phillips and Schweisfurth (2014, p10) and Marshall (2019, p15)

The diagram demonstrates Halls' understanding of international education as *one part* of comparative education. While Halls also includes education abroad and development education in this diagram, for now we are interested in the boxes A, A.1 and A.2, and C, C.1 and C.2 as these specifically refer to comparative and international education.

Comparative studies (boxes A, A.1 and A.2) is the study of two or more education systems that aims to better understand their differences and similarities. There are many reasons for making such comparisons: to understand possible alternative ways to approach education in our country, to gather evidence from other countries to support changes to our education system, or to anticipate what might happen if we make specific changes (Sharp et al., 2006). Comparative studies focuses on what can be learned from comparing education systems, *not* on declaring one education system as better or worse than another (Phillips and Schweisfurth, 2014).

KEY QUESTIONS

Have you ever experienced education outside your home country? What was it like? How was it different?

Comparative education can focus specifically on the teaching methods used in different countries (box A.1) in order to explore whether one type of pedagogy results in higher grades, happier students or more fulfilled teachers. Alternatively, we could focus on the interaction between education and wider society in different countries (box A.2). This is the point at which comparative studies, and comparative education, can carry us into a variety of academic areas:

- We can study politics by looking at educational policy.

- We can study sociology by looking at the treatment of different genders in education.

- We can study history by looking at the development of education systems, and so on.

However, when we compare different countries with different cultures in order to understand and develop our education system, we have to be mindful of cultural differences: what works in one country may not work in another.

LEARNING TO BE INTERNATIONAL OR INTERNATIONAL LEARNING?

As with comparative studies, international education is split into two sections in Halls' typology: international pedagogy (box C.1) and the study of international educational institutions (box C.2).

International pedagogy investigates how education can deal with increasingly diverse national populations. These diverse populations require tolerance and acceptance of cultural and social variations on the part of students and teachers alike (Marshall, 2019). The focus on teaching students to be tolerant, considerate and accepting of diverse groups of people can be characterised as learning to be international. In addition to promoting tolerance and acceptance within a specific country, international pedagogy also promotes education for global citizenship. Global citizenship education aims to teach pupils about human rights, social justice and climate change, and the impact of these on people around the world (McMahon, 2011; Phillips and Schweisfurth, 2014).

The study of educational institutions considers elements of education that extend beyond the borders of countries. This can include the question of how qualifications from one country are accepted in another or establishing student exchanges between different countries (Marshall, 2019). The focus in international education is on learning as an international endeavour, something that takes place across the world and has recognisable shared features wherever you go. An example of this is the Bologna Process, which introduced equivalent degree levels (bachelor, master, doctorate) across Europe, making it possible for students to study in different countries and receive the same qualifications (Marshall, 2019).

KEY QUESTIONS

Have you had classes on citizenship? What aspects did you cover? What did you discuss? Did you talk about issues that exist on an international scale?

Comparative education is the direct comparison of two or more education systems, or elements of education systems. International education is the inclusion of international perspectives in teaching and learning and the study of cross-border education issues. As Bray (2010) suggests, each field supports the other, complementing and overlapping areas of study. This chapter now brings together comparative and international education by looking specifically at how we compare education systems at the international scale with the example of Finland and the UK. The comparison undertaken includes specific teaching practices (box A.1) and wider social issues (box A.2), and some of the information we use comes from international educational institutions (box C.2) that compare similar skills and capacities of students across the world (box C.1).

KEY INFORMATION

Marshall, J. (2019) *Introduction to Comparative and International Education*, 2nd edn. London: SAGE.

Marshall's book is a detailed starting point for students of comparative and international education.

HOW DO WE COMPARE APPLES AND ORANGES?

Our next step is to explore *how* we can make comparisons between countries. To do this, we can use the analogy of apples and oranges. There is a saying that you cannot compare apples and oranges, meaning that it's not possible to compare two very different things. Why can't we compare apples and oranges? The simple answer is that we can, but we have to be clear about what we are comparing, why, and how we draw these comparisons. Although apples and oranges are obviously different, they share certain categories, and by carefully choosing those categories we can compare them to each other. While comparing shape or colour might not tell us anything particularly interesting or useful, there are other categories that can be more revealing (e.g. average size, average weight, growing season, growing conditions, texture, sweetness, average price, etc.). By carefully selecting some of these categories, we are able to learn more about both apples and oranges, not with the aim of deciding which is better, but in order to have a greater understanding of their differences.

We can apply the same process to a study of two different countries and their education systems. It is important to use the same categories (there is no use in describing and analysing the climate apples need to grow and comparing it with the average price of oranges). Knowing about the test results of Finnish 10-year-olds in maths cannot tell us anything about the performance of British 15-year-olds in science. The broad category of testing may be the same, but we need the details to make the comparison useful. We need to compare like for like, and would therefore need to compare the science test scores of Finnish 15-year-olds with the science test scores of British 15-year-olds. This comparison would help us to see what differences there are in the scores of Finnish and British 15-year-olds, which we could use as a starting point for asking further questions about why those test scores are different.

AN EXAMPLE: COMPARING TEACHER EDUCATION

If we find that one country's test results are better, we could ask whether a difference in teacher education can explain it. We would need to find details within this broad category that can help us make some comparisons. Knowing that teachers in Finland study up to MA level and teachers in the UK do at least 120 days of in-school experience is not helpful. Instead, we need to gather the same information for both countries (e.g. we could compare how long Finnish and British teaching students spend in school during their programme). Comparing like for like details within the same category enables us to understand the differences and similarities and to see what can be learned from that comparison.

KEY QUESTIONS

What other areas of education could we compare? How many can you think of?

When conducting comparative and international research, we first need to think carefully about what exactly we want to know about, and then work through the categories and detailed information we need to make a comparison. Once we have decided on the appropriate categories, we can gather the relevant data, and there are two main ways to approach this in comparative and international education: qualitative and quantitative research.

STATISTICS OR STORIES?

The type of data you collect depends on what you are trying to find out. Do you collect numerical/quantitative data (statistics) or do you collect non-numerical/qualitative data (stories)?

Quantitative data

Quantitative data gathers large amounts of statistical data with the aim of providing insights into large-scale patterns or trends. For this reason, studies using statistical data often take place at the national or international level and use large statistical databases from international organisations. One of the most frequently used sets of statistical data in comparative and international education is the Programme for International Student Assessment (PISA). PISA has been operating every three years since 2000 and tests a selection of 15-year-olds in language, maths, science, problem-solving, teamwork and financial literacy. The PISA tests are not designed to test subject knowledge, but are designed to test pupils' skills in the subject (e.g. can students do addition, subtraction, etc.). For this reason, the tests are not identical from country to country, but test the skills of the students in a similar way (OECD, 2019, box C.1). Once the tests have been completed, the data is collected in order to provide country-level average scores that can be easily compared to the data from another country.

Although the public focus on PISA results tends to be on the headline figures of overall averages in maths, reading and science, PISA gathers a vast array of additional interesting data for comparative and international education. For example, PISA also collects data ranging from parental education levels, to the number of brothers and sisters students have, to the students' home language (PISA, 2017). Thus, PISA can help us to make connections between education and wider society *within* a country (box A.2), as well as helping us compare information *between* countries (box A.1).

STUDY SKILLS

Should you use absolute numbers or percentages?

Statistics in education research can be presented in two main ways: either as an absolute number (e.g. 'In 2015, 57 million children were not in primary education worldwide') or as a percentage (e.g. 'In 2015, 9 per cent of children were not in primary education worldwide') (UN, 2015). Both numbers illustrate the same information, but one is more helpful than the other – it is easier to make comparisons between countries or across time if we use percentages.

We know that in the year 2000, 100 million children were not in primary education worldwide. This is a huge number, and knowing that 15 years later that number has dropped to 57 million is interesting, but all the absolute numbers can tell us is that 57 million is a smaller number than 100 million.

STATISTICS OR STORIES?

THE TYPE OF DATA YOU COLLECT DEPENDS ON WHAT YOU ARE TRYING TO FIND OUT.

DO YOU COLLECT NUMERICAL DATA/QUANTITATIVE DATA (STATISTICS)
OR
NON-NUMERICAL DATA/QUALITATIVE DATA (STORIES)?

QUANTITATIVE DATA

Quantitative data gathers large amounts of statistical data with the aim of providing insights into large-scale patterns or trends. Studies using statistical data often take place at the national or international level and use large statistical databases from international organisations.

QUALITATIVE DATA

Qualitative data is information that is non-numerical and can include a wide range of material ranging from written words, to video, to observations. Information (in education) can come from interviews with teachers or students, government documents and policy about education, or visits to different education institutions.

(Continued)

But what if the world population got a lot smaller over the past 15 years and there were simply less children who needed primary education? In this example, it is easier to see an improvement over time by using percentages: in 2000, 17 per cent of children were not in primary education worldwide, but by 2015 this figure had dropped to 9 per cent. This figure tells us that no matter how the world population changed over the 15 years, there was a comparatively lower number of children not in primary education in 2015.

However, this does not mean that absolute numbers cannot be useful, only that we must be careful to use numbers on the same scale - and this is where PISA is particularly helpful. PISA collects statistical data and presents the average scores of countries on the same scale. PISA uses a scale from 0 to 1,000 for all countries, so when we look at the results for Finland and maths we can see that they scored 511 in 2015, while the UK scored 492. Because we know the scale and that the countries are on the *same scale*, we know that the difference between Finland and the UK is 19 and that both sit about halfway on the PISA scale.

So, absolute numbers are useful if we know the scale and countries use the same scale, while percentages are useful for everything else.

Qualitative data

Qualitative data is information that is non-numerical and can include a wide range of material, ranging from written words, to video, to observations. Information (in education) can come from interviews with teachers or students, government documents and policy about education, or visits to different educational institutions. While statistical data can tell us that Finland outperformed the UK in maths in 2015 (511 points and 492 points, respectively), it cannot tell us why. The advantage of gathering qualitative in-depth data is that we can gain a better understanding of *why* certain patterns or trends are occurring.

If we want to find out why students in the UK scored lower in maths than students in Finland, we need to take a closer look at maths classes in Finland and the UK and explore whether the difference in PISA scores is a result of a difference in the curriculum, the delivery of the content, teacher training, or something else.

In order to explore any of these aspects, we need to engage with qualitative data. If we wanted to explore the impact of teacher training, we could use the materials from teacher training courses in each country to see how new teachers are taught to teach maths. This research would involve carefully reading the documentation on teacher education and analysing the different approaches contained within them. Or we could interview teachers in both countries to better understand how they teach maths once they are in the classroom faced with a room of (un)enthusiastic students. The use of qualitative data requires attention to detail and description of the practices of the teachers in Finland and the UK; it focuses on the individual, school or national level, in contrast to the national and international scale of statistical data explored above.

KEY QUESTIONS

What can quantitative data tell us, and at what point does it stop being useful? Is there anything that qualitative data can tell us that quantitative data cannot?

Although we have looked at quantitative and qualitative information separately, they can also be used together to great effect. The large-scale studies that use quantitative data are excellent at showing patterns at the national and international level, helping us to see some of the differences and similarities. When we are aware of these patterns, we can use qualitative data to investigate why those differences occur at the individual, school or national level.

KEY INFORMATION

Crehan, L. (2016) *Clever Lands: The Secrets Behind the Success of the World's Education Superpowers*. London: Unbound.

While much of the public conversation concerning international education is limited to the headline results of testing systems such as PISA, which allow easy-to-report comparisons, Crehan takes a decidedly different approach in focusing on the people behind the headline figures.

WHAT'S SO GREAT ABOUT FINLAND?

Comparative and international education are great tools in helping us understand how different countries' education systems operate and what we can learn from them. Finland is routinely held up as an international example of great education. Why is this?

Table 7.1 The overall PISA 2015 scores for Finland and the OECD in science, maths and reading

PISA 2015	Science	Maths	Reading
Finland	531	511	526
OECD average	493	490	493

Source: Adapted from OECD (2018)

Table 7.1 demonstrates the comparison between the OECD average (the OECD is the group of coun- tries that runs PISA) and Finland, and we can see that Finland scores higher than the OECD average by *at least* 21 points.

By moving beyond the quantitative data of the PISA results and looking at a range of qualitative data, we are better able to describe the details of the Finnish education system. We can draw on academic literature about Finnish education and documents published by the Finnish Ministry of Education and Culture. The Ministry of Education and Culture (2019) describes education as a fundamental part of Finnish society. The Finnish education system is characterised by:

- compulsory schooling runs from the age of 7 to 16 (Andere M., 2014);

- all schoolteachers require a bachelor's degree (level 6) (Andere M., 2014);

- all schoolteachers in compulsory schooling and vocational education require a master's degree (level 7) (Andere M., 2014); and

- there are few national-level examinations (Niemi et al., 2016).

These and many other elements combine in the Finnish approach to education, which centres on stu- dent learning and well-being (Ministry of Education and Culture, 2019) rather than the repeated use of testing as a way to measure academic progress and achievement. Despite the focus on well-being and a lack of testing, Finland scores highly in international tests such as PISA, leading us to question why that is.

WHAT CAN WE LEARN FROM FINLAND?

Our next step is to compare some of these key features with the UK. Keeping the same categories and types of data used in the case study of Finland, we start with the UK's position in the PISA 2015 test results. Table 7.2 shows that while the UK performs above the OECD average, it is still some way behind Finland.

Table 7.2 The overall PISA 2015 scores for Finland, the UK and the OECD in science, maths and reading

PISA 2015	Science	Maths	Reading
Finland	531	511	526
UK	509	492	498
OECD average	493	490	493

Source: Adapted from OECD (2018)

Other categories of comparison with Finland are starting and leaving age for compulsory education, the qualifications required for teachers, and the presence of national-level student tests. In the UK, these are as follows:

- Compulsory schooling from ages 5 to 16, followed by further or higher education, or apprenticeship, until the age of 18.

- To work in early years (ages 0–5), practitioners need a level 2 qualification or above (although they require a level 3 qualification to be included in staff-to-student ratio figures).

- All teachers from primary to secondary schooling require a bachelor's degree (level 6).

- National examinations are held in Key Stage 1, Key Stage 2, GCSE, and A levels or similar (BTEC, NVQ).

At first glance, there are several points of comparison to be made. While the Finnish focus is on the well-being of the student and the professional capacity of the teacher, in the UK there is a far greater focus on assessment and evaluation of the students and teachers.

Given that the school starting age in the UK is two years earlier than in Finland and UK students have more experience in sitting examinations, it would be reasonable to assume that UK students would perform higher in PISA testing than Finnish students, but we know from the data that this is not the case.

Maybe the difference lies in the teachers' qualification levels? Finnish teachers need a level 7 qualification (master's level) to work at all levels of compulsory schooling, but the UK requires a level 6 qualification for all levels of compulsory schooling.

A hastily drawn conclusion from this comparison would be that if the UK wanted to follow Finland and increase its average scores on international testing such as PISA, it should shorten the compulsory schooling age, remove national testing and increase the required teaching qualifications. The reason we should be cautious of such a hasty conclusion takes us back to one of the earliest warnings about comparative and international education: different countries have different cultures, and what might work in one country may not automatically work in another.

KEY QUESTIONS

Do you think there are any elements of the Finnish education system the UK should adopt? Which ones, and why? Can you foresee any problems with doing this?

ANY MORE LESSONS?

Before arguing that the UK should adopt all elements of the Finnish education system as it appears to work so well, it is important to go beyond the headline figures and ask some critical questions that would provide us with a more holistic picture. While Finland certainly does well on average, these high scores can mask issues in the interaction between education and wider society. In order to explore this issue further, let us have a closer look at two areas: the role of gender and the country of birth. What differences are there between boys and girls in Finland and the UK, and what difference does it make if you were born in the country you are tested in or if you are an immigrant? A closer look into either of these areas might change our perception of Finnish and British education.

Gender

Within those countries taking part in PISA testing, there is a gender difference in the three main subject areas, with boys scoring a higher average than girls in science and maths, and girls scoring higher in reading (OECD, 2018). In the 2015 PISA tests, Finnish girls scored higher than boys in each subject. Sometimes this difference was small (only 8 points in maths) and sometimes it was far bigger (47 points in reading). Data for the UK paints a different picture and shows girls scoring higher than boys only in reading (22 points' difference), with boys scoring higher by 11 points in maths and only 1 point higher in science. What is particularly interesting in the UK results is that the differences between the average scores of boys and girls are smaller than they are in Finland. Put another way, the results of girls and boys are more equal in the UK than in Finland (see Table 7.3).

Table 7.3 The PISA 2015 scores for Finland and the UK in science, maths and reading, sorted by gender

PISA 2015	Science		Maths		Reading	
	Girls	Boys	Girls	Boys	Girls	Boys
Finland	541	521	515	507	551	504
UK	509	510	487	498	509	487

Source: Adapted from OECD (2018)

Students' birthplace

PISA collects data about the home country of the student and splits this into two groups, 'country of test' and 'other country'. Those in the 'country of test' category were born in the country in which they took the PISA test, while those in the 'other country' category were born elsewhere. Internationally, the average score of a student who takes a PISA test in a country other than the one they were born in is lower than the average score of students who take the test in their home country (OECD, 2018). Accounting for this when comparing Finland to the UK reveals some interesting results. In Finland, students born outside Finland have a significantly lower average score than those born in Finland: 49 points lower for maths, 63 points lower for science, and 75 points lower for reading. In contrast, in the UK, students born outside the UK score an average of 15 points lower in maths, 24 points lower in science, and 26 points lower in reading. To summarise, according to the PISA results from 2015, immigrant children in the UK appear to be at less of a disadvantage than those in Finland (see Table 7.4).

Table 7.4 *The PISA 2015 scores for Finland and the UK in science, maths and reading, sorted by country of test versus other country*

PISA 2015	Science		Maths		Reading	
	Country of test	Other country	Country of test	Other country	Country of test	Other country
Finland	534	471	514	465	530	455
UK	514	490	496	481	503	477

Source: Adapted from OECD (2018)

Taking a closer look

The aim of taking a closer look at gender and students' birthplace was not to deny the successes of the Finnish education system, but to add to our understanding of it. While it is easy to stop our look at the Finnish education system at the headline figures and eye-catching policies, to do so would miss some important issues. Finland's education system has excellent average results, but the PISA data suggests that there are social issues in Finland that education does not fully address.

What we should take away from this example is the importance of asking questions about the data we gather and the need to go further than often-repeated assertions about a country's education system. Asking these questions and going into more detail with the information is vital for better understanding the complexities of education systems.

KEY QUESTIONS

What limits are there to what we have learned about the education system in Finland and what we can carry over into British education?

TO CONCLUDE

This chapter has introduced you to comparative and international education and taken you through an example case study of Finland and the UK. In doing so, we have used shared categories between the two countries, gathered like-for-like data within these categories, and analysed this data to better understand the ways in which the two countries are different and explored why this might be the case.

RESOURCES FOR FURTHER LEARNING

McMahon, M. (2011) *International Education: Education for a Global Future*. Edinburgh: Dunedin.

McMahon explores how international education is understood through various UK policies relating to teacher education, pedagogy, and professional learning that aim to educate pupils as global citizens.

Phillips, D. and Schweisfurth, M. (2014) *Comparative and International Education: An Introduction to Theory, Method, and Practice*, 2nd edn. London: Bloomsbury.

This text explores the development of comparative and international education as a method of research. If you are conducting a piece of comparative research for an assignment, this is a very useful book.

Spring, J. (2009) *Globalization of Education: An Introduction*. London: Routledge.

This wide-ranging work includes analysis of dominant approaches to international education through the World Bank, the OECD and the UN, as well as alternative progressive, religious and indigenous models of education. It is particularly useful for specific examples of different approaches to international education.

REFERENCES

Andere M., E. (2014) *Teachers' Perspectives on Finnish School Education: Creating Learning Environments*. London: Springer.

Bray, M. (2010) Comparative education and international education in the history of *Compare*: boundaries, overlaps and ambiguities. *Compare*, 40(6): 711–25.

Crehan, L. (2016) *Clever Lands: The Secrets Behind the Success of the World's Education Superpowers*. London: Unbound.

Halls, W.D. (ed.) (1990) *Comparative Education: Contemporary Issues and Trends*. London: Jessica Kingsley/ UNESCO.

Marshall, J. (2019) *Introduction to Comparative and International Education*, 2nd edn. London: SAGE.

McMahon, M. (2011) *International Education: Education for a Global Future*. Edinburgh: Dunedin.

Ministry of Education and Culture (2019) *Finnish Education System*. Available at: https://minedu.fi/en/education-system

Niemi, H., Toom, A. and Kallioniemi, A. (eds) (2016) *Miracle of Education: The Principles and Practices of Teaching and Learning in Finnish Schools*. Rotterdam: Sense Publishers.

Organisation for Economic Co-operation and Development (OECD) (2018) *PISA 2015: Results in Focus*. Paris: OECD.

Organisation for Economic Co-operation and Development (OECD) (2019) *About PISA*. Available at: www.oecd.org/pisa/aboutpisa/

Phillips, D. and Schweisfurth, M. (2014) *Comparative and International Education: An Introduction to Theory, Method, and Practice*, 2nd edn. London: Bloomsbury.

Programme for International Student Assessment (PISA) (2017) *Student Questionnaire for PISA 2018: Main Survey Version*. Available at: www.oecd.org/pisa/data/2018database/CY7_201710_QST_MS_STQ_NoNotes_final.pdf

Sharp, J., Ward, S. and Hankin, L. (eds) (2006) *Education Studies: An Issue-Based Approach*. Exeter: Learning Matters.

Spring, J. (2009) *Globalization of Education: An Introduction*. London: Routledge.

United Nations (UN) (2015) *The Millennium Development Goals Report 2015*. New York: UN.

8

WHAT ARE THEORIES OF LEARNING, AND HOW CAN WE USE THEM?

LIZ GREGORY

KEY WORDS

- THEORIES OF LEARNING
- BEHAVIOURISM
- COGNITIVISM
- NEUROSCIENCE

- CONSTRUCTIVISM
- EXPERIENTIAL LEARNING
- HUMANISM

- TWENTY-FIRST-CENTURY SKILLS

KEY NOTES

- Theories of learning refer to the different ideas about how people learn.
- An understanding of the ways in which learners take on board and retain new information is important if we are to begin to understand learning and education.
- Theories overlap and challenge each other. A critical approach is needed when studying learning theories.
- Every classroom is different, just as every learner is an individual – no one approach will work in all settings or with all learners.

INTRODUCTION

This chapter introduces learning theories and their use within education. It discusses what is meant by 'theories of learning' and how they might apply to the study of education, before exploring a range of theories from both a psychological and a social perspective. The chapter outlines the key ideas and research associated with each **learning theory**.

WHAT ARE THEORIES OF LEARNING?

Theories of learning refer to the different ideas about how people learn. An understanding of the ways in which we take on board and retain new information is important if we are to begin to understand learning and education. This chapter provides an outline of the most well-known theories and explores what each involves, as well as some of the key thinkers. Each of these theories is discussed individually, but there are inevitable crossovers and oppositions between ideas.

It is important that you do not passively absorb the information in this chapter, but instead actively consider and question the different learning theories presented here. Each of these theories has attracted objections, opposition and criticism, and none of them should be viewed as a neat or simple explanation of how students learn. Indeed, the fact that some of these theories have been developed or deconstructed since their introduction should alert you to the need for criticality. You should use the key questions to help you consider the limitations of the different schools of thought.

BEHAVIOURISM

Behaviourism is one of the best-known psychological theories of learning. It originated in the early 1900s, although its ideas have been refined and developed since. This school of thought suggests that behaviour – both animal and human – can be explained in terms of *conditioning* (the idea that behaviour is a response to external environmental factors). Much of the early work in this field consisted of testing with animals and the way in which they could be observed to respond to stimuli, Pavlov's dog being perhaps the most famous example (Pavlov, 1902). Russian psychologist Ivan Pavlov's study of the nervous systems of animals led him to the idea of conditioning – the notion that behaviour is dependent upon the existence of external environmental stimuli:

1. Pavlov exposed the dog to a stimulus – such as a bell – to which it did not initially respond. This response, or lack of it, was measured via the dog's salivary secretions.

2. The next stage of the experiment was to give the dog powdered meat soon after the noise had sounded.

3. Eventually, hearing the sound alone was enough to produce a response in which the dog salivated in anticipation of what was to come; in other words, the animal had become conditioned to associate the food with the sound, even when the second stimulus (the food) did not appear.

The process is summarised in Table 8.1.

Table 8.1 Summary of Pavlov's concept of conditioning

Before conditioning Unconditioned stimulus (food) = unconditioned response (dog salivates) Neutral stimulus (bell) = no response
During conditioning Unconditioned stimulus (food) + neutral stimulus (bell) = unconditioned response (dog salivates)
After conditioning Conditioned stimulus (bell) = unconditioned response (dog salivates)

But what does this tell us about how humans learn? Pavlov's notion of **classical conditioning** suggests that learners can begin to associate an unconditioned stimulus (one that automatically causes a particular response) with a new, conditioned stimulus, with the result that both stimuli bring about the same response. Thus, a student who has a negative classroom experience (such as feelings of humiliation) may forever associate future educational experiences with those original negative emotions.

KEY QUESTIONS

How might behaviourism be criticised for its interpretation of how humans learn?

Neo-behaviourism

The neo-behaviourist school offered an extension of behaviourist ideas. Skinner (1938) developed the stimulus–response model proposed by Pavlov by suggesting that the human brain is selective in its response to stimuli and can be influenced through a process of **operant conditioning**. Like Pavlov, many of Skinner's experiments involved animals; in Skinner's case, pigeons, dogs, monkeys and rats were used during the following sequence of events:

1.   An animal would be placed in a box, at this stage both unconditioned and hungry.

2.   Eventually, through chance, the animal would press a lever that would prompt a pellet of food to drop into a food tray.

3.   After repetition of this process, the animal would soon learn to go to the tray when it heard the sound of the food moving down the cartridge in which it was stored.

4.   Finally, the lever would be directly attached to the cartridge, allowing the animal to access food by itself by pressing the lever. The animal's ability to do this reflects the process of learning achieved through its conditioning.

Despite the non-human nature of many of Skinner's research subjects (a frequent criticism of early behaviourist studies), the idea of operant conditioning has been highly influential on educational practice. 'Operant' refers to a series of actions completed by a learner – a series that can be structured and reinforced for more effective learning to take place. Thus, as well as identifying the learning to take place, the teacher must also use 'reinforcers' or rewards (e.g. praise) to reinforce positive learning behaviours and encourage students to maintain these behaviours.

Skinner identified that such reinforcement was particularly important in the early stages of the learning process, when students should be rewarded as often as possible for each (often small) step achieved, and then at regular intervals later in the process. These ideas suggest that learner behaviour can be moulded in order to make particular responses more likely.

KEY QUESTIONS

What are the implications of behaviourist theories for classroom management?

Comparing classical and operant conditioning

The differences can be summed up as in Table 8.2.

Table 8.2 Summary of the differences between classical and operant conditioning

	Classical conditioning	Operant conditioning
Nature of response	Involuntary/reflexive	Generally voluntary (but can be involuntary)
Timing of stimulus	Comes before the response	Comes after the response (positive or negative reinforcement)
Timing of response	Comes after the stimulus	Comes before the stimulus
Learner role	Passive	Active

COGNITIVISM

Cognitivism refers to the idea that successful learning takes place thanks to internal processes and connections made by individual learners; in other words, learners must learn to think and reflect rather than simply complete the tasks asked of them.

KEY INFORMATION

Dewey, J. (1933) *How We Think: A Restatement of the Relation of Reflective Thinking to the Educative Process.* New York: D.C. Heath & Company.

Dewey defined this concept as 'active, persistent, and careful consideration of any belief or supposed form of knowledge in the light of the grounds that support it and the further conclusions to which it tends' (p118), and outlined five different stages of thought within the learning process:

1. suggestions;

2. intellectualisation of difficulties into a problem to be solved;

3. development of one suggestion into a hypothesis;

4. mental elaboration of this idea; and

5. testing the hypothesis through action.

KEY QUESTIONS

How could a teaching session be planned to incorporate these five different stages of thought?

While Dewey's model has attracted criticism (including from Dewey himself) for being too simplistically linear, it emphasises the active nature of learning. Dewey's ideas were highly influential on subsequent notions of the importance of reflection to the learning process. Other models outlining the cognitive aspects of learning have since been proposed (e.g. Norman, 1978).

While these models feature different terminologies and elements, what is consistent is the idea of the learner moving through different stages of thought. The inevitable transitions which exist between stages mean that at times the learner will be moving beyond their comfort zone; it is part of the educator's role to remind the learner that mistakes which may occur at such times are all part of the learning process.

Piaget

Also working in the field of cognitive development in the 1930s was psychologist Jean Piaget, whose work focused specifically on children's learning processes rather than those of all learners. Piaget

(1936) disagreed with the notion prevalent at the time that children were essentially less-competent versions of adults in their cognitive ability; instead, he suggested that children's cognitive processes are completely different from those of older learners.

Piaget believed that children are born with a basic mental structure upon which all future knowledge is based and built, as they construct a version of the world around them and then revise this as they gain further experience of the world and discover discrepancies between what they already know and what they discover. Piaget called these different units of knowledge *schemas*. Thus, cognitive growth is gained through a process of adaptation or adjustment to the world, achieved through these three stages.

KEY INFORMATION

Piaget, J. (1936) *Origins of Intelligence in the Child*. London: Routledge & Kegan Paul.

Piaget's three stages of adaptation:

1. assimilation;
2. accommodation; and
3. equilibration.

Disequilibration occurs when a child cannot process new information via existing schemas and must overcome the new challenge through the process of accommodation in order to restore the state of equilibrium.

Piaget also proposed that children progress through four stages of cognitive development:

1. sensorimotor stage (birth-2 years);
2. preoperational stage (2-7 years);
3. concrete operational stage (7-11 years); and
4. formal operational stage (11 years-adolescence and adulthood).

KEY QUESTIONS

Is there a danger that by focusing on cognitive development and process, the impact of environment and cultural factors is overlooked?

While Piaget did not explicitly link his ideas to education, his work has been highly influential on classroom practice. The notion that children must be active rather than passive learners can be seen in the prevalence of **discovery learning**, with its emphasis on play, the environment and peer-to-peer collaboration, as well as the concept of a child being 'ready' for certain tasks and concepts only when they have reached the relevant level of cognitive development.

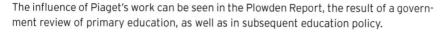

KEY INFORMATION

Central Advisory Council for Education (1967) *The Plowden Report: Children and Their Primary Schools*. London: HMSO.

The influence of Piaget's work can be seen in the Plowden Report, the result of a government review of primary education, as well as in subsequent education policy.

There is also a growing focus on the concept of **metacognition**, which recognises the understanding a learner may have of their own cognition and the role it plays in their own personal learning process. There is some disagreement over whether this is a purely conscious process or whether some of this knowledge lies within the subconscious; either way, learners should be encouraged to reflect upon the way they learn and recognise that challenges and mistakes are an inevitable (and important) part of the process.

KEY QUESTIONS

How often do you reflect on your own learning and the cognitive processes through which you acquire new knowledge, meaning and understanding? How could you do this more?

SOCIAL DEVELOPMENT THEORY

Another influential theory of learning is that it is socially mediated, with learners benefiting from the support of a more knowledgeable other (MKO). Russian psychologist Lev Vygotsky (1978) proposed the existence of a **zone of proximal development (ZPD)**, defined as the distance between a learner's current level of knowledge and ability and their potential level. This suggests that rather than teaching to the learner's current level, an educator should teach within the ZPD and support the learner to move through this zone to reach their potential. This can only be done through the **scaffolding** provided by more knowledgeable others (MKOs) – usually teachers – support that is gradually lessened and removed to allow the student to become an independent and autonomous learner.

Vygotsky conducted his work in the 1920s and 1930s, and was thus an approximate contemporary of Piaget. While both were concerned with cognitive development, they differed in their perceptions of this process. Piaget believed that children's cognitive development comes before their learning, whereas for Vygotsky the process was the other way around – meaning comes from social interaction, and thus learning from social situations and experience comes before development.

While Vygotsky agreed with Piaget's notion that children are born with basic abilities (Vygotsky refers to these as attention, sensation, perception and memory), he believed a learner could only develop more advanced and sophisticated thought processes through social learning gained by interacting with the environment. An MKO can help this process by working with the learner within their ZPD, thereby helping them achieve more than they would be able to independently, as in Figure 8.1.

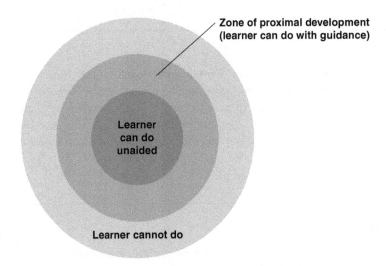

Figure 8.1 Visual representation of Vygotsky's zone of proximal development

CONSTRUCTIVISM

The constructivist viewpoint suggests that humans construct meaning from their own experiences, and places significant value on the existing ideas that the learner has. The educator must therefore identify these ideas in order to help students change, abandon or build on them, and thus construct new knowledge. Understanding what students know and think about a topic is important not only in terms of challenging misconceptions that could get in the way of acquiring new and correct knowledge, but as a means of explaining how every student will construct their own individual meanings despite a shared learning experience. Under this model, students are active rather than passive, and must take responsibility for their own learning through a process of discovery learning, drawing upon their existing knowledge and experience. The role of the teacher is to facilitate this by leading students to undertake the process shown in Figure 8.2.

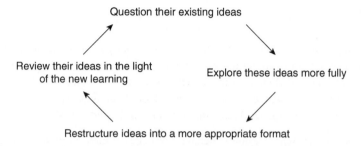

Question their existing ideas

Review their ideas in the light of the new learning

Explore these ideas more fully

Restructure ideas into a more appropriate format

Figure 8.2 Visual representation of the discovery learning process

This process can be encouraged through means of discussion and practical activities that allow students to try applying their ideas in new situations.

KEY QUESTIONS

What types of activities could an educator use to identify and explore learners' existing ideas and understanding?

Constructivism is a key theme in the work of Bruner, who believed that the role of an educator was to facilitate students to discover meaning for themselves by helping them to construct this new knowledge based upon what they already know or what they have learned in the past. There are overlaps here with both the cognitive model discussed above and the experiential model outlined below, as the learner's process of knowledge construction relies upon a cognitive structure (such as transforming information and formulating and testing a hypothesis) in order to make the given information meaningful to their own experiences.

According to Bruner (1966), an effective educator addresses the following four aspects of instruction in their teaching:

1. a learner's predisposition towards learning;

2. how to structure knowledge in such a way as to be most easily grasped by the learner;

3. the most effective sequences in which to present material, using a spiral structure to ensure the learner continually builds on what they have already learned; and

4. the nature of rewards and punishments (including how often they are used).

Bruner became increasingly interested in the role of social interactions in shaping learning, and he is often associated with the ideas of scaffolding discussed earlier in this chapter.

HUMANISM

Humanism became popular as an idea in the 1960s, and many of its basic premises remain highly influential today. This school of thought – as its name suggests – places the emphasis on the person at the centre of learning and their feelings of self-worth and self-esteem. In some ways, this new person-centred focus was a challenge to the prevalent ideas of behaviourism, which humanists saw as essentially belittling human dignity and reducing the value of the individual.

You may already be familiar with Maslow's hierarchy of needs, which proposed that basic needs must be met before an individual can move on to satisfying higher-level requirements (Maslow, 1943). This hierarchy is often represented as the pyramid illustrated in Figure 8.3, with fundamental needs (psychological needs, such as sufficient food, water and sleep) at the bottom and the need for self-actualisation as the pinnacle.

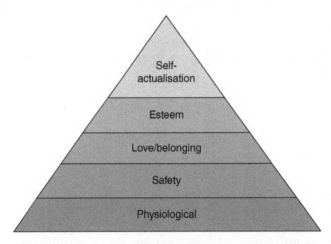

Figure 8.3 Visual representation of Maslow's hierarchy of needs

KEY QUESTIONS

Can you think of areas that are not represented in Maslow's hierarchy of needs? Do you agree with the order of the needs? Is there an argument that the order can be reversed?

Maslow's ideas have been highly influential, with a recognition that individuals have different levels of needs and that successful learning depends on each of these being met before the next level can be achieved. However, while Maslow believed that an individual must completely satisfy a level of needs before moving on to the next, modern interpretations suggest a less linear approach, with more overlapping of levels more likely (Maslow, 1954). Indeed, the model has been increasingly questioned in recent years, with *post-humanist* theories of learning suggesting that education is not something that can be so neatly achieved.

KEY QUESTIONS

What practical difficulties might the implementation of the humanistic model present in a modern classroom?

EXPERIENTIAL APPROACHES

Perhaps the best-known exponent of the **experiential** approach is David Kolb (1984), whose experiential learning cycle encompasses four different stages of learning, as illustrated in Figure 8.4.

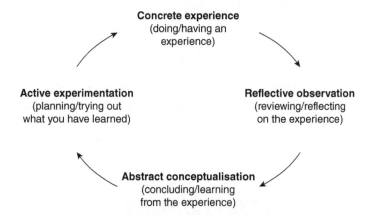

Figure 8.4 Visual representation of Kolb's experiential learning cycle

For successful learning to take place, the learner must progress through all four stages: having the experience, reflecting upon it, conceptualising the experience to form generalisations, and then testing these in future situations. A learner can enter the cycle at any point, and thus the teacher must be mindful of providing learning opportunities in which the whole process can be successfully completed.

KEY QUESTIONS

Think about your own educational experiences. Can you identify Kolb's four stages in the learning process in your experience? What did you learn from this?

Experiential learning has ideas in common with humanism, suggesting that meaningful learning only occurs when an individual perceives that their studies are satisfying their particular needs. Another figure associated with experiential learning is Carl Rogers, a humanist who shared many of Maslow's ideas, in his belief that for a learner to achieve their potential, a number of factors needed to be met.

However, Rogers emphasised that potential is unique to each individual and that people develop in different ways specific to their own particular goals and wishes. Rogers believed that humans had an inherent desire and potential to learn – to *self-actualise* – but that their potential to do so is threatened by traditional forms of teaching that fail to focus on the learner, and thus fail to provide a sufficiently motivating goal. Instead, the experiential approach suggests that the most successful learning is self-initiated and directly relevant to the learner's own interests. Thus, according to Rogers (1959), for self-actualisation to occur, the learner requires a learning environment that provides elements such as:

- genuineness (a sense of openness that encourages self-disclosure);

- acceptance (being viewed and treated in an unconditionally positive way); and

- empathy (the expectation of being listened to and having one's views understood).

The focus in Rogers' theory of learning is very much on discovery and exploration – an active process in which students will learn from their failures as well as their successes. This approach places the teacher in the role of facilitator, encouraging students to achieve self-discovery through activities involving problem-solving, cooperation, collaboration and self-reflection, rather than transmitting knowledge and information to students as passive recipients.

TWENTY-FIRST-CENTURY SKILLS APPROACHES

In an ever-changing educational context, it is vital for theories of learning to develop alongside the environment. The idea that certain skills (sometimes known as global professional skills) are essential for success in the modern world has come to the fore in recent years, with key competencies including:

- collaboration;

- communication;

- digital literacy;

- critical and analytic thinking;

- problem-solving;

- creativity and innovation; and

- accountability.

Many of these are nothing new, of course, but this particular learning theory considers how these skills might be promoted within a classroom setting in order to equip students for a world driven not only by knowledge, but by technology. In particular, this means a move away from more transitional models of education where the teacher transmits information and knowledge to students who passively receive it, and as such has much in common with constructivist and experiential approaches, in which learners are required to actively construct and develop their own understanding.

Pedagogical approaches have changed in the last few decades, making use of technological advances, with many educators adopting *blended learning* – a combination of learning via electronic and online resources along with more traditional classroom-based teaching. Learners are increasingly being assessed in ways other than traditional essay-based formats, such as being asked to produce a website or make a short film. However, the breadth of **twenty-first-century skills** goes far beyond technology, requiring students to successfully collaborate, to develop skills of metacognition and higher-level thinking, and to be able to transfer knowledge from one discipline to another, as well as to other areas of their lives.

The twenty-first-century skills approach is, as its name suggests, relatively new. However, its impact is beginning to be felt in the classroom, meaning that an effective teacher must be familiar with a range of different approaches, such as project-based and blended learning, and crucially be able to make these relevant to the skills students will need in their future lives.

KEY QUESTIONS

How can educators assess competency levels in the twenty-first-century skills discussed above?

NEUROSCIENTIFIC THEORIES OF LEARNING

The **neuroscience** of learning is an area that has been the subject of some debate in recent years. Neuroscience is the study of how the brain works, and the last 20 years have seen the rise of 'brain-based learning', which attempts to apply the knowledge gained from this branch of study to the field of education. This has attracted some criticism for its assumption that better learning can be achieved through the application of scientific rather than educational principles; in other words, using new scientific knowledge about the brain rather than drawing upon educator experience and tradition.

Neuroscience suggests that for successful learning to occur, changes within the brain are necessary – the production of new neurons in response to stimuli is what facilitates the absorption and retention of new knowledge and understanding. Learning is particularly effective when many different parts of the brain contribute to this process; for example, brain functions such as memory must be stimulated in conjunction with cognitive functioning if the new information is to be retained. This notion of *neuroplasticity* – the idea that the brain's neural connections have the capacity to change when encountering new concepts or experiences – has been highly influential in recent research.

While neuroscientific theories of learning are not without controversy, this area of learning is important in considering how you might improve your own study skills. The idea of *growth mindset*, for example, has been popular in educational discourse in recent years, suggesting that intelligence is not a fixed characteristic, as previously thought. Fixed and growth mindsets might be compared as in Table 8.3.

Table 8.3 Comparison of fixed and growth mindset

Fixed mindset	Growth mindset
Compares self (often negatively) to others	Compares self to own potential
Dislikes challenges	Embraces challenges
Gives up easily	Keeps striving for improvement
Afraid to make mistakes	Embraces mistakes and tries to learn from them
Reluctant to ask for help	Quick to ask for help

KEY INFORMATION

Have a look at the work of Carol Dweck (e.g. Dweck, 2012, 2014) for an accessible introduction to ideas about growth mindset. Dweck is an American psychologist who has researched and written widely on the impact of fixed and growth mindsets in educational environments, defining the latter as the belief that one's intelligence can be developed and improved.

Neuroscience emphasises the significant impact of contextual and external factors upon the learning process, such as how the human brain learns differently as it ages and matures, as well as how factors such as stress, poor diet, lack of sleep and lack of exercise can all play a part in restricting the absorption and retention of knowledge.

Cognitive neuroscience is a research area that is expanding and developing rapidly in line with advances in medical knowledge, but there is much that is not yet known about aspects of the brain that affect key elements of the learning process, such as memory, language, perception and attention. There also remains some doubt about the usefulness or validity of applying scientific knowledge to educational practice. However, this is an area of research set to grow, and one that educators can make use of in questioning their own capacity for learning and the efficacy of their own learning habits, as well as those of their learners.

KEY QUESTIONS

How can you draw upon a neuroscientific approach in adopting new study skills and making your own learning more effective?

LEARNING THEORIES IN THE CLASSROOM

It is important to remember that theory should underpin practice rather than dictate it. Every classroom is different, just as every learner is an individual – no one approach will work in all settings or with all learners. Instead, educators should draw upon the ideas presented here as a way of embracing a range of approaches, not losing sight of doing what is best for learners.

TO CONCLUDE

In this chapter, we have discussed what is meant by theories of learning. We have explored some examples. We have focused on the fact that while an understanding of a range of ways in which learners might acquire and retain information is useful, there is no one-size-fits-all approach to learning.

GLOSSARY/KEY TERMS

behaviourism A theory of learning that suggests behaviour occurs in response to stimuli.

classical conditioning The notion that two stimuli can eventually elicit the same response if repeatedly associated with each other.

cognitivism The study of mental processes and development.

constructivism The idea that humans construct their own meanings based on their experiences.

discovery learning A form of learning where the learner draws on their existing experience and knowledge to problem-solve.

experientialism A theory of learning that values experience as the source of knowledge.

humanism A theory of learning that places emphasis on the value of human needs and wishes.

learning theory An understanding of how learners acquire, process and retain new information and knowledge.

metacognition The understanding a learner has of their own cognition.

neuroscience The study of how the brain works, and how it acquires, processes and stores knowledge.

operant conditioning The notion that an association between a behaviour and its consequences can be modified through reinforcement or punishment.

scaffolding Support given (and gradually removed) by a more knowledgeable other.

social development theory The idea that learning is socially mediated.

twenty-first-century skills The skills needed to thrive in a technological age, and the pedagogical competencies needed to exploit these.

zone of proximal development (ZPD) The distance between a learner's current level of knowledge and ability and their potential level.

REFERENCES

Bruner, J. (1966) *Toward a Theory of Instruction*. Cambridge, MA: Harvard University Press.

Central Advisory Council for Education (1967) *The Plowden Report: Children and Their Primary Schools*. London: HMSO.

Dewey, J. (1933) *How We Think: A Restatement of the Relation of Reflective Thinking to the Educative Process*. New York: D.C. Heath & Company.

Dweck, C. (2012) *Mindset: How You Can Fulfil Your Potential*. London: Constable & Robinson.

Dweck, C. (2014) *The Power of Believing You Can Improve*. Available at: www.ted.com/talks/carol_dweck_the_power_of_believing_that_you_can_improve?language=en

Kolb, D.A. (1984) *Experiential Learning: Experience as the Source of Learning and Development. Vol. 1*. Englewood Cliffs, NJ: Prentice Hall.

Maslow, A.H. (1943) A theory of human motivation. *Psychological Review*, 50(4): 370–96.

Maslow, A.H. (1954) *Motivation and Personality*. New York: Harper & Row.

Norman, D. (1978) Notes towards a theory of complex learning. In A. Lesgold, J. Pellegrino and S. Fokkena (eds), *Cognitive Psychology and Instruction*. New York: Plenum, pp39–48.

Pavlov, I.P. (1902) *The Work of the Digestive Glands*. London: Griffin.

Piaget, J. (1936) *Origins of Intelligence in the Child*. London: Routledge & Kegan Paul.

Rogers, C. (1959) A theory of therapy, personality and interpersonal relationships as developed in the client-centred framework. In S. Koch (ed.), *Psychology: A Study of a Science. Vol. 3: Formulations of the Person and the Social Context*. New York: McGraw-Hill.

Skinner, B.F. (1938) *The Behavior of Organisms: An Experimental Analysis*. New York: Appleton-Century.

Vygotsky, L.S. (1978) *Mind in Society: The Development of Higher Psychological Processes*. Cambridge, MA: Harvard University Press.

9

WHAT ARE SCHOOLS FOR?

KATE BACON AND ZOE O'RIORDAN

KEY WORDS

- CHILDREN'S PERSPECTIVES
- SCHOOL
- MARKETISATION

- POLITICAL
- POWER
- CHILDHOOD STUDIES

- SPACE
- CHILDREN'S RIGHTS
- HISTORY

KEY NOTES

- The idea that all children should receive some formal schooling only became widely accepted from the early nineteenth century.
- When exploring the purposes of school, we find that schools are about more than just 'transferring knowledge' to children.
- Schooling is political. Education policy is shaped and debated by political parties.
- Children have very different experiences at school, based on their gender, age, social class, (dis)advantage, ethnicity and (dis)ability, as well as their individual characteristics, and these differences result in different outcomes and different life chances.
- Children have the right to express their views on all matters concerning them and to participate effectively in decision-making processes concerning them.

INTRODUCTION

This chapter examines children's experiences of schooling. It introduces you to some key ideas and theories, and challenges you to think about what children's experiences of school reveal about the purpose of schooling. We begin with a brief history of mass schooling and draw your attention to some different political and academic perspectives on the purposes of school. We then move on to discuss children's perspectives and experiences of school.

THE EMERGENCE OF MASS SCHOOLING

KEY QUESTIONS

How does your experience of compulsory schooling compare to your parents'/ guardians'? What does this start to tell you about the extent to which schooling has changed?

Although in everyday life we might use the terms 'school' and 'education' interchangeably, school is just one place where education and learning happen. Worldwide, around 91 per cent of primary school-age children are enrolled in school (UNICEF, 2018).

The history of mass schooling in the Western world is relatively short. The idea that all children should receive some formal schooling only became widely accepted from the early nineteenth century. In pre-industrial Britain, children worked from an early age (e.g. on farms or as apprentices) (Cunningham, 2003). Education was largely linked to religious 'salvation' – reading the Bible (e.g. at Sunday school) was vital to developing a virtuous life (McDowall Clark, 2016).

Industrialisation brought new modes of industry – mills, factories and mines. Families began moving from the country to work in towns and cities:

> For the great mass of the population of Western European countries like Britain and France, children's lives were characterised by poverty, hard labour and exploitation.

> (Clarke, 2010, p9)

Over time, labour reformers, concerned for the child's moral character and the impact of the harsh conditions on the child's mind and body, helped to fuel legislative changes (e.g. various Factory Acts and Mines Acts) that reduced the child's working day (Cunningham, 2003).

STUDY SKILLS

Choosing credible media sources to support your learning

When studying education, you will find a wealth of sources of information available to you. Some of these you will find in your institution's library and some from the media. It is important to always be aware of the credibility of the sources of information.

Watch *The Children Who Built Victorian Britain*: **www.bbc.co.uk/programmes/b00t6t3r**

As you watch, you will notice some clues to how credible/believable this information is. This is a BBC documentary narrated by historian Professor Jane Humphries. You can find out more about Jane Humphries online and see that she has published work on child labour, so we can assume the source is using evidence and relaying trustworthy information.

Some questions to think/watch with:

1. What does it tell you about how children experienced life and work during the industrial era?

2. Is there anything that surprised you? If so, think about why it did. What assumptions and ideas were you already carrying?

Adult work moved out of the home and child labour was becoming more restricted, so more children became visible on the streets. Compulsory schooling in England was largely a response to the perceived 'social problems' that these 'street' children presented. There were concerns about the threats to order posed by children who were not in school or work, and concerns that – left unregulated – the impoverished 'dangerous classes' would reproduce their delinquent habits, values and lifestyle (Hendrick, 1996). Compulsory schooling was one way that large populations (of children, but also indirectly parents) could be controlled and supervised (Boronski and Hassan, 2015).

In England and Wales, schooling became compulsory for children aged 5 to 10 in 1880. Bolstered by child study 'scientific' research, the advent of compulsory schooling helped to position children as ignorant apprentices who, through formal schooling, would be regulated and reshaped to fit a civilised and Christian nation (Hendrick, 1996; McNamee, 2016). 'Childhood' was being reconstructed as a time 'requiring protection and fostering through school education' (Hendrick, 1996, p39). Now designated as 'pupils', the school conferred on all children and all parents a national (British) childhood. Children were deemed to be 'in need' of regulation and control. Investing in this control and regulation of future adult citizens was important (Hendrick, 1996).

THE PURPOSES OF MASS EDUCATION

We tend to think of school as a natural place for children to be, and assume that children are learning things they need to know while they are there. However, schools are built on *ideas* about what children need to know, and these ideas can change.

Schiro (2012) identifies four purposes of mass education. Each purpose is linked to a world view, or ideology, which in turn leads to particular methods of teaching and learning:

1. *Transmitting knowledge to children.* Schiro calls this a 'scholar academic' ideology. Achieving this purpose involves deciding what children need to know, dividing this knowledge into subjects, and teaching children in a way that values memorisation and understanding.

2. *Training children to become contributors to society.* This is a 'social efficiency' ideology, which prioritises children's future role in society. Children are provided with the skills and knowledge required for employment, and the curriculum is directly related to developing these skills.

3. *Supporting children's growth as individuals.* This is a 'learner-centred' ideology. The aim is to develop a child's unique attributes, taking a holistic approach to the child, with a curriculum focused on their social, emotional and cognitive development.

4. *Turning children into critically educated citizens.* This is a 'social reconstruction' ideology. The aim is not just to develop children's sense of themselves and to help them to flourish, but also to give them a sense of the wider context within which they exist and encourage them to critically reflect on the power structures that shape their lives.

KEY QUESTIONS

Think back to your own experiences of school.

Which of these ideas can you see in the ways that education was provided to you in school?

How were these ideas put into practice?

Is there evidence of more than one of these ideas in your experience?

What was your role in school (e.g. learner of facts, apprentice for future employment, unique and nurtured being, critical citizen in the making)?

You may find that there are conflicting ideas in your experience of education. Perhaps different ideas seemed to dominate at different points in your school life, or maybe you went to different schools that had different approaches to education or some teachers who seemed to have different ideas about education than others. This should give you the opportunity to reflect on how your status in the school/classroom was shaped by the ideas that your schooling was built upon.

SCHOOLING IS POLITICAL

It should be becoming clear to you that schooling is political. Education policy is shaped and debated by political parties. Describing the political spectrum is complex, but one way to do this for the UK is to offer some simplified categorisations of the two different 'wings' of thought that exist.

The left-wing Labour Party has traditionally been inclined towards state intervention and publicly funded services such as schools and hospitals. This political perspective has been associated with the view that schools are there to promote social justice – to tackle inequality by ensuring equal opportunities to access and getting the most out of education. The right-wing Conservative Party has tended to promote lower rates of taxation and less state involvement in public services (Ward, 2013). Traditionally, this political perspective has been associated with promoting school discipline, a conservative curriculum of traditional subjects, increased autonomy for head teachers, and selective schooling and grammar schools (including privately funded schools) as routes through which some children can reach their full potential.

KEY QUESTIONS

How do these political views relate to Schiro's philosophies about the purpose of education?

Of course, these general categorisations oversimplify, and in reality education policy agendas reflect stronger and weaker versions of 'left' and 'right', and can also combine elements of both. For example, very much in line with a traditional left-wing perspective, in 1965 the Labour government moved towards comprehensive education (where all types of students are educated together). However, under Tony Blair, New Labour often combined elements of these two perspectives together to create a 'third way' (Evans, 2002). Tony Blair helped to build a post-comprehensive era where specialist schools – schools with a special focus on their chosen subject area (e.g. sports, technology, etc.) – funded by the government and private business could recruit a small proportion of pupils based on ability.

It is also fair to say that some principles relating to education are adhered to, to varying degrees, by parties from across the UK political spectrum. For example, reflecting broader global trends, recent Labour and Conservative governments have both, to some degree, argued that education provision should be guided by market forces. Two important market forces are *choice* and *competition*. Under the current system, schools are externally monitored by Ofsted and through league tables (which show data such as SATs results), which enables the public to assess the 'quality' of schooling on offer (see Ward, 2013). Families are able to use this information to 'choose' the school their child goes to, and unpopular schools that do not recruit and schools deemed to be 'failing' can go 'out of business'/close down. In reality, some families have more 'choice' than others, and middle-class parents are more likely to have the knowledge and resources to help them make the most of this system (not least because they may be able to move into 'catchment areas' that have 'better' schools). When education operates along market principles, theorists talk about the **marketisation of education**.

CHILDREN'S EXPERIENCES OF SCHOOL

There is an abundance of research, especially from within **childhood studies** and education studies, that provides insight into children's experiences of school. Childhood studies has done much to draw attention to how children's lives are shaped and constrained by adults/society and how children can – and do – shape their own lives as well as the lives of others (see Prout and James, 1997). You will see examples of this below.

When we explore research on children's experiences of school, some interesting points emerge. While there is evidence that children identify some 'good sides' to school, there is also evidence that some children find schools oppressive, boring and alienating places that restrict their voices and citizenship (e.g. Hughes, 2011). These findings contradict some of the 'functions' of schooling outlined earlier. We explore these themes below.

KEY QUESTIONS

What do children's experiences of school tell us about what schools do for/to children?

The good things about school

Research reveals that children associate school with a number of positive things/benefits. School can help prepare them for work (Davis, 2015), and they can spend time with friends, do sports and enjoy particular lessons (Alderson, 1999). In some studies, children report liking doing things and achieving things, as well as being active and energetic (Mayall, 2002). Children enjoy receiving praise in school, being challenged, working together, and finding ways to exercise some power over their learning and their lives (though not always in ways that their teachers know about) (Hargreaves, 2017). So, there is evidence that schools are preparing children for the future and providing them with positive learning experiences. However, some children have less-positive experiences of school.

Schools can be oppressive, boring and scary

Schools are places where adults have more power and authority than children (Mayall, 2002). Many children find schools oppressive places where they have limited autonomy (little freedom to make choices or use their own initiative to set/achieve goals). Research highlights how the physical design of schools can be used to regulate and control children. Pike (2008) shows how schools have a role to play in monitoring children's manners, food intake and opportunities for social interaction. Similarly, Devine's (2002) study with 133 primary school children, as well as their teachers and head teachers, in

Ireland showed how the organisation of tables in the classroom prevented children from socialising with friends.

This lack of control over time and space at school is, according to Christensen and James (2001), one of the main reasons why children find school 'boring'. In his cross-national study (comparing England, Australia and New Zealand), Sargeant (2014) linked children's boredom to distractions, poor concentration and the role of the teacher. As one child put it, 'If kids aren't interested they get bored, and when they get bored they don't do their work' (p196).

Hargreaves (2017) goes further, drawing on a range of research from the UK, Palestine and Egypt, to say that schools are often experienced by children as authoritarian regimes, sometimes characterised by coercion, physical control and (for the children) fear. Children were afraid of disappointing their teachers, failing, being shouted at (or beaten in Palestine), being punished or humiliated, and of their parents being told about misdemeanours. Even teachers who cared about their pupils and wanted them to have a happy and productive time in school became more authoritarian as they came under increased pressure to 'perform' – to ensure they hit attainment targets. Fear seemed to be a normal part of school lives for the children, and they were clear that fear made it harder for them to learn.

KEY INFORMATION

Christensen, P. and James, A. (2001) What are schools for? The temporal experience of children's learning in Northern England. In L. Alanen and B. Mayall (eds), *Conceptualizing Child–Adult Relations*. London: Routledge Falmer, pp84–99.

This book chapter, written by two key thinkers within childhood studies, relays key findings from an ethnographic study of three primary schools in England with teachers and children. The findings reveal that despite wanting to offer children a 'rounded' education, the teachers often felt under pressure to use classroom teaching to help children achieve the specified literacy/numeracy targets. For the children, school was often regarded as necessary preparation for future work. When exploring children's and teachers' control of time and space at school, the researchers found that teachers had more control over the use of school space. Some buildings were designated as 'adult spaces' and teachers also used time to penalise children (e.g. by restricting the time children had to play). In contrast, children had less control over their time – who to talk to, what to wear, where to go – and often described school as 'boring'.

Children pushing back

Although children may be subject to adult regulation and control, the research shows that they still find ways of pushing back. In her study of two schools (one primary, one secondary) in Northern England, Simpson (2000) found that while strict uniform policies were in place and enforced, students developed 'micro' strategies of resistance to adult authority:

> *Boys and girls habitually flouted the dress code by wearing plastic 'friendship bands' on their wrists, sometimes up to a dozen on each arm and these were a source of real contention among the staff.*

> (p72)

In their study cited above, Christensen and James (2001) found that children developed strategies that helped them to gain some degree of control over time: not looking at the clock and fast writing were used by children to help school time to pass more quickly. Children in Hargreaves' (2017) studies took pleasure in playing 'tricks' on their teachers, finding ways of appearing to comply while actually doing what they chose to do. Exercising power in this way made the children feel good; as one child said:

> *It makes me feel like I'm the cleverest boy in the whole school … and that I can do anything I want!*

> (p45)

Schools can be alienating for some and beneficial for others

So far in this chapter, we have talked – for the most part – about schooling as if it is the same for everyone. This is not the case. Children have very different experiences at school, based on their gender, age, social class, (dis)advantage, ethnicity and (dis)ability, as well as their individual characteristics, and these differences result in different outcomes and different life chances. This makes us question if schools are **meritocracies** – institutions that reward students based on merit alone.

To demonstrate this, we will focus on social class/disadvantage, as this is one of the strongest and most persistent influences on children's experiences and achievement in school in the developed world (Perry and Francis, 2010). Social class is difficult to define, so we tend to use disadvantage as a 'proxy' measure, and a key measure of disadvantage in England is eligibility for free school meals (FSM). In England, children who are assessed as being entitled to FSM achieve much less in secondary school than children who are not (DfE, 2019).

Research exploring working- and middle-class children's experiences of school life suggests that many working-class children feel out of place at school. Even at a young age, children are aware of social differences between themselves and others, and the implications this has for the ways they are treated at school (Hirsch, 2007). Middle-class children are 'trained' for school from an early age, spending leisure time on 'school-like' activities (e.g. reading, writing, playing educational games) and building school-oriented skills (e.g. listening to adults, following instructions, performing in front of others). School, for them, is a comfortable and familiar place. Working-class children tend to spend their free time in unstructured activities with peers and siblings, and develop a different set of skills that are not as valued in school (Lareau, 2000).

When working-class children talk about how they are viewed by their teachers in school, they sometimes say that they feel they are not respected by their teachers. Two boys in Reay's (2006) study capture this particularly well:

Martin: Those teachers look down on you.

Kenny: Yeah, like they think you're dumb … we don't expect them to treat us like their own children. We're not … you don't need to love us. All you need to do is treat us like humans.

> (p297)

These attitudes to working-class children can result in them being disproportionately placed in lower sets in school, sometimes as a result of **unconscious bias** rather than an objective measure of their ability (Crenna-Jennings, 2018). This leads to lower-ability groups being dominated by working-class children while top sets are dominated by middle-class children. The children in the lower sets know that they have less value than those in the higher sets and are more likely to find school alienating (Reay, 2012; Hargreaves, 2017). Some of the working-class children that Reay (2006) spoke to wondered if there was any point in trying:

Neil: It's too easy, it's like they think you're stupid or something.

Sean: Yeah, like 'How do you write "the"'?

(p298)

Schools can be places that highlight the material differences between children. Some schools choose expensive school uniforms that can only be bought from certain shops while some offer costly extra-curricular trips (skiing, theatre, sports events). Further expense can also be incurred when buying equipment and materials for study, coursework projects and exams. Not all families will be able to afford all these things. This can make some children feel like they don't belong. However, rather than just being passively affected by poverty, children actively find strategies to deal with the inequalities and stigma they face, such as:

- Trying to remain invisible so that their peers do not notice/comment on their appearance:

  My sleeves were all wrecked and that so I was nervous ... of what they thought ... So I went into my new class and ... and ... then I just got on like with my work real quiet. (Helen)

  (Brown, 2018, p51)

- Not telling their parents about school trips, because they know that they cannot afford them and want to protect their parents from worry or guilt:

  I don't usually go on trips 'cos they are expensive and that ... At our school they do loads of activities and they go to loads of different places ... I don't bother asking. (Martin)

  (Ridge, 2003, p8)

While these strategies may help children to cope with the day-to-day reality of school, they also deepen children's social exclusion, reinforcing the divide between those who 'have' and those who 'have not'.

Unable to belong in school in an approved way, many seek belonging in 'anti-school' friendship groups (e.g. see Willis, 1977; Macleod, 2009; Brown, 2018). This goes some way to explaining why rather than being 'engines of mobility, helping children to overcome the accidents of birth and background ... our schools system does not close the gaps, it widens them' (DfE, 2010, p6). In fact, data shows us that disadvantaged children are, on average, 4.3 months behind their non-disadvantaged peers when in their early years, but in secondary school they are 19.3 months behind (Andrews et al., 2017).

Schools can restrict children's voices and participation

In 1989, the UK along with almost every other nation in the world signed up to the United Nations Convention on the Rights of the Child (UNCRC). This international treaty contains a wide range of rights, covering many aspects of children's lives. One of the most important is Article 12, which says children have the right to express their views on all matters concerning them (their views being given due weight in accordance with their age and maturity) and to participate effectively in decision-making processes concerning them. These kinds of rights are often referred to as participation rights, and they seem to be particularly difficult to incorporate into everyday school life. Teachers' perceptions of children, concerns about their own lack of voice in the school, and feeling that this is just *another* initiative being imposed on them can act as barriers to teachers engaging with student voice (Lundy, 2007). Sometimes, perhaps as a result, capturing and responding to students' voices becomes the responsibility of a few key members of staff rather than the whole school (Whitty and Wisby, 2007).

STUDY SKILLS

Building your skills as an independent learner

You may not be familiar with the idea of children's rights. You can learn more about them here: **www.open.edu/openlearn/people-politics-law/politics-policy-people/sociology/childrens-rights/content-section-0?active-tab=description-tab**

This is one of many 'open' learning courses you can find on the internet. If you are introduced to a new idea or want to understand something in more depth, then you can often find courses such as this online to supplement your learning. Sometimes you can get a certificate to show that you have completed the course. These are usually not recognised by employers as qualifications, but they show that you are self-motivated and interested in learning, and employers value these qualities.

DEMOCRACY IN SCHOOLS

Children's right to participate in decision-making in school is often enacted through the use of school councils. These are now a common feature of schools and could be an effective way for schools to support participation. However, councils are limited in their effectiveness by the issues they are allowed to consider (which generally do not include teaching and learning, school rules or timetables), the way they are run (often with adult facilitators, who lead the discussion) and because of the way councillors are selected (Wyness, 2005, 2009).

It is usual for schools to use representative democratic processes to select children for the council – potential councillors put themselves forward and are then elected by the other children to represent them. The children who get elected are often those who are most articulate and confident, resulting in academically able children, who are best served by the school as it is, representing their peers (Alderson, 2000; Wyness, 2009). This may go some way to explaining the findings of the Good Childhood Report, which suggests that less than half of all children feel they have a say in the running of their school (Pople, 2009).

Schools in Sweden as 'democratic places'

KEY INFORMATION

Thornberg, R. and Elvstrand, H. (2012) Children's experiences of democracy, participation and trust in school. *International Journal of Educational Research*, 53: 44-54.

This journal article reports the findings of an ethnographic study with 183 children and 26 teachers conducted in three schools in Sweden. The researchers collected data using observations and informal conversations, and interviewed children and teachers. The children were asked to draw pictures of 'a day in my school' as part of their interviews.

In Sweden, schools are required to be democratic places that explicitly teach citizenship. Schools are expected to work with their pupils and develop an agreed set of norms and values through listening and discussion. However, even when this is embedded in law and teachers are committed to practising in this way, this study reveals how participation is still limited by:

- discontinuity - changes in teachers led to changes in rules that had previously been agreed with pupils;
- power relations that teach compliance - children learn through interactions with teachers that they will be rewarded for contributions that the teacher agrees with;
- naïve trust in teachers - based on their status as teachers rather than on their actions;
- school processes suppressing children's voices - weekly class councils that become places for reinforcing rules rather than democratic discussions; and
- lack of fairness - different rules for some children than others, and for teachers, as well as rules that are unwritten.

The researchers concluded that the ways the power of adults, as well as beliefs about children's incompetence (in the eyes of both adults and children), are enacted through the school day has a greater influence on children's ability to experience democracy, participation and trust in schools than the law that is supposed to direct and shape their lives.

TO CONCLUDE

In trying to understand the purpose of schools, this chapter has asked two key questions. First, what are adults trying to achieve through the ways that they have created and developed the state school system? We have shown that this varies, depending on the perspective of the adult, ideology and political stance. Common purposes of education are to:

- provide children with a moral education;
- keep them busy and out of trouble;

- prepare them for the routines of work; and

- provide them with skills and knowledge for work.

Importantly, as the aims of schooling change, so does what (and how) children are taught.

Second, we have explored children's perspectives to find out how they experience school. While some children enjoy their classes and value schools as a route into work, others find it a boring, alienating place that offers limited opportunities for meaningful participation, and a place where they may face (further) inequality and stigma. Ultimately, the chapter encourages you to be cautious about assuming too much! We may think we 'know' what schools are for, but we need to question where these ideas come from and recognise that, in reality, these ideas and ideals may not be borne out or reflected in children's lives. In fact, children may be learning a range of 'subliminal' messages through the **hidden curriculum** that contravene the dominant, 'obvious' purposes of schooling.

RESOURCES FOR FURTHER LEARNING

Hargreaves, E. (2017) *Children's Experiences of Classrooms: Talking About Being Pupils in the Classroom.* London: SAGE.

This book offers rare insights into children's experiences of classrooms. It mixes academic discussion of children's school lives with the children's own words to show how the way we set up and manage our schools and classrooms affects children. It prioritises the children's view of the classroom and pushes us to take them seriously.

McNamee, S. (2016) *The Social Study of Childhood.* London: Palgrave Macmillan.

This book offers a really thorough overview of research within childhood studies. It outlines the main defining features of childhood studies and then helps you to see what researchers have found out. It's really readable.

Frankel, S. (2018) *Giving Children a Voice: A Step-by-Step Guide to Promoting Child-Centred Practice.* London: Jessica Kingsley.

This book is centrally concerned with how settings can build cultures of advocacy where children's voices are respected, heard and taken seriously. It encourages you to think about how ideas from childhood studies can feed into and shape your professional practice. It's not a boring book; it's a practical (but passionate) book with a range of well-designed exercises to help you figure things out for yourself.

GLOSSARY OF KEY TERMS

childhood studies An interdisciplinary field of research that focuses on gathering children's perspectives and showing how they participate in shaping everyday social life.

hidden curriculum The things that are learned as a by-product of being in the education system (e.g. it's good to be on time, it's good to do as you are told, you should obey authority figures, etc.).

marketisation of education When education is treated like a product in a market – something that that can be selected, 'bought' and 'sold', shaped by the laws of supply and demand (bad products get discontinued, good ones get investment), choice and competition.

meritocracy A system that rewards people based on merit rather than social background.

unconscious bias We tend to find people who are similar to ourselves easier to be with, and this can lead to us thinking favourably about people who are most like us. When we encounter people who are different to us, we can rely on stereotypes or past experience of people 'like them' (e.g. 'children from that estate are always trouble'), and we can find ourselves looking for the characteristics we associate with that group rather than seeing the person as an individual.

REFERENCES

Alderson, P. (1999) Human rights and democracy in schools: do they mean more than picking up litter and not killing whales? *International Journal of Children's Rights*, 7(2): 185–205.

Alderson, P. (2000) Students' views on school councils and daily life at school. *Children and Society*, 14(2): 121–34.

Andrews, J., Robinson, D. and Hutchinson, J. (2017) *Closing the Gap? Trends in Educational Attainment and Disadvantage*. Available at: https://epi.org.uk/wp-content/uploads/2017/08/Closing-the-Gap_EPI.pdf

Boronski, T. and Hassan, N. (2015) *Sociology and Education*. London: SAGE.

Brown, C. (2018) Education policy and the binds of poverty: lack of aspiration or a failure of the imagination? In I. Gilbert (ed.), *The Working Class: Poverty, Education and Alternative Voices*. Camarthen: Independent Thinking Press, pp41–63.

Christensen, P. and James, A. (2001) What are schools for? The temporal experience of children's learning in Northern England. In L. Alanen and B. Mayall (eds), *Conceptualizing Child–Adult Relations*. London: Routledge Falmer, pp84–99.

Clarke, J. (2010) The origins of childhood. In D. Kassem, L. Murphy and E. Taylor (eds), *Key Issues in Childhood and Youth Studies*. London: Routledge, pp3–13.

Crenna-Jennings, W. (2018) *Key Drivers of the Disadvantage Gap: Literature Review*. Available at: https://epi.org.uk/wp-content/uploads/2018/07/EPI-Annual-Report-2018-Lit-review.pdf

Cunningham, H. (2003) Children's changing lives from 1800 to 2000. In J. Maybin and M. Woodhead (eds), *Childhood in Context*. Milton Keynes: John Wiley & Sons in association with The Open University, pp81–119.

Davis, R. (2015) The child's voice. In D. Wyse, R. Davis, P. Jones and S. Rogers (eds), *Exploring Education and Childhood*. London: Routledge, pp30–40.

Department for Education (DfE) (2010) *The Importance of Teaching: The Schools White Paper 2010*. London: Her Majesty's Stationery Office.

Department for Education (DfE) (2019) *Revised GCSE and Equivalent Results in England: 2016 to 2017*. Available at: www.gov.uk/government/statistics/revised-gcse-and-equivalent-results-in-england-2016-to-2017

Devine, D. (2002) Children's citizenship and the structuring of adult–child relations in the primary school. *Childhood*, 9(3): 303–20.

Evans, B. (2002) The third way. In G. Blakeley and V. Bryson (eds), *Contemporary Political Concepts*. London: Pluto, pp145–60.

Frankel, S. (2018) *Giving Children a Voice: A Step-by-Step Guide to Promoting Child-Centred Practice*. London: Jessica Kingsley.

Hargreaves, E. (2017) *Children's Experiences of Classrooms: Talking About Being Pupils in the Classroom*. London: SAGE.

Hendrick, H. (1996) Constructions and reconstructions of British childhood: an interpretive survey from 1880 to the present. In A. James and A. Prout (eds), *Constructing and Reconstructing Childhood*. London: Falmer, pp29–53.

Hirsch, D. (2007) *Experiences of Poverty and Educational Disadvantage*. York: Joseph Rowntree Foundation.

Hughes, C. (2011) *Schools as Prisons*. IBAEM Regional Conference, The Hague, Netherlands.

Lareau, A. (2000) Social class and the daily lives of children: a study from the United States. *Childhood*, 7(2): 155–71.

Lundy, L. (2007) 'Voice' is not enough: conceptualising Article 12 of the United Nations Convention on the Rights of the Child. *British Educational Research Journal*, 33(6): 927–42.

Macleod, J. (2009) *Ain't No Makin' It: Aspirations and Attainment in a Low-Income Neighborhood*, 3rd edn. New York: Routledge.

Mayall, B. (2002) *Towards a Sociology for Childhood: Thinking from Children's Lives*. Maidenhead: Open University Press.

McDowall Clark, R. (2016) *Childhood in Society for the Early Years*, 3rd edn. London: SAGE.

McNamee, S. (2016) *The Social Study of Childhood*. London: Palgrave Macmillan.

Perry, E. and Francis, B. (2010) *The Social Class Gap for Educational Achievement: A Review of the Literature*. London: RSA.

Pike, J. (2008) Foucault, space and primary school dining rooms. *Children's Geographies*, 6(4): 413–22.

Pople, L. (2009) *The Good Childhood Inquiry: Lifestyles – A Summary of Themes Emerging from Children and Young People's Evidence*. London: Children's Society.

Prout, A. and James, A. (1997) A new paradigm for the sociology of childhood? Provenance, promise and problems. In A. James and A. Prout (eds), *Constructing and Reconstructing Childhood*. London: Falmer, pp6–28.

Reay, D. (2006) The zombie stalking English schools: social class and educational inequality. *British Journal of Educational Studies*, 54(3): 288–307.

Reay, D. (2012) What would a socially just education system look like? Saving the minnows from the pike. *Journal of Education Policy*, 27(5): 587–99.

Ridge, T. (2003) Listening to children. *Family Matters*, 65: 4–9.

Sargeant, J. (2014) Prioritising student voice: tween children's perspectives on school success. *Education 3–13*, 42(2): 190–200.

Schiro, M. (2012). *Curriculum Theory: Conflicting Visions and Enduring Concerns*, 2nd edn. London: SAGE.

Simpson, B. (2000) The body as a site of contestation in school. In A. Prout (ed.), *The Body, Childhood and Society*, Basingstoke: Macmillan, pp60–78.

Thornberg, R. and Elvstrand, H. (2012) Children's experiences of democracy, participation and trust in school. *International Journal of Educational Research*, 53: 44–54.

United Nations Children's Fund (UNICEF) (2018) *Primary Education*. Available at: https://data.unicef.org/topic/education/primary-education/

Ward, S. (2013) Education policy and the marketization of education. In S. Ward (ed.), *A Student's Guide to Education Studies*. London: Routledge, pp3–11.

Whitty, G. and Wisby, E. (2007) Whose voice? An exploration of the current policy interest in pupil involvement in school decision-making. *International Studies in Sociology of Education*, 17(3): 303–19.

Willis, P. (1977) *Learning to Labour*. Farnborough: Saxon House.

Wyness, M. (2005) Regulating participation: the possibilities and limits of children and young people's councils. *Journal of Social Sciences*, 9(7): 2–18.

Wyness, M. (2009) Children representing children: participation and the problem of diversity in UK youth councils. *Childhood*, 16(4): 535–52.

10

WHAT IS LEARNING OUTSIDE THE CLASSROOM?

ELIZABETH PARR

KEY WORDS

- **LEARNING OUTSIDE THE CLASSROOM (LOTC)**
- **OUTDOOR LEARNING**
- **FORMAL, NON-FORMAL AND INFORMAL LEARNING**
- **VISITS**
- **EXCURSIONS**
- **RESIDENTIAL EXPERIENCES**

KEY NOTES

- Learning outside the classroom (LOtC) has been widely advocated in the UK and internationally for its positive impacts on children's academic outcomes.

- It is useful to view LOtC as a tool for teaching and learning, rather than a 'subject' to teach.

- There is a range of terminology used for ideas relating to LOtC.

- Place is crucial as it plays a vital and active role in learning.

- The spectrum of LOtC experiences range from within the school grounds, the local neighbourhood, and day visits to residential experiences and expeditions.

- One area of particular development in recent years has been interest in Forest Schools.

- There is evidence to show that residential experiences have specific and positive benefits for learning.

INTRODUCTION

This chapter explores what constitutes learning outside the classroom by considering what it means as well as its benefits. To explore this contemporary theme in depth, the chapter focuses on learning that would otherwise take place in a classroom setting, specifically the learning of school-aged children and the practice of their educators (teachers). It considers how learning outside the classroom fits with related ideas and terminology such as formal, non-formal and informal learning. It discusses places for learning outside the classroom and will use a model for organising places as a tool for thinking about the range of opportunities that could be harnessed to enhance learning.

LEARNING OUTSIDE THE CLASSROOM

Learning outside the classroom (LOtC) has been widely advocated in the UK and internationally for its positive impacts on children's academic outcomes, physical fitness, confidence, self-esteem, mental health and social skills, among many others (Malone, 2008). However, this is at a time when children are spending ever-decreasing amounts of time outside. The Natural Environment White Paper went as far as to say:

> Children are becoming disconnected from the natural environment. They are spending less and less time outdoors. In fact, the likelihood of children visiting any green space at all has halved in a generation.

> (HM Government, 2011, p12)

We will consider what constitutes learning outside the classroom, how it can be utilised across a range of age ranges and subjects, and why it can be such a useful teaching and learning tool.

KEY INFORMATION

HM Government (2011) *The Natural Choice: Securing the Value of Nature*. Natural Environment White Paper, HM Government CM8082.

In this White Paper, the government pledges to remove barriers to children learning outdoors, increase schools' ability to teach outdoors and encourage fairer access to outdoor learning for all children. In reading this, you will see how the government sets out to promote more learning outside the classroom and a greater connection for children with nature.

WHAT IS LEARNING OUTSIDE THE CLASSROOM?

Many would argue that rather than seeing LOtC as a subject, it is much more useful to view it as a tool for teaching and learning. In doing this, it can then be applied across a range of contexts and subjects. The Council for Learning Outside the Classroom (2019) defines LOtC as:

The use of places other than the classroom for teaching and learning. It is about getting children and young people out and about, providing them with challenging, exciting and different experiences to help them learn.

This is to say that it should not be considered an 'add-on' to the curriculum, but rather an integral part of planning for all learners, in all subject areas, all year round. In doing this, further relevance and depth to the learning is created, something that it is challenging to replicate within the confines of a classroom. The places that can be used for LOtC range from the immediate grounds of a school to the local area, day trips within a region, and excursions much further afield.

There is a range of terminology used for ideas relating to LOtC, as follows.

Outdoor learning

Outdoor learning is a broad term that includes discovery, experimentation, learning about and connecting to the natural world, and engaging in adventure activities and outdoor sports.

(Institute for Outdoor Learning, 2019)

Outdoor learning encompasses learning outdoors outside of a school context (e.g. outdoor learning undertaken by professional adults).

Fieldwork

'Fieldwork' is much more restrictive and focuses on collecting data about people, cultures and natural environments. While LOtC could include fieldwork, it does not need to involve any data collection. Instead, learners could be visiting museums, galleries and places of worship, for example.

Place-based education

Much of the literature from Australia and North America uses the term 'place-based education' to focus on learning outside of the classroom, particularly focusing on connecting learners with their local communities. Place-based learning uses the local area as the catalyst for curriculum development and encourages learners to be creators of knowledge rather than consumers as determined by others, such as a teacher.

Formal, non-formal and informal learning

The distinctions between these three areas are much discussed in the literature, and clear definitions are hard to establish. Gerber et al. (2001), for example, argue that 'informal learning can be defined as the sum of the activities that comprise the time individuals are not in the formal classroom in the presence of a teacher' (p570). This suggests that informal learning is anything that happens outside the classroom. However, Gilbert and Priest (1997) highlight that 'if teachers ... during museum visits see themselves promoting meaningful activity by means of focused conversation, then it does seem very likely that the learning taking place would be similar in type and quality' (p750) to that in the classroom. This would then suggest that there is more to distinguishing between formal and informal learning by means of the location of the learning. Formal learning could happen in informal contexts such as a museum.

In order to resolve this, Eshach (2007) proposes three types of learning: formal, informal and non-formal. Table 10.1 summarises the differences between these three terms.

Table 10.1 Differences between formal, non-formal and informal learning

Formal	Non-formal	Informal
Usually at school	At an institution out of school	Everywhere
May be repressive	Usually supportive	Supportive
Structured	Structured	Unstructured
Usually prearranged	Usually prearranged	Spontaneous
Motivation is typically more extrinsic	Motivation may be extrinsic but typically more intrinsic	Motivation is mainly intrinsic
Compulsory	Usually voluntary	Voluntary
Teacher-led	May be guided or teacher-led	Usually learner-led
Learning is evaluated	Learning is usually not evaluated	Learning is not evaluated
Sequential	Typically non-sequential	Non-sequential

Source: Eshach (2007, p174)

Eshach's table does suggest that there are three clear distinctions here where the reality of LOtC involves much more fluidity. For example, in many non-formal learning contexts, learning is thoroughly evaluated and is compulsory for all learners. This is why Eshach goes on to discuss how to bridge the gaps between these three types of learning, ensuring that there is progression, clear links to the curriculum and close assessment of the learning. We will go on to consider some of the places in which LOtC, in terms of both non-formal and informal learning, might happen in the next section.

KEY QUESTIONS

Consider Eshach's table of formal, non-formal and informal learning. Can you think of examples of when you have learned something in a formal, non-formal or informal context?

What are the benefits and challenges for teachers in each of these contexts?

What types of learning do you think is best suited to a formal, non-formal or informal learning context?

PLACES TO LEARN OUTSIDE OF THE CLASSROOM

In thinking about LOtC, the idea of place is crucial. It plays a vital and active role in the learning as the learners will be engaged in and influenced by their surroundings. Places not only have their own geographical boundaries, but also their own cultures, histories, expectations and social relations. Learners within these places have a personal and emotional response to their surroundings. So, learners attach their own meanings to places, finding relevance in places to their own lives and making connections with their existing knowledge and understanding. These ideas are developed by Waite and Pratt (2011) when they explored a relational model for LOtC (see Figure 10.1). In this model, they propose that there is a relationship between the national context (e.g. curriculum, standards, strategies), the local context (cultural norms and expectations of a setting), and the child, place and others (mainly adults) who are operating within the place. Their work suggests that it is within the triangle that learning opportunities are created as a result of the interactions between child, other and place. These learning opportunities are set in the local and national contexts that surround them.

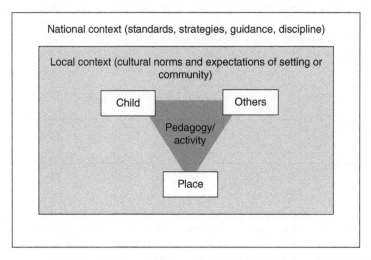

Figure 10.1 The possibility space in relations between place, pedagogy and learning

Source: Waite and Pratt (in Waite, 2017)

It is important to remember that this model only presents a snapshot of the learning at one point in time. In reality, this is a dynamic system of interactions. The learning and cultural expectations may be revised and built upon if the place is revisited, for example. This would be the case for Forest Schools, which we will explore later. Histories and associations of a place may also be developed over time as these places become meaningful to the child and others. The unpredictability of places outside the classroom may mean that the conventional relationships between the child and others – particularly teachers – may be disrupted and shift the power dynamics, leading to different opportunities for learning. Each of these situations sees the place in the model as an active partner in the learning, engaging the child and being fundamental to the learning.

KEY QUESTIONS

Look at Figure 10.1 and think about a learning opportunity that you have been involved with outside of the classroom. It might be your own experience of learning or you looking at someone else's learning experience.

What interactions happened between each of the components?

For example, how did the child interact with the place?

How did the expectations of the setting influence the behaviour of the child or others?

It is important to think about what LOtC means in terms of the places this encompasses. LOtC involves 'the use of places other than the classroom for teaching and learning' (Council for Learning Outside the Classroom, 2019). In an attempt to categorise these places, Beames et al. (2012) suggested four zones in which LOtC occurs (see Figure 10.2). The 'school grounds' are central to the model, with learners being able to explore these on a daily basis during curriculum time as well as break times. This might include outdoor provision for children in the early years, Forest School provision and an outdoor classroom. Beyond this is the 'local neighbourhood', which comprises the area that can be explored by learners on foot or local public transport (places such as local allotments, libraries and places of worship would be included in this zone). Further still are 'day excursions', which would require a greater level of organisation and group transport. Places that would be in this zone include museums, national parks and zoos.

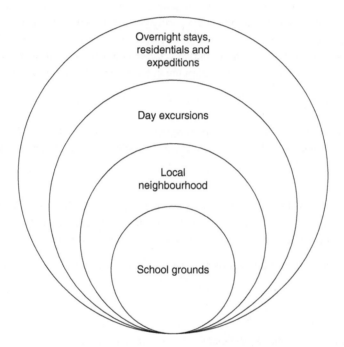

Figure 10.2 The four 'zones' of outdoor learning

Source: Beames et al. (2012)

The fourth zone is 'overnight stays, residentials and expeditions'. LOtC in these places requires significant organisation of transport, accommodation, equipment and food. Field trips, language exchanges and outdoor adventure centres would be in this zone. Since proposing this model, Higgins et al. (2013) have suggested a further fifth zone, 'Planet Earth'. They argue that this final zone reflects the recent interest and developments in understanding the importance of LOtC in relation to sustainability, health and well-being.

While each of these zones is crucial to providing rich learning experiences, the model is designed to be progressive. This means that it is recommended that learners fully explore their own surroundings and local area prior to moving further afield.

Within the school grounds

LOtC is most easily organised by taking advantage of the rich potential for learning opportunities within the school grounds. Children in the early years are most likely to be engaging in LOtC as the statutory framework for the Early Years Foundation Stage highlights that 'providers must provide access to an outdoor play area or, if that is not possible, ensure that outdoor activities are planned and taken on a daily basis' (DfE, 2017, p30). This might include using an outdoor storytelling area, an outdoor classroom or school gardens. One area of particular development in recent years has been the interest in Forest Schools, with many schools investing in their own Forest School provision.

While Forest Schools have not received formal recognition in policy documents or been endorsed by the Department for Education, their rapid growth in popularity points to their potential – a distinctive process by which learners engage with the natural environment. The term 'Forest School' was introduced in 1993 by Bridgwater College practitioners after researching early years pedagogy and practices in Denmark. Soon after, their training college was launched, and as interest in Forest Schools grew, clearly defined principles and training criteria developed. There are currently over 40 Forest School training providers across the UK and an estimated 10,000 educational settings engaging in Forest Schools (Waite, 2017).

A Forest School is distinct from other forms of outdoor play and learning as it:

is an inspirational process that offers ALL learners regular opportunities to achieve and develop confidence and self-esteem through hand-on learning experiences in a woodland or natural environment with trees.

(Wellings, 2012)

This definition emphasises the importance of all learners engaging in the Forest School experience. It is not an intervention for specific pupils. It also stresses the importance of a natural environment with trees or a woodland, as well as active engagement in this natural environment.

Alongside this definition, the Forest School Association has produced a set of six principles that underpin the approach:

A Forest School:

1. *Is a long term process with frequent and regular sessions in a local natural space, not a one-off visit. Planning, adaptation, observations and reviewing are integral elements.*

2. *Takes place in a woodland or natural wooded environment to support the development of a relationship between the learner and the natural world.*

3. *Aims to promote the holistic development of all those involved, fostering resilient, confident, independent and creative learners.*

4. *Offers learners the opportunity to take supported risks appropriate to the environment and themselves.*

5. *Is run by qualified Forest School Practitioners who continuously develop their professional practice.*

6. *Uses a range of learner-centred processes to create a community for development and learning.*

(Wellings, 2012)

Much of the Forest School research focuses on the positive impact on children of using this approach. A range of benefits, including increased self-confidence, improved relationships, greater interest in learning, enhanced psychological well-being, more sophisticated language skills and improved behaviour, have all been observed.

KEY INFORMATION

Knight, S. (2013) *Forest School and Outdoor Learning in the Early Years.* London: SAGE.

Sara Knight's book presents a detailed and comprehensive overview of Forest Schools. Topics such as the effects of Forest Schools on behaviour and social development, working with parents and carers, and developing a Forest School ethos are explored and exemplified using a range of case studies.

Local neighbourhood

LOtC in the local neighbourhood embraces learners' natural interest in where and how they live and uses this as a source of learning and activity (Melaville et al., 2006). Local neighbourhoods are often rich in history, culture and resources, which can all be useful in providing meaningful contexts and relevance to learning. Places that might be included are:

- local businesses;

- gardens/allotments;

- libraries;

- places of worship;

- arts venues;

- neighbouring schools; and

- community groups and facilities.

The curricula used in schools that aim to engage with the local community are broadly modelled on the notion of an area-based curriculum. Area-based curricula draw on communities' resources to provide a curriculum tailored to the history and experience of people living in the school's surrounding areas. In this sense, the aim of community-responsive curricula and pedagogy is to make learning relevant to the lives of young people living in the community (Dyson et al., 2011, p5). Examples of this include the Disadvantaged Schools Programme in Australia (Connell et al., 1982) and the RSA area-based curricula.

The Royal Society for the Encouragement of Arts, Manufactures and Commerce (RSA) aims to find innovative and practical solutions to social challenges. One such challenge was being able to engage all children in education and their wider society. Thus, the RSA aim to 'develop engaging curricula that meet the learning, wellbeing and civic needs of learners, and is fit for the social and economic demands of contemporary society' (RSA, 2012).

The Peterborough Curriculum was developed as part of the wider Citizen Power project in the local Peterborough area. The project aimed 'to shape the way in which young people learn and alter the relationship between schools and their communities' (O'Brien, 2011, p19). The project increased links between schools and local businesses, heritage sites, arts centres, and public services by increasing civic participation among pupils, parents and the wider community. The intention was to strengthen young people's capacity to thrive in their future work and in life.

KEY QUESTIONS

Think about your own local area. What resources are available within the community that could be harnessed in teaching and for learning experiences?

What learning could happen in these places?

What historical, social and cultural experiences might these places provide?

What impact could this type of LOtC have on the learners?

Day excursions

Day excursions provide an entirely different context in which to learn. For some learners, this may be the first time they have visited this place. As a result, there is potential for a wide range of new learning to occur. LOtC through day excursions might include places such as:

- museums;
- theatres;
- nature reserves;
- galleries;
- heritage sites;
- national parks;
- zoos and aquaria;
- nature reserves; and
- science/discovery centres.

Much of the literature highlights the increased planning and preparation that is required. Research shows that students who are fully prepared for their visit and who have clear links between the work completed in the classroom and on the day excursion learn most from their experiences (Jensen, 1994). This includes preparing for the more informal nature of learning in this context rather than mirroring classroom behaviours (e.g. preparing for first-hand experiences and observations rather than completing worksheets) (Price and Hein, 1991). This then enables the learners to not only develop knowledge and understanding of the topic studied, but also negotiate some of the difference in cultural and social expectations within the context.

One example that we will look at in some detail is the use of museums in LOtC. Increasingly, museums offer a broad range of learning methods, such as interactive exhibits, demonstrations, videos, experts, specimens and displays. Outreach sessions, learning resources and professional development for teachers are also offered. While the majority of school visits to museums are made by primary school children, there has been a recent drive to engage secondary schools, which has positively impacted on routes to higher education and careers (Arts Council England, 2016). Museums must also be responsive to curriculum change and development. During the most recent changes to the national curriculum, topics such as the Victorians and the Second World War were no longer in as much demand, requiring museums to be flexible and develop new sessions to support the curriculum.

For learning during museum visits to be most productive, Guisasola et al. (2005) suggest these three principles:

1. integrating school learning into museum learning;

2. guiding students towards development and contrasting of their own ideas; and

3. facilitating strategies that are appropriate to the museum's context.

This is to say that preparation and a different way of facilitating learning in museums is crucial to ensuring learners gain the most from the experience. Research from the Research Centre for Museums and Galleries (RCMG) provides evidence of the positive impact of museums on pupils' motivation, emotional and social well-being, and improved attainment (measured as increase in assessment grades) (Watson et al., 2007).

KEY INFORMATION

Ofsted (2008) *Learning Outside the Classroom: How Far Should You Go?* London: Crown.

This Ofsted document was written in response to the then government's publication *Learning Outside the Classroom Manifesto* (DfES, 2006). This document evaluates the impact of LOtC in a range of contexts, such as museums, art galleries and field centres across a small number of case study primary, secondary and special schools.

Overnight stays, residential experiences and expeditions

LOtC through overnight stays, residential experiences and expeditions is comparatively more complex to organise. When planning, teachers need to think about transport, accommodation and provision for food, in addition to all of the other components necessary for LOtC. Having said that, there is a wealth of possibilities and opportunities for learning when travelling further afield. Examples include:

- outdoor centres;
- field trips;
- residential experiences;
- overseas trips; and
- language exchanges.

Recent research findings have demonstrated that although the number of schools which offer residential experiences and visits further from school is increasing, fewer opportunities are available in schools with more deprived catchment areas (Williams, 2013), and it is those children from advantaged backgrounds who tend to access these activities to a greater extent (Hirch, 2007). This could be in part due to the considerable costs incurred for such visits or limitations in terms of a school's timetable or curriculum as a result of accountability measures such as testing.

Residential experiences involve being away from home overnight and are a useful way of providing opportunities to foster new relationships because they allow greater time, space and depth of experience. A recent report by Learning Away (Hamlyn, 2015) evaluated the impact of residential experiences on learners and concluded that there were benefits in terms of:

- relationships (between peers and between students and staff);
- resilience;
- self-confidence;
- engagement with learning;
- achievement;
- knowledge;
- cohesion; and
- transition between Key Stages.

The report found that these benefits were a result of the following distinctive aspects of a residential experience:

- The time, space and intensity of the residential experience.
- Residentials were a leveller: residentials provided a new space and context where participants were equal and existing barriers and hierarchies could be broken down.

- Relationships developed through a sense of community/living together.

- Challenging activities and opportunities to experience success (e.g. a range of practical and physical challenges).

- New ways of learning/ownership of and engagement with learning.

(adapted from Hamlyn, 2015)

The above aspects of a residential experience highlight the unique way in which learners can not only develop academically, but also their personal and social skills. In order for these outcomes to be achieved, residential experiences need to be progressive. This is to say that such experiences should be planned on an ongoing basis throughout the school career of a child to ensure the knowledge, skills and understandings that have been developed can be built upon. In addition, teachers who design and facilitate such LOtC need to consider how to make meaningful links to other areas of the curriculum, engaging learners in this planning and ensuring that learning is reinforced and embedded following the experience.

KEY QUESTIONS

Have you ever participated in a residential experience while in school?

What memories do you have of it?

What do you think you learned as a result of the experience?

What impact did the experience have on your relationships with peers and/or staff?

PLANNING, FACILITATING AND ASSESSING LEARNING OUTSIDE THE CLASSROOM

All LOtC experiences need to be carefully planned, facilitated and assessed. When planning, teachers must consider issues such as the learning that is intended, how this fits within the curriculum, the budget for the activity, the risk assessments needed, and the school's policy on LOtC. When completing the planned experience, the leader also needs to ensure the potential for learning is maximised. This can be done through pre-visit work in the classroom as well as embedding the learning following the experience. Assessing and evaluating LOtC is more challenging than within the classroom as there is much more than just academic knowledge, skills and understanding to consider. Some of this assessment happens during the LOtC experience and some will be through reflections afterwards. This includes assessment as learning, assessment for learning and evaluation.

KEY INFORMATION

Department for Education (DfE) (2018) *Health and Safety on Educational Visits*. Available at: www.gov.uk/government/publications/health-and-safety-on-educational-visits/

This guidance from the DfE highlights the types of activities outside the classroom that require risk assessments and extra planning. This includes when to seek consent from parents, what questions to ask other organisations and what to do in an emergency outside the classroom.

TO CONCLUDE

In this chapter, we have seen the wide variety of opportunities and places for LOtC. The spectrum of LOtC experiences can range from within the school grounds, to the local neighbourhood, to day visits, all the way to residential experiences and expeditions. While careful consideration is required to plan meaningful and relevant experiences in any of these places, the benefits to learners are seen to be plentiful. These benefits can be seen through academic achievement as well as social and emotional skills. This is most effectively done when LOtC is incorporated progressively throughout a child's school career and an appreciation for LOtC is nurtured in all learners.

RESOURCES FOR FURTHER LEARNING

Council for Learning Outside the Classroom: **www.lotc.org.uk**

The Council for Learning Outside the Classroom is a registered charity existing to champion learning outside the classroom (LOtC). Their website provides a range of documents, case studies and creative ideas for working outside of the classroom.

Forest School Association: **www.forestschoolassociation.org**

The Forest School Association is the professional body and UK-wide voice for Forest Schools, promoting best practice, cohesion and 'quality Forest School for all'. Their website provides advice for professionals, a comprehensive reading list and information about the history of Forest Schools.

Grigg, R. and Lewis, H. (2016) *A–Z of Learning Outside the Classroom*. London: Bloomsbury.

This book explores an A to Z of places for LOtC. Guidance for teachers is provided for each location, including links to numeracy and literacy, suggested activities, and ways to effectively prepare learners prior to the visit.

Waite, S. (2017) *Children Learning Outside the Classroom: From Birth to Eleven*. London: SAGE.

Sue Waite's book considers the how, why and what of outdoor learning to help students understand the importance of learning beyond the classroom. The companion website contains useful annotated reading lists, links to additional readings and weblinks to a variety of resources. This is especially useful if you are completing an assignment focusing on how to creatively incorporate outdoor activities in the primary curriculum.

REFERENCES

Arts Council England (2016) *Now and the Future: A Review of Formal Learning in Museums*. Available at: www.artscouncil.org.uk/sites/default/files/download-file/Now_and_the_future_formal_learning_in_museums_NOV2016.pdf

Beames, S., Higgins, P. and Nicol, R. (2012) *Learning Outside the Classroom: Theory and Guidelines for Practice*. London: Routledge.

Bentley, T. (1998) *Learning Beyond the Classroom: Education for a Changing World*. London: Routledge.

Coffield, F. (2000) *The Necessity of Informal Learning*. Bristol: Policy Press.

Connell, R.W., Ashenden, D., Kessler, S. and Dowsett, G. (1982) *Making the Difference: Schools, Families and Social Division*. Sydney: Allen & Unwin.

Council for Learning Outside the Classroom (2019) *About LOtC*. Available at: www.lotc.org.uk

Department for Education (DfE) (2017) *Statutory Framework for the Early Years Foundation Stage*. London: Crown.

Department for Education (DfE) (2018) *Health and Safety on Educational Visits*. Available at: www.gov.uk/government/publications/health-and-safety-on-educational-visits/

Department for Education and Skills (DfES) (2006) *Learning Outside the Classroom Manifesto*. London: Crown.

Dyson, A., Gallannaugh, F. and Kerr, K. (2011) *Conceptualising School–Community Relations in Disadvantaged Areas*. London: Arts and Humanities Research Council, Connected Communities.

Eshach, E. (2007) Bridging in-school and out-of-school learning: formal, non-formal, and informal education. *Journal of Science Education and Technology*, 16(2): 171–90.

Gerber, B.L., Marek, E.A. and Cavallo, A.M.L. (2001) Development of an informal learning opportunities essay. *International Journal of Science Education*, 23(6): 569–83.

Gilbert, J. and Priest, M. (1997) Models and discourse: a primary school science class visit to a museum. *Science Education*, 81(6): 749–62.

Green, L. (2017) *Music, Informal Learning and the School: A New Classroom Pedagogy*. London: Routledge.

Greenhow, C. and Lewin, C. (2016) Social media and education: reconceptualizing the boundaries of formal and informal learning. *Learning, Media and Technology*, 41(1): 6–30.

Grigg, R. and Lewis, H. (2016) *A–Z of Learning Outside the Classroom*. London: Bloomsbury.

Guisasola, J., Morentin, M. and Zuza, K. (2005) School visits to science museums and learning sciences: a complex relationship. *Physics Education*, 40(6): 544–9.

Hamlyn, P. (2015) *Evaluation of Learning Away: Final Report*. Leeds: York Consulting.

Higgins, S., Katsipataki, M., Kokotsaki, D., Coe, R., Major, L.E. and Coleman, R. (2013) *The Sutton Trust-Education Endowment Foundation Teaching and Learning Toolkit: Technical Appendices*. London: Education Endowment Foundation.

Hirch, D. (2007) *Experiences of Poverty and Educational Disadvantage: Reviewing the Evidence*. Leeds: Joseph Rowntree Foundation.

HM Government (2011) *The Natural Choice: Securing the Value of Nature*. Natural Environment White Paper, HM Government CM8082.

Institute for Outdoor Learning (2019) *What Is Outdoor Learning?* Available at: www.outdoor-learning.org

Jensen, N. (1994) Children's perceptions of their museum experiences: a contextual perspective. *Children's Environments*, 11(4): 300–24.

Knight, S. (2013) *Forest School and Outdoor Learning in the Early Years*. London: SAGE.

Malone, K. (2008) *Every Experience Matters: An Evidence Based Research Report on the Role of Learning Outside the Classroom for Children's Whole Development from Birth to Eighteen Years*. Report commissioned by Farming and Countryside Education for UK Department Children, School and Families, University of Wollongong, Australia.

Melaville, A., Berg, A.C. and Blank, M.J. (2006) *Community-Based Learning: Engaging Students for Success and Citizenship*. Washington, DC: Coalition for Community Schools.

O'Brien, R. (2011) *Citizen Power in Peterborough One Year On*. London: Royal Society of Arts.

Ofsted (2008) *Learning Outside the Classroom: How Far Should You Go?* London: Crown.

Price, S. and Hein, G.E. (1991) More than a field trip: science programmes for elementary school groups at museums. *International Journal of Science Education*, 13(5): 505–19.

Royal Society for the Encouragement of Arts, Manufactures and Commerce (RSA) (2012) *Citizen Power*. Available at: www.thersa.org/projects/citizen-power/civic-commons

Waite, S. (2017) *Children Learning Outside the Classroom: From Birth to Eleven*. London: SAGE.

Waite, S. and Pratt, N. (2011) Theoretical perspectives on learning outside the classroom: relationships between learning and place. In S. Waite (ed.), *Children Learning Outside the Classroom: From Birth to Eleven*. London: Sage, pp1–18.

Watson, S., Dodd, J. and Jones, C. (2007) *Engage, Learn, Achieve: The Impact of Museum Visits on the Attainment of Secondary Pupils in the East of England 2006–2007*. Leicester: Research Centre for Museums and Galleries, University of Leicester, Museum Libraries Archives East of England, Renaissance East of England.

Wellings, E. (2012) *Forest School National Governing Body Business Plan 2012*. Available at: www.outdoor-learning.org

Williams, R. (2013) Woven into the fabric of experience: residential adventure education and complexity. *Journal of Adventure Education and Outdoor Learning*, 13(2): 107–24.

11

WHY DO SOME CHILDREN IN THE UK DO BETTER AT SCHOOL THAN OTHERS?

JAYSHREE PATEL

KEY WORDS

- INTELLIGENCE
- MERITOCRACY
- SOCIAL CLASS
- SOCIAL MOBILITY
- EQUALITY OF OPPORTUNITY
- CULTURAL CAPITAL

KEY NOTES

- The UK has the highest social gap for educational achievement in the developed world.
- The impact of social class remains the strongest predictor of educational achievement in the UK.
- Sociologists reject the idea that intelligence cannot be improved upon.
- Family and cultural issues impact educational achievement.
- Schools with similar intakes can have different outcomes for pupils.
- The relationship between ethnicity and achievement is complex but is strongly related to class.
- All 'disadvantaged' ethnic minority groups achieve greater success than 'disadvantaged' white British pupils.

INTRODUCTION

One of the most enduring debates within education is, quite simply, why do some pupils do better than others? Richer children outperform their less-wealthy counterparts. Girls have outperformed boys for a number of years, at every age phase. There are some very wide gaps between different ethnic groups, while the performance of white working-class children has – despite some improvement – pretty much remained static.

Exploring this, sociologists of education began by focusing on the point of education, its purpose and values. The thinking then moved on to examining why children from middle-class backgrounds consistently outperformed their working-class counterparts. Could children from middle-class backgrounds simply be more intelligent and hard-working? Sociology, as a discipline, is rarely satisfied with simplistic explanations. So, when it comes to the underachievement of any group, where does the responsibility lie? Parents? Schools? Wider society? Or the child? Many sociologists argue that social class is the single most defining factor when it comes to our life chances, determining how many children we may choose to have, how many teeth we may be left with in our sixties, and whether we're brought up on a diet of either halloumi or string cheese.

This chapter examines the relationship between class, ethnicity and gender with educational achievement. We'll start by defining the concept of social class, then move on to exploring explanations for differential educational achievement. From early theories on intelligence, to the myth of meritocracy, we will critically explore some of the key arguments that have shaped debate for decades.

KEY QUESTIONS

The idea that everybody has an equal chance to succeed is referred to as a meritocracy. Do you think the UK is a meritocracy?

THE EDUCATION GAP IN THE UK

The UK has the highest social gap for educational achievement in the developed world (see **www.equalityhumanrights.com/en/britain-fairer**). The Equality and Human Rights Commission (EHRC) concluded in 2010 that the impact of social class remains the strongest predictor of educational achievement in the UK. Think about that. The second you are born, we can predict how well you will probably do at school. This is astounding. And it is echoed by the later report in 2018, which indicated that poverty continues to have a huge impact on educational achievement (EHRC, 2018).

The
Education Gap
in the UK

The UK has the highest social
gap for educational achievement
in the developed world.

(Source: www.equalityhumanrights.com/en/britain-fairer).

The Equality and Human Rights Commission (EHRC)
concluded in 2010 that the impact of social class remains the
strongest predictor of educational achievement in the UK.

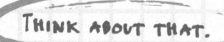

THINK ABOUT THAT.

THE SECOND YOU ARE BORN, WE
CAN PREDICT HOW WELL YOU WILL
PROBABLY DO AT SCHOOL.

★ THIS IS ASTOUNDING. ★

KEY INFORMATION

Equality and Human Rights Commission (EHRC) (2018) *Is Britain Fairer? The State of Equality and Human Rights 2018*. Available at: www.equalityhumanrights.com/en/publication-download/britain-fairer-2018

How can we start unpicking these findings? In order for us to understand education as a whole, and ultimately become better practitioners, it's essential for us to uncover some of the reasons behind the education gap.

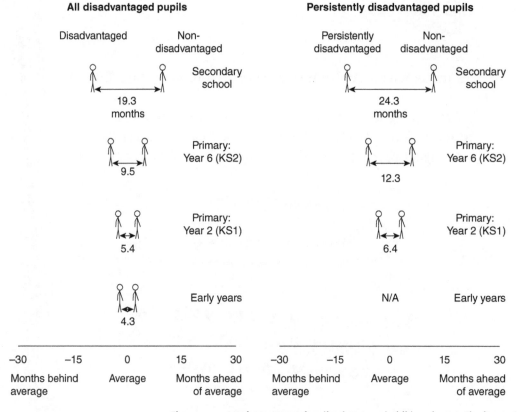

Figure 11.1 Attainment gap for disadvantaged children in months in 2016

Source: https://epi.org.uk/wp-content/uploads/2017/08/Closing-the-Gap_EPI-.pdf

Note: Disadvantaged pupils are those who are in receipt of free school meals (disadvantaged includes CLA children and children of the armed forces). Persistently disadvantaged pupils are those who have been in receipt of free school meals for more than 80 per cent of their school life.

Figure 11.1 demonstrates that the attainment gap gets wider as children progress up the system. The 'All disadvantaged pupils' part of the graphic shows that the gap (in months) is 4.3 in the early years, rising to 19.3 at secondary school. By the time children leave secondary school, there is a more than two years' difference between persistently disadvantaged pupils and non-disadvantaged pupils (the non-disadvantaged group is represented on the graphic at the 'Average' point on the *x*-axis). Or, put another way, a non-disadvantaged pupil in Year 9 can outperform a persistently disadvantaged pupil in Year 11.

The question of why this happens has perplexed academics, practitioners, school leaders and the government.

KEY INFORMATION

https://epi.org.uk/wp-content/uploads/2017/08/Closing-the-Gap_EPI-.pdf

This report from the Education Policy Institute (EPI) looks at the educational achievement gaps between children from disadvantaged backgrounds and their peers. It is a long report but useful reading. Published in 2017, it helps you to get a detailed picture of the current situation.

HOW CAN WE START TO EXPLAIN WHY SOME PUPILS OUTPERFORM OTHERS?

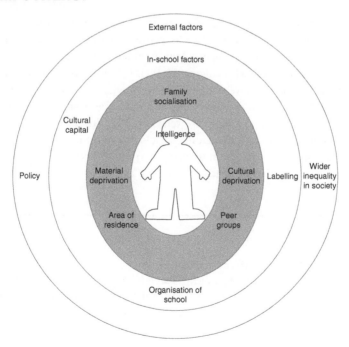

Figure 11.2 What makes us who we are?

Figure 11.2 demonstrates how we might start to think about explanations for differential educational attainment according to social class, ethnicity or gender. We can start with explanations that focus on the individual, moving on to the family, then school, and finally wider societal factors. This model opens up a complex debate about what contributory factors are there when it comes to underachievement.

The intelligence debate

The idea of meritocracy is that everyone has an equal chance to succeed. In the UK we are all entitled to a free education, so if there are differences in outcome, some would suggest that they can only be put down to the individual. Are some individuals more intelligent than others?

KEY QUESTIONS

What is intelligence?

How do we measure it?

Intelligence is often defined as a person's capacity to learn rather than a measure of what they already know. Therefore, it is important to recognise that knowledge doesn't equate to intelligence, more our ability to acquire it, understand it and perhaps retain it. IQ tests were designed to take the guesswork out of assessing abilities. Although much maligned for their cultural bias (Klineberg, 1935), IQ tests are an impressively accurate predictor of levels of performance. Children from poorer backgrounds tend to have lower IQ scores and then go on to achieve less well than their wealthier counterparts. This does not mean intelligence is predetermined, nor can we assume that we can't improve our own levels of intelligence or that of children we want to educate. Sociologists reject the idea that intelligence cannot be improved upon. Countless studies on nature versus nurture indicate that our upbringing is much more likely to dictate our levels of intelligence.

KEY INFORMATION

See **www.simplypsychology.org/naturevsnurture.html** for examples suggesting that our primary socialisation (the process by which children learn the norms and values of society, usually in the family home) is a major factor in determining how well we do at school.

Furthermore, sociologists are particularly cautious when using genetic and biological theories as these standpoints have been used to justify the ideology of oppressive regimes, such as Nazi Germany, apartheid in South Africa and racial segregation in the US. The idea that there is a biological justification for inequality is certainly not dead. Saunders (2012) suggests that children from wealthier backgrounds inherit intelligence from their parents, thus suggesting that limited social mobility among the working classes is inevitable.

KEY QUESTIONS

How might educationalists refute the idea that some groups of people are 'simply more talented than others'?

Cultural deprivation theory

How might family and cultural issues impact educational achievement? Some academics argue that primary socialisation may impact attitudes towards education, and therefore school performance – middle-class children are brought up with a particular set of norms and values, which subsequently allow them to outperform their working-class counterparts. In particular, it is suggested that middle-class households are generally more supportive of education. Hartas (2015) suggests that parental influence is a determining factor:

> *Although good school systems make a difference, the biggest influence on educational attainment is family background, so disadvantaged children do less well at school and miss out on the benefits of education.*

KEY QUESTIONS

How do positive attitudes towards education manifest themselves through parenting?

Table 11.1 highlights some of these different norms and the theorists that explore them.

Table 11.1 *The attainment gap*

Classic theoretical stances		
Working-class characteristics	**Middle-class characteristics**	**Theorist**
Immediate gratification (wanting your rewards immediately)	Deferred gratification (waiting for your rewards)	Sugarman (1970)
Restricted code (context-bound language, use of simple sentences and narrow vocabulary)	Elaborated code (non-context-bound language, use of more complex language)	Bernstein (1964)
Lack of interest in education	Keen interest in education	Douglas (1964)
Unable to help with homework	Have the knowledge, skills and confidence to help with homework	Leibowitz (1977)
Fatalistic (belief that life is predetermined, people are powerless to change things)	Optimistic (hopeful and confident about the future)	Sugarman (1970)
Dependent	Independent	Murray (1990)

Cycle of poverty

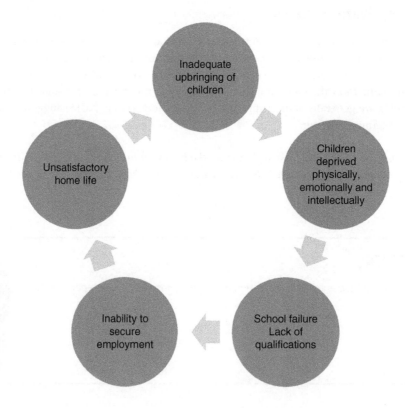

Figure 11.3

By pointing to the transmission of particular values, these classic arguments seem to blame the working class for their own underachievement. Murray (1990) argues that the 'underclass' have become dependent on benefits, and as a result have no incentive to either work or take control over their own lives.

Cultural capital and habitus

Bourdieu (1973) suggests that groups at the top of the hierarchy possess the skills, knowledge, norms and values to 'get ahead'. Those at the very top are also in possession of social capital; the old adage 'It's not *what* you know, it's *who* you know' describes this well. In contrast to cycle of poverty arguments, this concept draws attention to the view that one form of knowledge or culture is not inferior to another. Consider these quiz questions:

- Who composed the opera *The Marriage of Figaro*? / Who sang the lyrics 'In a street brawl, I strike men quicker than lightning'?

- When did *Death of a Salesman* first open in the UK? / Name four men Mercedes McQueen has had a relationship with in the past three years.

Bordieu's concept of habitus describes how upbringing defines you. This is often seen as the physical embodiment of cultural capital – the skills, knowledge, experiences. It is suggested that the middle and upper classes decide which forms of knowledge or culture are considered worthy, giving their children an unfair advantage within the education system. In order for working-class children to succeed in school, they need to adopt middle-class habitus. Even more controversial is the suggestion that in order for black children to succeed, they need to 'act white'.

Material deprivation theory

Material deprivation is the idea that some people in society are unable to afford the basic resources or have access to services that allow them to maintain a life that is custom in any particular society.

KEY QUESTIONS

How might poverty impact educational performance?

In some ways, material deprivation theory covers similar themes to the cycle of poverty. However, the focus of 'blame' is not on the working class or the 'underclass'.

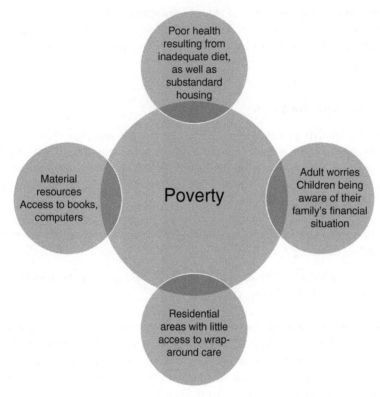

Figure 11.4 Poverty and educational performance

In-school factors

From Matilda's Miss Honey to Lisa Simpson's Mr Bergstrom, the idea that teachers can make a huge difference to the lives of children remains a rather romantic notion. In reality, we need to consider whether teachers and schools, as a whole, can break the cycle of deprivation and make a genuine difference to the lives of children. Or, in fact, is the opposite true, and schools and teachers merely reinforce class inequalities through processes such as labelling? This labelling can be based on class, gender or ethnicity.

Are working-class and disadvantaged pupils seen as being inferior to their wealthier counterparts? As suggested above, being working-class is often associated with *lacking* something:

> *Middle-class parents very often have respect for teachers ... in a way that working-class parents will not.*

> (Teacher)

Whereas being middle-class is often associated with the possession of a *more positive attitude* to education:

Middle-class students on the whole value ideas as they have been taught to do so before they even reach the school gates.

(Trainee teacher)

(Dunne and Gazeley, 2008)

KEY QUESTIONS

Do teachers label children from different class groups?

Some studies suggest that working-class parents are just as interested in their children's education as middle-class parents are. However, a number of contributing factors may ensure the reproduction of inequalities (see Table 11.2).

Table 11.2 Explanations for differential educational attainment

Middle-class parents	Working-class parents
Likely to be proactive in addressing concerns and are able to use their knowledge of the education system to their advantage.	Likely to be as focused on the advantages of a 'good' education as middle-class parents.
Likely to make active choices when selecting a school and to be influenced by league tables and Ofsted reports.	Less likely to have knowledge and experience of the education system to use to their advantage. Unable to relocate to catchment areas of 'better' schools.
Likely to be viewed as an equal when talking with teachers and other professionals and to make effective challenges to practice.	Less likely to be viewed as an equal partner when dealing with professionals and teachers.
For a further account of these issues, see Gewirtz (2001).	For more on this, see Todd and Higgins (1998).

In 1966, Coleman's 'Equality of Educational Opportunity' report came to the conclusion that schools made little difference when it came to educational outcomes (Coleman, 1975). In his seminal text *Fifteen Thousand Hours*, so named after the number of hours the average child spends in school, Rutter (1979) presents a more optimistic view. He identified a number of factors that some schools possessed which allowed them to make a difference. His research into school effectiveness identified a number of schools who had more success than others with similar intakes. These schools shared certain characteristics with each other. These characteristics included good leadership that provides strategic vision, which is shared by all effective home–school partnerships. While some of Rutter's methodology was called into question, this study as well as a later one (Rutter and Maughan, 2002) partly established the idea that school ethos is a powerful force which is able to transform the lives of children.

CASE STUDY

KIPP Schools USA

The Knowledge Is Power Program (KIPP) has achieved an impressive set of results in some of its schools. The schools are based on a clear ethos of, 'work hard, be nice'. The mission for these schools is to get all pupils into higher education. Expectations are high; indeed, the phrase 'high expectations, no excuses' is proudly displayed in corridors. Around 95 per cent of KIPP schools are made up of 95 per cent African-American and Latino children from economically deprived backgrounds, and they are regularly outstripping their counterparts. For how these schools have made an impact on the educational outcomes of children, see: **www.kipp.org/schools/**

KEY QUESTIONS

Are there any ethical issues raised by the Knowledge Is Power Program for teachers or pupils?

Is the ethnic make-up of KIPP schools a significant factor in their success?

Wider societal factors

The gap between rich and poor in the UK is high (e.g. see **http://theconversation.com/inequality-of-education-in-the-uk-among-highest-of-rich-nations-105519**). Private schooling continues to exist, allowing advantage to be passed on. Successive governments have placed high expectations on schools to increase social mobility. The question posed by Wilkinson and Pickett (2009) is: How realistic is it to expect schools to compensate for the vast inequalities in society?

KEY QUESTIONS

Can schools really make up for these kinds of entrenched inequalities in society?

A focus on 'high standards' in education, as suggested by successive education secretaries, has meant that the 'blame' lies firmly at the door of educational establishments. While there are examples of schools and academies in the UK, particularly in London, that have succeeded despite the odds, they are few and far between. As Bangs et al. (2010) suggest, factors such as family, peer groups, area of residence, and most of all social class largely dictate how well a child will achieve in education.

DIFFERENTIATION ACCORDING TO ETHNICITY

Early studies of differential educational attainment were somewhat rudimentary in terms of methodology and analysis. Biological explanations have been long dismissed from British sociological thinking, but some American studies (Jensen, 1969; Pinker, 2005) still hold on to the idea that some ethnic groups are intellectually superior to others due to genetics. Here, we will focus largely on the influence of labelling, peer groups and culture as major contributors in the understanding of the different levels of attainment according to ethnicity, now and through recent history.

In 1985, the Swann Report found significant attainment differences between children of Afro-Caribbean origin and their white counterparts:

> *West Indian children as a group are underachieving in our education system ... [this] is a reinforcement of a stereotype that black people are academically challenged.*

> (Verma, 1985)

Explanations for these differences often focused on the concept of labelling. What is 'labelling'?

The term 'labelling' was popularised by Becker (1963). He suggested that the behaviour of human beings is influenced significantly by the way other members in society label them. Originally used to understand deviance, the concept is widely used in education to help explain how teacher expectations of pupils may impact actual performance.

KEY INFORMATION

Rosenthal, R. and Jacobson, L. (1968) *Pygmalion in the Classroom: Teacher Expectation and Pupils' Intellectual Development*. New York: Holt, Rinehart & Winston.

This classic study offers an understanding of how perceptions can lead to labelling, which in turn leads to self-fulfilling prophecy.

In a damning criticism of the British education system, Coard (1971) insisted that the curriculum reflected 'whiteness' as the norm and failed black pupils by ignoring their histories and accomplishments in literature and music. This compounded the idea that black pupils experienced exclusion from the education system. The issue of race in the classroom was a clear focus for researchers in the 1980s. Stone (1981) suggested that this exclusion led these pupils to feelings of hostility towards their teachers. Indeed, in a later study, Green (1991) found that teachers had lower academic expectations of black Afro-Caribbean pupils. This lowered levels of self-esteem as these boys felt they were not receiving the same levels of encouragement. Tomlinson (2005) suggested that teachers often stereotyped these children as being 'slow learners' as well as being poorly behaved. These arguments helped to raise the profile of the issue of racism in schools, both in the form of overt racism from pupils and covert from staff; however, some of these works did not fully recognise the intricacies of the whole picture.

More recent data presents a much more complex picture regarding the relationship between ethnicity and achievement. Part of this is due to the fact that the categorisation of ethnic groups is more specific and therefore more useful than it was in the past. For example, the term 'Asian' included pupils from India, Pakistan and Bangladesh. Their performance level averaged out as being similar to that of white pupils. However, if we separate these groups, huge differences in levels of achievement are apparent. Figure 11.5 demonstrates this. It traces GCSE achievement levels of nine different ethnic groups. The threshold is five GCSEs A*–C, including English and maths. A grade C is roughly equivalent to a current grade 4.

Identified trends

All ethnic groups have improved, but the rise was particularly steep from 2006 to 2011:

- There is a significant gap between Chinese and Indian pupils and all other ethnic groups.

- Black African students have shown substantial increases in their educational achievement.

- Bangladeshi pupils have shown the highest levels of improvement.

- There has been a significant closing of the gap for black Caribbean, mixed white and black Caribbean, and Pakistani students.

- Only one ethnic group has seen performance decline relative to white British over the period – white other groups (predominantly from Europe, including Polish, Turkish and Portuguese).

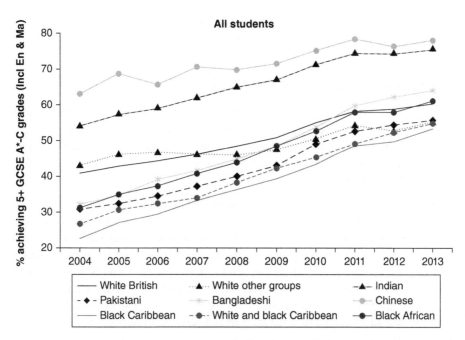

Figure 11.5 Percentage of all students achieving 5EM by ethnic group, 2004–2013

Source: https://assets.publishing.service.gov.uk/government/uploads/system/uploads/attachment_data/file/439867/RR439B-
Ethnic_minorities_and_attainment_the_effects_of_poverty_annex.pdf.pdf

How do we go about trying to analyse this sort of data? More importantly, how can we focus on concepts such as culture without falling into stereotypical assumptions about the home lives of children?

KEY QUESTIONS

Why are levels of achievement among Chinese and Indian pupils so high?

Why have the achievement levels of Bangladeshi pupils increased so significantly?

Why is there such a significant difference between black Caribbean pupils and black African pupils?

Culture is linked to material factors. It's important to recognise at this stage that differences in achievement between Chinese, Indian and black African pupils compared to black Caribbean, Bangladeshi and Pakistani pupils have been put down to social class. With separate waves of immigration, we found that most Bangladeshi families, for example, were migrant labourers, whereas most Indians were professionals who had been expelled from North Africa in the 1960s and 1970s. Class seemed to be the logical explanation until poor children from Bangladeshi backgrounds started to do well in terms of educational attainment; therefore, things couldn't be put down to class alone.

Cultural and in-school factors revisited

While much academic space has been given to problematising the issue of race and achievement, little time has been given to aiming to understand why British Chinese and British Indian pupils do so well at school. Political discourse has largely focused on how achievement levels could be raised among some ethnic groups. As Chinese and Indian pupils don't seem to be presenting a problem for society, key issues or even learning points have been ignored.

Stand-up comedians of Indian origin often focus on the difference between Indian and Western discipline. The idea that Indian children have strict upbringings is something that goes beyond comedy. Much has been attributed to the idea that parents from Indian and Chinese backgrounds value education highly, but comparatively little research has been done in this area. This is particularly the case with British Chinese parents and children. Archer and Frances (2005) suggest that seemingly positive stereotypes of these pupils can be damaging. Teachers often view Chinese pupils as being well behaved. Gillborn and Mirza (2000) suggests that it's crucial to avoid stereotypical perceptions that 'some groups are naturally talented in some areas or inherently culturally disposed to learning whilst others are not' (p56).

Similarly, when it is implied that Chinese and Indian parents are supportive of education, is there a suggestion that other ethnic groups are not? Tizard et al. (1982) argue that black parents do support the educational needs of their children through reading at home and other behaviours. This suggests that black Caribbean parents want their children to do well, but they do not see school as a supportive environment for their children. Gillborn and Mirza (2000) found that in some local education authorities, black children were the highest achievers upon entry to primary school, but year on year their performance dwindled, resulting in their marks being 21 points below the average. In a later study, Strand (2010) supports this finding by stating that more able black pupils from more economically successful backgrounds in the end made less progress then their white peers. This leads us to a strong suggestion that schools are failing to deal with the destructive influences of labelling, racism and misinterpretation of culture. There have been similar findings in the US. Interestingly, an evaluation of KIPP schools' success stories suggests that when black children are equally invested in, they get to where they should be.

Undoubtedly, prejudice and discrimination in school is damaging for all concerned. And yet in isolation from wider societal factors, it can only explain so much. As Sewell (1997) suggested, there are a multitude of other factors that need to be considered. These may include negative media representations that emphasise sporting prowess, natural rhythm or criminality. We could also consider anti-school masculine culture as well as the absence of male role models at school and home. There's further complexity in that some aspects of culture may be wrongly misinterpreted as anti-school. My own experience as an assistant head teacher illustrates this point. During the 1990s, black boys often got 'tracks' in their hair. This was interpreted as part of an anti-school subculture, and subsequently these pupils were asked to shave off the offending lines. Conversely, white middle-class boys who grew their hair were afforded the luxury of 'self-expression'. This sort of basic unfairness, arguably a form of institutional racism, may well help to explain the huge disparity in exclusion rates. Much attention has been devoted to the levels of underachievement of black Caribbean boys; however, an examination of data based on gender provides some interesting reading.

ETHNICITY AND GENDER

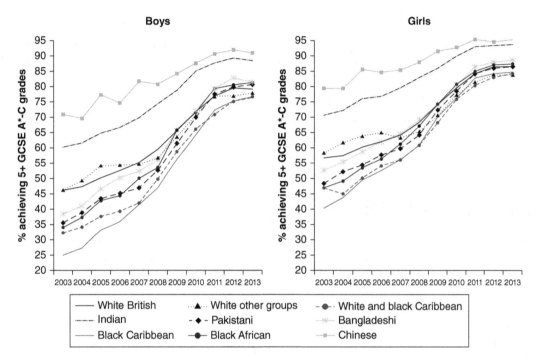

Figure 11.6 Educational performance according to gender

Girls outperform boys at every level in education. In every ethnic group, girls outperform boys. This is particularly the case when it comes to black Caribbean girls. Research has tended to focus on boys rather than girls. Early studies from the likes of Moynihan (1965) popularised the idea that the lack of male role models in the home has an impact, although this argument doesn't help to explain why black children have such high reading ages on entry to school and it's only subsequently they underachieve. Nevertheless, later studies make similar claims. Sewell (1997) suggests that the lack of male role models starts to present a problem during adolescence. When male role models in the home or school don't exist, some black boys may look elsewhere. Elsewhere could be the media, which often presents a very narrow form of black masculinity, or even street gangs that offer an alternative narrative to the conformist culture demanded at school. Thus, peer influence demands a rejection of these 'white' values and instead offers 'loyalty and love' through a different means. A sense of belonging is important to humans. If there is no sense of this in the school, then arguably it's a natural reaction for boys to seek validation and gain status in an alternative structure. In contrast, Driver and Ballard (1981) suggest that family structure provides girls with an extremely positive role model. A working woman, single-handedly bringing up her children, the image of black women in the media, and particularly music, also present this picture of the strong independent woman.

Family structure aside, there is a suggestion that black female peer groups perform an entirely different role to male groups. Fuller (1984) suggests that Afro-Caribbean girls feel the same level of discrimination, and as a result are hardly pro-school; however, their responses are different. Fuller describes how instead of accepting negative stereotypes of themselves, the girls channelled their anger about being labelled into the pursuit of educational success. They refused to seek approval from teachers, but instead worked independently, supporting each other. Unlike many high achievers, they did not seek company with other (white) high achievers, and instead maintained strong friendships with black girls from lower sets. The role of peer group here is an interesting one, a suggestion that these girls had more faith in each other than their white teachers. This also challenges the common notion that labelling automatically leads to self-fulfilling prophecy.

Thus far, it is clear that we cannot understand ethnicity and achievement in isolation. It has to be understood in terms of gender too as experiences are so radically different. Indeed, when compared, ethnicity gaps are not as great as gender ones.

ETHNICITY AND SOCIAL CLASS

Figure 11.7 brings social class into this – already complex – equation. It shows the percentage of free school meals (FSM) pupils gaining 5A*–C, including English and maths, according to ethnicity.

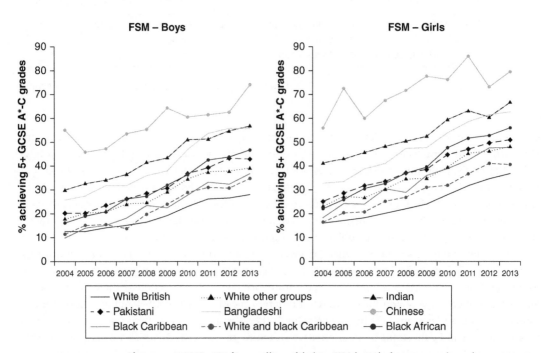

Figure 11.7 GCSE 5EM for pupils entitled to FSM by ethnic group and gender, 2004–2013

The most defining point is that *all* FSM ethnic minority groups achieve greater success than FSM white British pupils. The suggestion here is that poverty seems to impact white British children (particularly boys) more than any other ethnic group. Uncovering why this is seems to throw up more questions than it answers. McCulloch (2014) suggested that poor ethnic minority pupils are more likely to aspire to go to university, as much a result of parental aspirations as their own. Education was seen as the way to climb the social ladder. Conversely, teachers saw poor white parents as having a negative attitude towards education (Lupton, 2004).

CASE STUDY

London

London has a particularly high concentration of non-white communities. It's interesting to note that London also has the best results in the country. While I'm not suggesting there is causality here, it is a situation that is worth researching. London schools get more funding per pupil, but costs, including teacher pay, are higher. It could be suggested that with the lure of living in the capital, London attracts more high-quality teachers. Like the KIPP schools in the US, children in London schools sharing the same characteristics as ethnic groups elsewhere do much better. The ethnic make-up in London has changed dramatically in recent years. Some local authorities are 90 per cent non-white, and these are the schools that black children do well in. This has led to some suggesting that black boys in particular should be taught in the same school. There is a similar argument with girls in that females that go to all-girl schools tend to perform better than those attending co-ed schools.

KEY QUESTIONS

Why do you think black boys in particular perform better in 'black' schools?

What can we learn from girls doing better in single-sex schools?

Would you support the idea of dividing schools up along race lines?

WHITE WORKING-CLASS BOYS

Research suggests that when ethnic minority children are invested in, they perform well. However, the group that remains a challenge is white working-class boys. This group has been ignored and marginalised more than any other. To focus on ethnic minority underachievement was seen as a priority, even though the class gap is far greater than ethnicity. As we have already established, ethnic minorities are still technically divided by class, but characteristics – and in particular aspirations – are still largely shared. This is not the case for majority white people. The division between the rich white and the poor white is astounding (see **https://epi.org.uk/wp-content/uploads/2017/08/Closing-the-Gap_EPI-.pdf**). White working-class males have become a marginalised ethnic minority (Jones, 2011), and indeed that's how they see themselves. Ironically, this group, thanks to media manipulation, tend to blame those who share most in common with them – immigrants. The educational success of immigrants and their children has compounded the view that white lower-class men are excluded from education as much as they are excluded from society.

TO CONCLUDE

In this chapter, we have seen that the educational attainment of pupils is not particularly dependent on intelligence or hard work. Social class, gender and ethnicity all have a huge impact on educational outcomes. Explanations for these differences are wide-ranging and complex. We have noted that these theoretical stances start with the individual and then move towards societal issues. For example, our work on poverty demonstrates that cultural explanations are linked to wider societal factors and cannot be understood in isolation. The study of ethnicity and attainment seemingly poses more questions than it answers. A cursory glance may suggest that the impact of social class is greater than ethnicity; however, evidence suggests that poverty seems to have much more of an impact on white pupils than any other ethnic group. The reasons for this seem to hark to cultural explanations, but there is something deeply unsatisfactory about returning to this sort of explanation. When gender is thrown into the mix and we start to compare why girls do better than boys in every category and subgroup (a dynamic that shows no indication of changing), it is obvious that the whole area of differential educational attainment is as complex as it is fascinating. Successive governments, nationally and internationally, have tried to narrow the achievement gap. While there have been some notable successes, overall it remains the case that our educational attainment, and ultimately our wealth, income, health and life chances, are largely set at birth. The job of the educator is to try to break this correlation.

REFERENCES

Archer, L. and Francis, B. (2005) Constructions of racism by British Chinese pupils and parents. *Race, Ethnicity and Education*, 8(4): 387–407.

Bangs, J., Macbeath, J. and Galton, M. (2010) *Reinventing Schools, Reforming Teaching: From Political Vision to Classroom Reality*. London: Routledge.

Becker, H. (1963) *Outsiders: Studies in the Sociology of Deviance*. Oxford: Free Press.

Bernstein, B (1964) Elaborated and restricted codes: their social origins and some consequences. *American Anthropologist*, 66(6): 55–69.

Bourdieu, P. (1973) Cultural reproduction and social reproduction. In R.K. Brown (ed.), *Knowledge, Education and Cultural Change*. London: Tavistock, pp71–84.

Coard, B. (1971) Making black children subnormal in Britain. *Equity & Excellence in Education*, 9(5): 49–52.

Coleman, J. (1975) Equal educational opportunity: a definition. *Oxford Review of Education*, 1(1): 25–9.

Douglas, J. (1964) *The Home and the School*. London: MacGibbon & Kee.

Driver, G. and Ballard, R. (1981) Comparing performances in multi-racial schools: South Asian pupils at 16-plus. In A. James and A. Jeffcoate (eds), *The School in a Multi-Cultural Society*. Open University Press.

Dunne, M. and Gazeley, L. (2008) Teachers, social class and underachievement. *British Journal of Sociology of Education*, 29(5): 451–63.

Equality and Human Rights Commission (EHRC) (2018) *Is Britain Fairer? The State of Equality and Human Rights 2018*. Available at: www.equalityhumanrights.com/en/publication-download/britain-fairer-2018

Fuller, M. (1984) Black girls in a London comprehensive school. In R. Deem (ed.), *Schooling for Women's Work*. London: Routledge, pp52–66.

Gewirtz, S. (2001) Cloning the Blairs: New Labour's programme for the re-socialization of working-class parents. *Journal of Education Policy*, 16(4): 365–78.

Gillborn, D. and Mirza, H.S. (2000) *Educational Inequality: Mapping Race, Class and Gender – A Synthesis of Research Evidence*. London: Office for Standards in Education.

Green, A. (1991) *The Peculiarities of English Education*. London: Unwin.

Hartas, D. (2015) Parenting for social mobility? Home learning, parental warmth, class and educational outcomes. *Journal of Education Policy*, 30(1): 21–38.

Jensen, A. (1969) How much can we boost IQ and scholastic achievement? *Harvard Educational Review*, 39(1): 1–123.

Jones, O. (2011) *Chavs: The Demonization of the Working Class*. London: Verso.

Klineberg, O. (1935) *Race Differences*. New York: Harper & Brothers.

Leibowitz, A. (1977) Parental inputs and children's achievement. *Journal of Human Resources*, 12(2): 242–51.

Lupton, R. (2004) *Schools in Disadvantaged Areas: Recognising Context and Raising Quality*. London: Centre for Analysis of Social Exclusion, London School of Economics and Political Science.

McCulloch, A. (2014) Regional differences in university admissions in England. *Graduate Market Trends*, Winter 2013/14: 4–7.

Moynihan, D. (1965) *The Negro Family: The Case for National Action by United States Department of Labor*. Washington, DC: United States Department of Labor.

Murray, C. (1990) *The Emerging British Underclass*. London: Institute of Economic Affairs.

Pinker, S. (2005) So how does the mind work? *Mind and Language*, 20(1): 1–24.

Rosenthal, R. and Jacobson, L. (1968) *Pygmalion in the Classroom: Teacher Expectation and Pupils' Intellectual Development*. New York: Holt, Rinehart & Winston.

Rutter, M. (1979) *Fifteen Thousand Hours: Secondary Schools and Their Effects on Children*. Cambridge, MA: Harvard University Press.

Rutter, M. and Maughan, B. (2002) School effectiveness findings 1979–2002. *Journal of School Psychology*, 40(6): 451–75.

Saunders, P. (2012) *Social Mobility Delusions*. London: Civitas.

Sewell, T. (1997) *Black Masculinities and Schooling: How Black Boys Survive Modern Schooling*. Stoke-on-Trent: Trentham Books.

Stone, M. (1981) *The Education of the Black Child in Britain: The Myth of Multiracial Education*. London: Collins Fontana.

Strand, S. (2010) The limits of social class in explaining ethnic gaps in educational attainment. *British Educational Research Journal*, 37(2): 197–229.

Sugarman, B. (1970) The cloistered elite. *Sociology*, 4(3): 434.

Tizard, J., Schofield, W.N. and Hewison, J. (1982) Collaboration between teachers and parents in assisting children's reading. *British Journal of Educational Psychology*, 52(1): 1–15.

Todd, E. and Higgins, S. (1998) Powerlessness in professional and parent partnerships. *British Journal of Sociology of Education*, 19(2): 227–36.

Tomlinson, S. (2005) *Education in a Post-Welfare Society*, 2nd edn. London: Routledge.

Verma, G. (1985) The Swann Report and ethnic achievement: a comment. *New Community*, 12(3): 470–5.

Wilkinson, R. and Pickett, K. (2009) The spirit level: why more equal societies almost always do better. *Leadership and Policy in Schools*, 11(1): 129–34.

WEBSITES

www.historylearningsite.co.uk/sociology/education-and-sociology/bernard-coard/

An easily accessible overview of Coad and his life and work.

https://epi.org.uk/wp-content/uploads/2017/08/Closing-the-Gap_EPI-.pdf

A 2017 paper from the Education Policy Institute on 'closing the gap'.

www.equalityhumanrights.com/en/publication-download/britain-fairer-2018

A comprehensive review of how Britain is performing on equality and human rights, dated 2018.

www.equalitytrust.org.uk

The Equality Trust analyses and disseminates the latest research, promotes robust evidence-based arguments, and supports a dynamic network of campaign groups across the country.

www.educationnext.org/moynihan-and-the-single-parent-family/

An interesting article about the Moynihan Report and single-parent families.

https://assets.publishing.service.gov.uk/government/uploads/system/uploads/attachment_data/file/439867/RR439B-Ethnic_minorities_and_attainment_the_effects_of_poverty_annex.pdf.pdf

Data about ethnicity, deprivation and educational achievement at age 16 in England – trends over time.

www.simplypsychology.org/naturevsnurture.html

An introduction to the nature versus nurture debate, considering the extent to which particular aspects of behaviour are a product of either inherited (i.e. genetic) or acquired (i.e. learned) influences.

www.educationengland.org.uk/documents/swann/swann1985.html

The Swann Report, *Education for All: The Report of the Committee of Enquiry into the Education of Children from Ethnic Minority Groups*.

www.theguardian.com/news/2018/mar/02/the-unwelcome-revival-of-race-science

An interesting article on race science from *The Guardian*.

12

HOW CAN WE PROVIDE CHILDREN WITH SPECIAL EDUCATIONAL NEEDS WITH A QUALITY LEARNING EXPERIENCE?

JONATHAN GLAZZARD AND SAMUEL STONES

KEY WORDS

- **SPECIAL EDUCATIONAL NEEDS**
- **DISABILITY**
- **INCLUSION**
- **INTEGRATION**
- **EXCLUSION**

KEY NOTES

- Definitions help identify children who are likely to have special educational needs and disabilities, but teachers are not qualified to diagnose conditions.
- Children with SEND do not necessarily have low levels of ability.
- 'Integration' and 'inclusion' are often used interchangeably, but they are quite different concepts.
- The medical model of disability has traditionally dominated special educational needs.

INTRODUCTION

In this chapter, we will explore how to provide learners with special educational needs with a quality learning experience. We will focus on the example of children as learners for this chapter, allowing us to look in depth at the special educational needs of this group. We will begin by asking what is meant by special educational needs and will go on to find out more about strategies for ensuring that learners with special educational needs are provided with a quality learning experience.

WHAT DO WE MEAN BY SPECIAL EDUCATIONAL NEEDS?

The code of practice for special educational needs and disabilities (SEND) is a statutory document that outlines the roles and responsibilities of schools and local authorities for meeting children's special educational needs. It states:

> A child or young person has SEN if they have a learning difficulty or disability which calls for special educational provision to be made for him or her.
> A child of compulsory school age or a young person has a learning difficulty or disability if he or she:
>
> * has a significantly greater difficulty in learning than the majority of others of the same age, or
> * has a disability which prevents or hinders him or her from making use of facilities of a kind generally provided for others of the same age in mainstream schools or mainstream post-16 institutions.

(DfE and DoH, 2015, pp15–16)

These definitions help identify children who are likely to have special educational needs and disabilities, although teachers are not qualified to diagnose conditions. It is important to remember that children with SEND do not necessarily have low levels of ability. Often it is assumed that these children are less able, and they are placed in groups with other children who are operating at lower stages of cognition. While some children with SEND do have learning and cognition needs, others have very specific sensory, physical, communication or learning needs, and they can be operating at higher levels of cognitive development.

KEY QUESTIONS

What are the issues associated with the use of the word 'special' in the label 'SEND'?

THE CATEGORIES OF NEED

There are four broad areas of need identified in the code of practice. These are:

1. communication and interaction needs;

2. cognition and learning needs;

3. social, emotional and mental health needs; and

4. sensory and physical needs.

KEY QUESTIONS

What are the problems with linking mental health needs to social and emotional needs?

KEY INFORMATION

Department for Education (DfE) (2014) *The Equality Act 2010 and Schools: Departmental Advice for School Leaders, School Staff, Governing Bodies and Local Authorities.* London: DfE.

The Equality Act 2010 identifies disability as a protected characteristic. This makes it unlawful for schools to discriminate against children with disabilities in their admissions arrangements and in teaching, learning and assessment policies and processes.

Communication and interaction needs

Children with communication and interaction needs may have speech, language or communication needs. These words are often used interchangeably but are different skills. Children with speech difficulties may have difficulties with pronunciation of sounds and words (e.g. those who stammer may struggle with speech production). Children with language difficulties may not have speech production difficulties but they may struggle with generating sentences that make sense. Communication involves more than speech and language. In fact, children can communicate in the absence of speech through sign language and through pressing switches, using visual symbols or pointing to make choices.

Communication is the interaction that occurs between two or more people. It involves various skills, including eye contact, turn-taking, taking pauses in conversation, and building on what another person has said. Some children may struggle to understand these 'rules' of communication, and although their speech and language skills may be secure, their communication skills may be lacking. Children may have deficits in only one area (i.e. either speech, language or communication) or they may have weaknesses in more than one area.

Children with autistic spectrum conditions experience difficulties with social communication. While some may have deficits in speech and language (e.g. those with classic autism), many children with high-functioning autism (e.g. Asperger's syndrome) have well-developed speech and language skills. The core deficit in all children with autistic spectrum conditions is social communication. They struggle to understand the rules of social communication and find skills such as maintaining eye contact or turn-taking extremely difficult.

KEY QUESTIONS

Should children with autism be included in mainstream schools? What might be the advantages and disadvantages of doing this?

Cognition and learning needs

Children with cognition and learning needs learn at a slower pace than their peers of the same age. They may have moderate learning difficulties (MLD), severe learning difficulties (SLD), where they need support in all areas of the curriculum, or profound and multiple learning difficulties (PMLD), where they have severe, multiple and complex learning needs. They may also have specific learning difficulties (SpLD), where their difficulties lie in one or more areas of the curriculum (e.g. dyslexia).

KEY QUESTIONS

Should children with MLD, SLD and PMLD be included in mainstream schools? Why or why not? Think about the impact that being in a mainstream school might have on children with learning difficulties, and then think about the impact of having children with learning difficulties in a class of children who mostly do not have learning difficulties.

Social, emotional and mental health needs

The introduction of 'mental health' within a category of need was new in the 2015 code of practice. Children can have mental health needs without social and emotional needs. However, some children experience social, emotional and mental health needs (SEMH). Children with SEMH may demonstrate challenging behaviour and they find it difficult to self-regulate their emotions. They may demonstrate a range of mental health needs, including anxiety, depression, self-harm, eating disorders, conduct disorders and substance abuse. This is not an exhaustive list.

KEY QUESTIONS

Should teachers be expected to support children's social, emotional and mental health needs?

What factors do you think might have an effect on children's mental health?

KEY INFORMATION

Department for Education (DfE) (2018a) *Mental Health and Behaviour in Schools.* London: DfE.

Department for Education (DfE) (2018b) *Mental Health and Wellbeing Provision in Schools: Review of Published Policies and Information.* London: DfE.

These documents will provide you with useful guidance on children's mental health needs. You can search for the documents on the internet.

Sensory and physical needs

Sensory needs include hearing impairment, visual impairment and multisensory impairment. Physical impairments can arise from a range of conditions. These needs can fluctuate over time, and children with sensory or physical needs often require the support of the health service to meet their needs.

KEY QUESTIONS

How can children with these needs be successfully included in physical education lessons? What might be the challenges in doing this? Can children with physical and sensory needs be included in every sort of physical education lesson?

INTEGRATION VERSUS INCLUSION

The terms 'integration' and 'inclusion' are often used interchangeably, but they are quite different concepts. Integration was common practice in the 1980s and involved children with SEND being placed within mainstream schools, often without appropriate provision and support to meet these needs. The practice of integration evolved from the Warnock Report (DES, 1978), which removed the term 'handicap' and replaced it with 'special educational needs'. Mary Warnock, the author of the report, advocated that children with special needs should, where possible, be integrated into mainstream schools, with financial aid to support the most vulnerable. This became known as the 'statement' of special educational needs, which was reserved only for those with the most severe needs. Following the publication of the Warnock Report, the recommendations of this report were made statutory in the Education Act 1981, and the practice of integration subsequently evolved.

The problem with integration is that it was largely a 'dump and hope' model. Children with special educational needs were placed in mainstream schools without any adaptations to the physical environment, curriculum or teaching. The child was expected to adapt to an unchanged system of education, rather than the education system adapting to meet the needs of the child.

Inclusion developed as a policy agenda in the 1990s to replace integration. In contrast, inclusion is a proactive response on the part of schools to meet children's special educational needs. It involves adapting the school policies, physical environment, curriculum, teaching and assessment processes to respond to children's needs. Inclusion places an onus on the school to adapt to meet the needs of the child, rather than the child adapting to meet the needs of the school.

KEY QUESTIONS

Do you think the national curriculum meets the needs of all learners? What kinds of learners may not be having their needs met by the national curriculum? In what ways might the national curriculum not be meeting the needs of every learner?

To what extent do you think that assessment processes in schools meet the needs of all learners?

To what extent do the curriculum and assessment processes in education promote exclusion rather than inclusion? What might we be able to do about this?

WHAT ARE TEACHERS' RESPONSIBILITIES?

The code of practice is clear that teachers are responsible for teaching children with special educational needs and meeting their needs. Children with special educational needs are often taught by teaching assistants (TAs) rather than teachers (Sharples et al., 2015), and too frequently they are subjected to low teacher expectations. They are placed in low-ability groups and the responsibility for their education is left to someone who is unqualified to teach. This results in children with SEND making less progress than their peers and developing dependency on the teaching assistant (Sharples et al., 2015).

Teachers must plan for all children. They are accountable for the progress and attainment of children with SEND. They should demonstrate high expectations of all the children they teach and ensure that they plan tasks which are sufficiently challenging for them. Children with SEND should not automatically be asked to complete easier tasks than their peers. This is because this widens the ability gap rather than closing it. Sometimes it will be necessary for children with SEND to work on separate learning objectives, and therefore to be assigned different tasks to those of their peers. However, this should be the exception, not the norm. Rather than automatically planning different learning objectives and different activities for learners with SEND, teachers should consider carefully how children with SEND might be able to access the same task as their peers by:

- providing them with additional adult support during the time they are working on the task;

- structuring the task carefully into a series of smaller, achievable steps;

- providing additional responses to enable them to complete the task;

- pre-teaching the knowledge, skills and concepts to these children before the lesson so that they are able to make greater progress during the lesson;

- providing frequent opportunities to revisit the learning so that they develop mastery;

- using effective modelling during the activity so that children understand what they need to do; and

- providing alternative ways for children to record their learning other than through writing (particularly if they have dyslexia).

Teachers should ask 'How can I structure or modify this task so that this group can achieve the same learning outcomes as their peers?' rather than 'How can I change the task for this group of children?'

> ## KEY QUESTIONS
>
> What are the effects of low teacher expectations on children with SEND? Are the effects on children with SEND more serious than the effects of low expectations on children who do not have SEND?

RESEARCH

Research has found:

- The typical deployment and use of TAs, under everyday conditions, is not leading to improvements in academic outcomes.

- There is mixed evidence to support the view that TA support has a positive impact on 'soft' outcomes. Some evidence suggests that TA support may increase dependency.

- Support from TAs tends to be more focused on task completion and less concerned with developing understanding.

- TAs are not adequately prepared for their role in classrooms and have little time for liaison with teachers.

(Sharples et al., 2015)

The research makes several recommendations to improve the deployment of teaching assistants in schools. According to the research, teachers should:

- not use TAs as an informal teaching resource for low-attaining pupils;

- use TAs to add value to what teachers do, not replace them;

- use TAs to help pupils develop independent learning skills and manage their own learning;

- ensure that TAs are fully prepared for their role in the classroom;

- use TAs to deliver high-quality one-to-one and small group support using structured interventions;

- adopt evidence-based interventions to support TAs in their small group and one-to-one instruction; and

- ensure explicit connections are made between learning from everyday classroom teaching structured interventions.

(Sharples et al., 2015)

Teachers therefore need to ensure that the teaching assistant is not always working with children with special educational needs. All children deserve to be taught by a teacher. One way that teachers can achieve this is to consider assigning TAs to support other groups while they work with children with SEND. The research highlights that TAs typically focus on asking children to complete tasks rather than on developing their independent learning skills. The research suggests that TAs have more impact on children's learning when they are trained to deliver evidence-based interventions with children that focus on developing specific skills. Careful monitoring of the progress that children are making in these interventions is essential to ensure that they can build on the skills they are learning through interventions. This will provide good reinforcement of the skills and help children to recognise that the learning they are undertaking outside of classrooms is related to what they are learning in lessons. Interventions outside of classrooms should be short, sharp and snappy so that children do not miss out on the learning in the classroom. Children learn more when they learn in the classroom with their peers.

KEY QUESTIONS

How can teachers cater for children's special educational needs at the same time as meeting the needs of all pupils?

Do children with special educational needs need a different kind of teaching to their peers?

THE GRADUATED APPROACH

Children who are identified as having SEND move onto a process known as *SEN support*. This means that teachers must follow a graduated approach to meet their needs. The graduated approach has four stages:

1. Assess: assess the child's current achievement and identify their next steps in learning.

2. Plan: plan how their needs will be best met.

3. Do: implement evidence-based interventions to meet their needs.

4. Review: evaluate the impact of the intervention on children's learning.

The graduated approach is best represented as a cycle (see Figure 12.1).

Figure 12.1 The graduated approach

WORKING IN PARTNERSHIP WITH PUPILS AND PARENTS

The code of practice emphasises the importance of working in partnership with children and parents to more effectively meet the needs of pupils with SEND. Often schools and teachers listen to the perspectives of external professionals without first asking the child for their perspectives on what might help them to learn more effectively. The following questions are useful prompts to explore the child's perspectives:

- What do you enjoy learning at school?

- What are you good at?

- What do you find difficult?

- What do you want to get better at?

- What do you think we can do to help you learn better?

- What do you think we can do to help you improve your behaviour/mental health?

- What would you like to get better at by next week/next term?

Parents have a unique knowledge of their child and are usually well placed to inform how you might support their child. The following questions might be useful to think about:

- What does your child enjoy doing outside of school?

- What are they good at?

- What do they find difficult?

- How do you think we can best support your child in school?

- How do you manage your child's behaviour at home? Is this working?

Working in partnership to meet the child's needs extends beyond these discussions. Children and parents should be given opportunities to contribute to identifying learning goals or targets and they should be asked to contribute to reviewing their child's progress during SEND review meetings. It is critical that they feel they are partners within this process, and all decisions that are taken should be made in conjunction with parents and, where possible, with children.

KEY QUESTIONS

The code of practice emphasises the importance of child voice but provides no guidance on how teachers can elicit the perspectives of children who do not have verbal communication. How can teachers give these children a voice?

The code of practice emphasises the need for schools to develop partnerships with parents, but some parents are reluctant to participate. How can schools develop productive partnerships with reluctant parents?

Why might some parents be reluctant to participate in decision-making processes?

THEORY

The medical model of disability has traditionally dominated special educational needs. It is a model that views disability as a personal tragedy and something which is located within the body. It assumes that individuals need to receive treatment or intervention to minimise the effects of the disability on the person's life.

In contrast, the social model of disability assumes that disability is socially constructed, and therefore results from the failure of society to make appropriate adjustments so that individuals with impairments can have equality of opportunity. The social model of disability distinguishes between 'impairment' and 'disability':

- Impairment is something within the body that limits typical functioning.

- Disability is defined as access to goods and services (including education).

The assumption of the social model is that although an individual may have an impairment, the impairment does not need to disable the individual from accessing goods and services, provided that society makes appropriate adjustments to facilitate access and participation. Examples of the social model 'in action' are presented below:

- A child has a physical impairment but is able to access the school building and classes through the provision of ramps and a lift. The child is able to access the service of education and is therefore not disabled from learning.

- A child has dyslexia (an impairment within brain functioning) but is able to learn to read due to a structured multisensory phonological awareness programme. This means that the child is not disadvantaged.

- A child has a hearing impairment but is able to enjoy full hearing as a result of a hearing aid. This enables them to learn effectively in school.

- A child has attention deficit hyperactivity disorder (ADHD). Their learning is adapted by organising tasks into shorter timed tasks within lessons. The teacher develops positive relationships with the child and teaching assistant support is deployed to keep the child focused. This combination of adaptations enables the child to reach their full educational potential.

- A child with autism struggles to understand other people's emotions as a result of lacking a theory of mind. A curriculum intervention is implemented that develops the child's emotional literacy and teaches the skills of emotional regulation. This enables the child to more effectively regulate their own emotions.

Figure 12.2 illustrates the range of adaptations that schools can use to prevent children from experiencing disability.

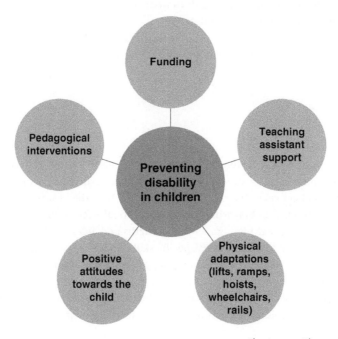

Figure 12.2 The social model in schools

189

The affirmative model of disability is an extension of the social model of disability. It provides a positive affirmation of disability by rejecting the assumption that disability is a negative aspect of someone's identity. The affirmative model was developed by disabled people and aims to create a proud disabled identity. It rejects the idea that disability should be removed from people's lives and it views disability as a positive rather than a negative aspect of a person's identity.

KEY QUESTIONS

What do you think are some of the limitations of the social model of disability?

STRATEGIES TO SUPPORT CHILDREN WITH SPECIAL EDUCATIONAL NEEDS

Evidence-based approaches

The teaching and learning toolkit from the Sutton Trust (**https://educationendowmentfoundation. org.uk/evidence-summaries/teaching-learning-toolkit**) demonstrates that the following strategies are effective in supporting pupil progress:

- developing metacognitive strategies and self-regulation skills;

- feedback;

- mastery learning; and

- peer tutoring.

Strategies that are less successful include teaching assistant intervention, the use of learning styles to support learning, and setting or streaming. Metacognition involves developing children's awareness of how they learn effectively. Once children understand how they learn, they can take increased ownership of their learning. Children with special educational needs will benefit from very specific feedback about their learning that highlights their strengths and areas for development. It is better to provide very focused feedback that addresses a specific skill rather than providing generic feedback that addresses several areas for development. Providing opportunities for children with special educational needs to learn from other peers through peer tutoring schemes has been proven to be highly effective. Mastery learning involves developing children's abilities to approach solving problems in different ways. In mastery learning, children are not accelerated on to the next stage of learning too quickly.

Mastery learning provides opportunities to consolidate and reinforce the learning by applying their understanding of the content in different ways.

Pre-teaching

Some children with special educational needs benefit from pre-teaching the key lesson content prior to a lesson. This provides an ideal opportunity for pupils to learn about, develop and understand:

- subject-specific vocabulary;

- subject-specific knowledge;

- subject-specific skills; and

- subject-specific texts that will be used in the lesson.

Pre-teaching this content enables these pupils to make greater progress during the lesson. Normally, pre-teaching inputs are relatively short. The purpose of these sessions is for pupils to master the essential subject content rather than go through the whole lesson prior to the lesson.

Multisensory

Multisensory approaches to learning provide opportunities for children to learn the lesson content using their senses (touch, smell, sight, sound and taste). The senses are used to reinforce the learning in different ways. For example, in a phonics lesson, the lesson plan could be developed to address the following senses:

- *Sight*: the children are introduced to the grapheme, which is visually represented.

- *Sound*: the children are introduced to the corresponding phoneme.

- *Touch*: the children trace the grapheme on the floor, in the air, on their hand, on their partner's back, in the sand or in a tray of glitter.

This example illustrates how the senses can be integrated into lesson planning to provide rich opportunities to consolidate the learning. This principle can be applied to other subjects.

Multisensory approaches can also be adopted when planning topics or themes. Take the topic of the Second World War. Rather than planning the topic through subject links, the topic can be planned through the senses. An example of multisensory planning is shown in Figure 12.3. This plan has been started for you, but it is not complete. Perhaps you could complete it?

Using resources

Children with SEND sometimes benefit from the use of concrete resources in lessons. Examples might include number lines, hundred squares, multiplication squares, vocabulary mats, formulae, definitions of subject-specific terms, sentence starters, spellcheckers and cubes.

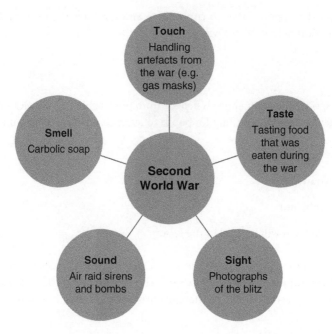

Figure 12.3 Multisensory planning

Graphic organisers

Graphic organisers can help children to capture their ideas and they are particularly useful to help children structure their writing. An example of a graphic organiser that could be used when planning a story is shown in Figure 12.4, in the form of a story mountain, but the principle of using graphic organisers can be used in a range of subjects.

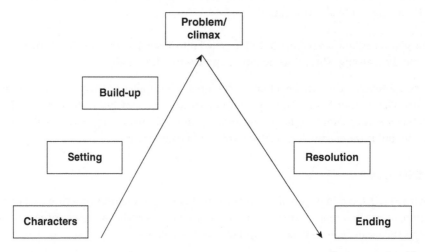

Figure 12.4 Graphic organisers

Now and next boards

Now and next boards are useful for children who require a sense of routine and need to know what is coming next. An example is shown in Figure 12.5.

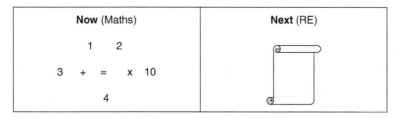

Figure 12.5 Now and next boards

Solution-focused approaches to behaviour

Solution-focused approaches to behaviour management are tools to build a positive sense of self within children and to set small, achievable goals rather than focusing on the consequences of poor behaviour. Using a range of questioning techniques, they attempt to build within the child a positive view of themselves. Techniques include:

- Complimenting. For example: 'I noticed in that lesson that you persevered with that question even though you found it difficult.'

- Exception finding. For example: 'Tell me about a time when you were a good team member.' (This is a good one if the child does not normally work well as part of a team. It is about focusing on exceptions to the usual behaviour.)

- Scaling. For example: 'On a scale of 1 to 10 (1 being very poor and 10 being excellent), how would you rate your behaviour? OK, so it is a 2. What are you doing to score a 2 because that is better than a 1? What score would you like to aim for if we repeated this is a few weeks' time? How would your behaviour be different then?'

Mindfulness

Mindfulness is an approach that supports children to enjoy being 'within the moment' by blocking out of their minds what has happened in the past and what might happen in the future. It facilitates them to enjoy being 'within the present' and it can be a useful relaxation tool for children who experience anxiety. There are various ways of implementing this approach, including:

- asking children to close their eyes or lie down and listen to calm, relaxing music;

- focusing their attention on glitter in a tube falling down through thick, clear liquid;

- focusing their attention on their breathing;

- focusing their attention on the taste and texture of an item of food (mindful eating); and

- talking them through an imaginary, calm, peaceful experience.

KEY QUESTIONS

Have you ever used any mindfulness techniques?

Do you think that mindfulness can divert children's attention away from adverse child-hood experiences? Why or why not?

CASE STUDY

Strategies to support children with autism

Sarah was a trainee primary teacher placed in a Year 2 class. During her placement, a child with a diagnosis of autism joined the class. His name was Jack. Sarah discussed with her mentor how she might address Jack's needs. They decided to speak to the parent about his needs and the parent felt strongly that Jack required a visual timetable so that he understood clearly the structure of the day. Sarah decided to implement a whole-class visual timetable rather than giving Jack a separate timetable. She created a timetable using pictures to denote the lessons. These were attached to the timetable using a Velcro strip so that the pictures could be removed as soon as the lesson had been taught. The timetable provided a clear structure and routine to each day. Sarah researched autism and discovered that visual approaches to teaching tended to be effective for children with autism. Following her research, she started to use photographs, objects, diagrams and other visual modes of representation in her teaching. Sarah noticed that all children benefited from this strategy.

Sarah noticed that Jack became distressed when he was asked to participate in an unfamiliar activity. She decided to use the technique of social stories to help prepare Jack for undertaking these experiences. In one physical education lesson, Sarah had planned for the children to use large equipment for the first time. The equipment included benches, beams, mats, trestles and ropes. This was the first time the class had used large apparatus. Sarah decided to construct a social story. Jack was named as a character in the story and the story was developed to capture Jack's experiences and feelings of using large equipment. Sarah read the story to Jack prior to the lesson. The story included photographs of the equipment in the hall. Key vocabulary (beam, mat, bench, rope swing) was emphasised next to the photographs. This helped to prepare Jack for an unfamiliar situation.

> ### KEY QUESTIONS
>
> What are the advantages and disadvantages of the approaches that Sarah uses with Jack?

TO CONCLUDE

This chapter has emphasised:

- the need for teachers to have high expectations of children with SEND;

- the importance of effectively deploying teaching assistants to maximise their impact on children with SEND;

- the implications of the models of disability for teachers; and

- strategies to support children with SEND in schools.

RESOURCES FOR FURTHER LEARNING

Glazzard, J. and Netherwood, A. (2019) *Teaching and Supporting Children with Special Educational Needs and Disabilities in Primary Schools*. London: SAGE.

This book provides a useful overview of the code of practice and practical strategies for addressing the main needs that you will be required to address.

Heaven, B. (2012) *The Mental Health Handbook for Primary School: Raising Awareness of Mental Health Issues and How to Deal with Them*. London: Routledge.

This book provides a useful overview of the common mental health needs that you might encounter in primary schools and strategies for addressing these.

REFERENCES

Department for Education (DfE) (2014) *The Equality Act 2010 and Schools: Departmental Advice for School Leaders, School Staff, Governing Bodies and Local Authorities*. London: DfE.

Department for Education (DfE) (2018a) *Mental Health and Behaviour in Schools*. London: DfE.

Department for Education (DfE) (2018b) *Mental Health and Wellbeing Provision in Schools: Review of Published Policies and Information.* London: DfE.

Department for Education (DfE) and Department of Health (DoH) (2015) *Special Educational Needs and Disability Code of Practice: 0 to 25 years Statutory Guidance for Organisations Which Work with and Support Children and Young People Who Have Special Educational Needs or Disabilities.* London: DfE and DoH.

Department of Education and Science (DES) (1978) *Special Educational Needs: Report of the Committee of Enquiry into the Education of Handicapped Children and Young People (The Warnock Report).* London: HMSO.

Glazzard, J. and Netherwood, A. (2019) *Teaching and Supporting Children with Special Educational Needs and Disabilities in Primary Schools.* London: SAGE.

Heaven, B. (2012) *The Mental Health Handbook for Primary School: Raising Awareness of Mental Health Issues and How to Deal with Them.* London: Routledge.

Sharples, J., Webster, R. and Blatchford, P. (2015) *Making the Best Use of Teaching Assistants: Guidance Report.* London: Education Endowment Foundation.

13

TEACHER IDENTITY, TEACHING AND PEDAGOGICAL APPROACHES

RACHEL STENHOUSE

KEY WORDS

- IDENTITY
- PEDAGOGY
- TEACHER-CENTRED PEDAGOGY

- STUDENT-CENTRED PEDAGOGY
- BLOOM'S TAXONOMY
- MASTERY

- QUESTIONING
- REFLECTION
- DIALOGIC
- LEARNING STYLES

KEY NOTES

- Teaching involves many things in addition to standing in front of a class.
- Teacher identity develops over time and is influenced by key others.
- Pedagogical approaches to teaching include behaviourism, constructivism and social constructivism.
- Student-centred pedagogies include co-constructed learning, dialogic pedagogies and inquiry-based learning.
- Teachers may develop their teaching by conducting research-informed teaching and team teaching.
- New ideas come and go in education. It is important to critically evaluate where a new idea has come from and if the research behind it is robust.

INTRODUCTION

This chapter begins by considering teachers as professionals. It looks at the importance of teacher identity in teaching. The chapter then goes on to consider some of the different approaches to teaching, or what we call 'pedagogies'. Each teacher may have a preferred pedagogical practice, and different pedagogies will be better suited to different age groups and the subject being taught. As you read this chapter, consider how each pedagogical practice might impact learning in the classroom.

TEACHERS

KEY QUESTIONS

What is involved in being a teacher?

Which of a teacher's activities directly impact learning either in a positive or a negative way? In what ways does the activity impact learning?

What do teachers do?

You would be forgiven for thinking that a teacher spends the majority of their working time in the classroom teaching. Yet there are many other elements that make up a teacher's workload. These include planning, marking, meetings, liaising with parents (emails, phone calls, parents' evenings), running extracurricular activities, spending extra time with struggling students, and so on.

CASE STUDY

Typical day of a secondary school teacher

Solomon is a secondary teacher in a state school. He has been teaching for over ten years. This is his typical day.

07:45 Arrive at school. Check emails. Look through timetable for the day to check over what I am doing for the day.

07:55 Marking. Creating more resources for the day, usually creating questions/activities for independent work.

08:30 Form group. This session usually revolves around admin: taking the register, notices, and other administrative tasks.

08:45 Lesson. Teaching.

09:45 Lesson. Teaching.

10:45 Break time. Spend between 5 and 15 minutes helping students from previous lesson. Grab a drink to avoid dehydration.

11:05 Lesson. Teaching A level. Although planned, A level lessons require a lot of responding and adjusting in the moment to meet the needs of the students; therefore, they require a lot of energy.

13:05 Lunchtime. Spend first 10 minutes with students. Spend a further 15 minutes dealing with admin.

13:50 Form time. Usually involves a PSHE-based activity. Resources provided by another member of staff, and vary in quality, so requires thinking on the spot as no time to plan for this session.

14:10 I might be lucky enough to have a free lesson. This is used for email management, marking, chasing students, dealing with detentions and parental contact.

15:10 End of the school day. Once a week, I run an after-school club for one hour. Once a week, there will be a department or pastoral meeting, varying in length from one to two hours. Otherwise, I am marking, supervising detentions or creating resources.

16:30 Go home.

19:00–21:00 Marking or creating resources.

Teaching is not a nine-to-five job. Managing workload can be an issue for many teachers as more and more demands are placed upon those in the profession. This case study shows how Solomon has to find time outside of lessons to plan, prepare and carry out other tasks required of a teacher.

KEY INFORMATION

To get a better understanding of some of the issues teachers face with workload, read the reports produced by teaching union NASUWT: **www.nasuwt.org.uk/ advice/conditions-of-service/workload.html**

Teacher identity

KEY QUESTIONS

What is meant by teacher identity?

How might teacher identity develop?

Everyone has one, or usually more than one, identity. A person might have an identity as a parent and another identity as a professional in the workplace. However, these identities feed into each other and are intertwined. A person's identity is shaped by their experiences and the people around them.

Every teacher has a teacher identity and a style of teaching that they have developed. Teacher identity is often fluid and changes over time. A trainee teacher will have a teacher identity that they are striving towards. This is based on their other identities (friend, student, colleague, relation, etc.) and their ideas of what a teacher should be. The trainee teacher will develop their teacher identity during their training and beyond. Even established teachers find that their teacher identity is still evolving (e.g. as they take on different roles in schools and develop their understandings of themselves and of the process and systems of education).

How does teacher identity develop?

Initially, teacher identity is based on a teacher's, or trainee teacher's, ideal of what makes the perfect teacher. This in turn will be based on their experiences of education: as a student, as an observer, as a parent, as a professional in another field. Everyone has an experience of being taught, or what we call an 'apprenticeship in the classroom'. They will have had positive and negative experiences. These experiences form the initial basis of what, in their opinion, a teacher should be, and hence form the basis of their teacher identity. This initial identity is then built on, developed or changed as a result of initial teacher education. During initial teacher education, trainee teachers are exposed to different styles of teaching through their training provider, their school mentor and the teachers they work with. These will all inform the teacher identity that a trainee teacher is forming. Through classroom practice, a trainee teacher tries out their emerging teacher identity and moulds it. They will also start to appreciate that their ideal teacher identity is not achievable and make compromises about the teacher identity they will take on.

TEACHING

KEY QUESTIONS

How do teachers develop their pedagogy? In answering this, consider when and where teachers develop their pedagogy.

From whom do teachers develop their pedagogy, and why?

Teaching involves a teacher and a learner. Many things will affect how subject matter is taught, including the age of the learner, the classroom and environment, the subject being taught, and so on.

Teachers will have a pedagogical approach based on their own experience of education. This will be built on during their initial teacher education. There will be a large input from subject mentors during teaching practice and university tutors during university-based sessions. As teachers progress through their careers, their teaching approach will only change if they have input from colleagues, engage in research, or engage in training that they then choose to act upon. Historically, a teacher's pedagogy would be based on their own experience of education and direct interaction with colleagues. As a result, longer-serving teachers tend to have a style of teaching that they stick to and do not often engage with 'new' methods of teaching. Some of these longer-serving teachers who have not engaged with research might tend to be resistant to change, with a view of 'if it isn't broke, don't fix it'. It is only recently, during the twentieth and twenty-first centuries, that trainee teachers have been actively encouraged to engage with research and to reflect on their teaching. This change in teacher education means that teachers new to the profession are more likely to engage in research about teaching and to experiment with different teaching approaches. As a result, their pedagogies are more likely to be informed by research and reflection, in addition to their colleagues. We are also seeing a wave of research-informed teaching in the twenty-first century, as teachers are being encouraged to take control of their profession.

An introduction to pedagogical approaches to teaching

KEY QUESTIONS

What are the main pedagogical approaches?

How do these relate to educational theories?

The main pedagogical approaches are behaviourism, constructivism and social constructivism. Refer to Chapter 8 to remind yourself of the theories relating to these approaches. The pedagogical approach a teacher takes will depend on what the teacher perceives their purpose to be. If a teacher sees their role as imparting knowledge, then they would be more likely to employ a behaviourist approach to teaching. However, if a teacher sees their role as guiding students' learning, then they would use a constructivist or social constructivist approach. A teacher might use a mix of approaches, or vary their approach based on the material they are teaching or the needs of a particular class.

Behaviourism

Learning is teacher-led, what we might refer to as 'chalk and talk', or historically a more traditional approach to teaching. The teacher is the knowledge provider in the lesson and the lesson is taught through direct instruction. The teacher lectures and models.

Constructivism

The student is at the centre of the learning. In the classroom, this might take the form of project work or inquiry-based learning. There would be less teacher talk than in a behaviourist approach.

Social constructivism

This is a mix of teacher-led and student-centred learning. In practice, you would see group work along-side teacher modelling.

KEY QUESTIONS

Think of your own experiences of learning (as a school student, as a university student, etc.). What pedagogical approaches were used? Reflect on how these supported or hindered your learning.

We now go on to look at some more specific pedagogies within these.

Student-centred pedagogies

KEY QUESTIONS

What student-centred pedagogies are there? How might these support learning?

What are the advantages and disadvantages of each approach?

How can research inform a teacher's pedagogical approach?

Co-constructed learning

Co-constructed learning (based on Vygotskian theory) (e.g. Vygotsky, 1978) is not only student-centred, but student-led. Students democratically decide on what topic they want to learn and might even plan out how they will learn it. In this pedagogy, students might research a topic and then present it to the rest of the class, sharing their learning with their peers.

Dialogic pedagogies

Dialogic pedagogies are based on ancient Greek philosophy (e.g. Socrates) and then on Bakhtin (1981) and Freire (1970). They emphasise the idea of an equitable relationship. They involve talk between teacher and student or student and student, as opposed to just the teacher talking at the students ('chalk and talk'). Different dialogic pedagogies will be useful at different points in a lesson. The initiation-feedback-response model is useful for ascertaining if a student knows a fact, whereas student–student dialogue can be used to develop ideas and understanding.

KEY QUESTIONS

How might dialogic pedagogies promote or hinder learning?

What might good dialogue look like?

Initiation-feedback-response

This idea draws on the work of Sinclair and Coulthard (1992). The teacher initiates a dialogue, often in the form of a question. A student then gives feedback in the form of an answer to the question. The cycle ends with the teacher responding to the student's answer, usually by confirming or correcting the answer given. The types of questions the teacher asks allow the students to respond in different ways. Types of questions are explored further in the key information box below. Initiation-feedback-response dialogue can take place as part of whole-class teaching or in one-to-one interaction between a teacher and a student.

Student–student dialogue

This is often seen when students work in pairs or small groups. Students are often more prepared to take risks when working in pairs or small groups than giving an answer in front of the whole class, so this type of dialogue can allow them to test their thinking with a peer. For this dialogue to be successful, students need the necessary skills to partake in rich dialogue. These skills include turn-taking, use of appropriate vocabulary, responding, and listening. A good dialogue between students will involve well-developed responses and students building on each other's ideas and arguments.

KEY INFORMATION

https://webarchive.nationalarchives.gov.uk/20090811091628/http://national-strategies.standards.dcsf.gov.uk/node/154685

This Department for Education publication gives guidance for developing questioning and dialogue in specific subjects.

There is a time and place for both teacher–student dialogue and student–student dialogue. The role of the teacher is to determine when each type of dialogue is appropriate and how long should be spent on each type of dialogue.

Inquiry-based learning

This approach has roots in constructivism; it is also called problem-based learning. A question or problem is posed, usually by the teacher (however, in a co-constructed learning environment, the problem would be posed by the students), and the students then conduct research that they think will help them to solve the problem. This is in contrast to a traditional approach, in which the teacher would present facts and then give the students questions to answer using these facts.

Research-informed teaching

As we see more schools being labelled 'research schools', we see teachers actively being asked to engage with research.

Teachers may engage in research through reading about effective practice and then trying it out in their own classroom. Alternatively, teachers might engage in action research; this involves teachers developing a strategy or classroom practice, trying it out in their own classrooms, reflecting on the results, and then adjusting their practice accordingly. Research-informed teaching should be a continuous cycle, as shown in Figure 13.1.

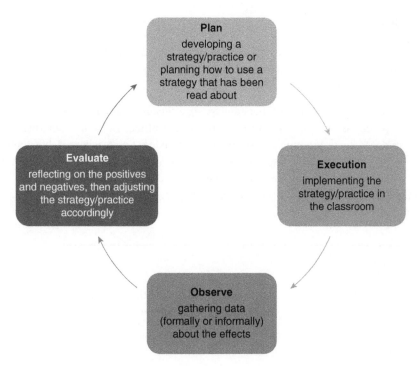

Figure 13.1 Example of a research cycle

This research cycle is often attributed to Lewin (1948), who suggested a spiralling process of planning, executing and fact-finding.

By engaging in research and trying out practices in their classroom, teachers are able to adjust practices accordingly to fit their students and school context. In theory, this should empower teachers to adapt pedagogies that are being pushed by the government rather than having new ways of teaching forced upon them.

KEY INFORMATION

**https://assets.publishing.service.gov.uk/government/uploads/system/uploads/attachment_
data/file/625007/Evidence-informed_teaching_-_an_evaluation_of_progress_in_
England.pdf**

This document reports on a study, commissioned by the Department for Education, to analyse the progress that schools had made developing research-informed practice. It considers the factors that influence teachers' engagement with research. It will help you to understand the complexities of developing teachers and schools into research-informed parties.

Team teaching

Team teaching is predominantly seen during initial teacher education, but opportunities for team teaching for experienced teachers can be valuable. There are a number of different ways of 'team teaching', as discussed by Friend and Cook (1996).

Team teaching means two or more teachers delivering a lesson. It provides an opportunity for professional development as the teachers can learn from each other. It can also demonstrate effective teamwork to students. Team teaching can simply be turn-taking: one teacher teaches the first part of the lesson, with the other teacher taking the next part, and so on. Team teaching is often most effective for teachers and students when the teachers chip in at different points in the lesson rather than waiting for their 'turn'. This prevents learning opportunities, for both the teachers and the students, from being missed.

STUDY SKILLS

As part of your course, you may spend time in a classroom, either observing or teaching. If this is not the case, consider a session you have as part of your university studies.

When you are observing a lesson, think about how the teacher uses pedagogical approaches to promote learning.

Use the following questions as prompts for your observation:

- What pedagogical approach, or approaches, is the teacher using?
- Why might the teacher have chosen to use a particular approach?

Reflect on this on your own to begin with and then ask the teacher what their rationale is.

Could the teacher have chosen to use a different approach? In your opinion, did the teacher use the right pedagogical approach? When answering this, consider the teacher, the learners, the subject matter and the learning environment.

Tools to support teaching

KEY QUESTIONS

What are the different types of questions a teacher might use?

Questioning is a key part of teaching. Questioning will be used differently in different pedagogies and at different times. Generally speaking, in a behaviourist approach, questioning would be used to determine if a student knows key facts, while in a constructivist approach questioning would be used to pose a problem and allow students to answer in a variety of ways.

Closed questions

These have a short, usually one-word, answer. A teacher uses these to ascertain if students can recall particular facts. For example: 'How many wives did Henry VIII have?'

Open questions

These questions allow for extended answers and often require more thought than closed questions. For example: 'How does a battery work?'

Diagnostic questions

These questions are used to identify students' mistakes or misconceptions and are often multiple-choice. Other than correct answers, each choice highlights a common mistake or misconception a student may have. Diagnostic questions may also be used at the start of a topic to determine what material needs to be covered. For example: 'What is {1/8} + {5/8}? A {6/16}, B {6/8}, C {5/8}, D {3/4}.'

Probing questions

A probing question allows a student to talk about their opinions and is intended to encourage a student to think critically. For example: 'Why do you agree with John's answer?'

Bloom's taxonomy of questioning (Bloom, 1968)

KEY QUESTIONS

How can Bloom's taxonomy help teachers develop their questioning?

Bloom's taxonomy was developed in the 1950s and 1960s by Benjamin Bloom and his colleagues. It is still widely used in education.

Bloom's taxonomy gives a comprehensive structure of different levels of questioning and is often represented as a pyramid (see Figure 13.2).

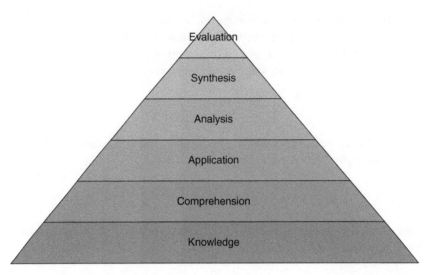

Figure 13.2 Bloom's taxonomy

The pyramid structure indicates that knowledge questions require lower-level thinking skills than understanding questions. The structure also indicates that knowledge is a prerequisite for understanding a subject matter (e.g. one cannot understand how a battery works without knowing what a battery is).

- *Knowledge*. These questions often take the form: Who? What? When? Where? Why? How? These are considered to be closed questions, which require a specific answer, and are used to elicit whether a student has knowledge of particular facts. For example: 'When was the Battle of Hastings?'

- *Comprehension*. These questions require students to explain an idea or concept in their own words, demonstrating understanding of a concept. For example: 'Can you explain the water cycle in your own words?'

- *Application*. These questions require students to apply their existing knowledge and skills to new situations. For example: 'What approach would you use to solve ...?'

- *Analysis*. These questions require a student to examine something in a critical way. For example: 'Why did the Second World War break out?'

- *Synthesis*. These questions require students to engage in original thinking. For example: 'What would the world be like if there was no gravitational force?'

- *Evaluation*. These questions require students to make a judgement about something. For example: 'Do you think communism is a good or a bad political system?'

Bloom's taxonomy suggests that there is a hierarchy of questioning, starting with facts at the base of the pyramid. However, in some pedagogies (e.g. inquiry-based learning), it might be more appropriate to start with the 'application' level of questioning.

REFLECTING ON PRACTICE

KEY QUESTIONS

What is meant by the discipline of noticing?

How can teachers use noticing and reflecting to improve their pedagogies?

Taking the time to reflect on practice allows a teacher to improve their practice. It can be difficult to become aware of things that are naturally in our unconscious. Longer-serving teachers could be described as unconsciously competent (i.e. they are able to teach well without really thinking about what they are doing). New teachers often strive towards this. However, to continue to develop as a teacher, it is helpful to be able to reflect on practice so that it can be improved. This requires teachers who are unconsciously competent to become conscious of what they are doing. We will look at two ways in which teachers might reflect on their practice.

Noticing in the classroom

Noticing as a discipline can be a useful tool for teachers to develop their classroom practice (Mason, 2002). John Mason developed the idea of noticing to be a discipline. Rather than just observing things around us, we begin to reflect on them (i.e. notice them). Noticing centres around a situation or incident. By noticing something, we give it attention. It can be difficult to notice things that are always around us or in our unconscious.

CASE STUDY

Noticing in a coffee shop

When we sit in a coffee shop with a friend, we rarely notice the passers-by as we are concentrating on the conversation. These passers-by are in our unconscious; we know they are there, but we are not consciously thinking about them. However, if we 'intentionally notice' them, we move them into our consciousness. We can then reflect on our own response to this. What are their interesting features? What are the similarities and differences between the passers-by? We can begin to theorise: Why might the person in the green coat be talking on his mobile phone?

NOTICING IN A COFFEE SHOP

WHEN WE SIT IN A COFFEE SHOP WITH A FRIEND, WE RARELY NOTICE THE PASSERS-BY, AS WE ARE CONCENTRATING ON THE CONVERSATION.

THESE PASSERS-BY ARE IN OUR UNCONSCIOUS, WE KNOW THEY ARE THERE BUT WE ARE NOT CONSCIOUSLY THINKING ABOUT THEM.

HOWEVER, IF WE "INTENTIONALLY NOTICE" THEM, WE MOVE THEM INTO OUR CONSCIOUSNESS.

<u>WE CAN THEN REFLECT ON OUR OWN RESPONSE TO THIS.</u>

 WHAT ARE THE INTERESTING FEATURES?

 WHAT ARE THE SIMILARITIES AND DIFFERENCES BETWEEN THE PASSERS-BY?

 WE CAN BEGIN TO THEORISE: WHY MIGHT THE PERSON IN THE GREEN COAT BE TALKING ON HIS MOBILE PHONE?

Noticing as a discipline can be a useful tool for teachers to develop their classroom practice (Mason, 2002). John Mason developed the idea of noticing to be a discipline. Rather than just observing things around us, we begin to reflect on them, that is, to notice them.

Mason, J. (2002). *Researching Your Own Practice: The Discipline of Noticing*. London: Routledge.

Gibbs' reflective cycle

Gibbs (1988) presented a reflective cycle with six stages: description, feelings, evaluation, analysis, conclusions, and action plan (see Figure 13.3).

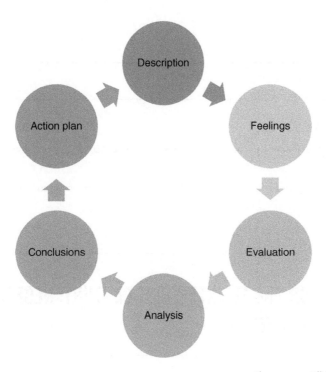

Figure 13.3 Gibbs' cycle of reflection

STUDY SKILLS

As part of an assignment, you might be asked to reflect on your experiences of education. You could use Mason's discipline of noticing or Gibbs' reflective cycle, or both, to help you critically reflect.

Rather than just describing what happened, Gibbs' reflective cycle gives structure and purpose to your reflection. You could follow Gibbs' cycle to give structure to your reflection as follows:

- *Description.* Describe what happened.
- *Feelings.* How did this make you feel?
- *Evaluation.* Make judgements about what was good and bad about your experience.
- *Analysis.* Analyse what was happening: Would other people act in a similar or different way, and why might this be the case?

(Continued)

(Continued)

- *Conclusions.* How else might you have acted or responded to the situation?
- *Action plan.* What would you do differently if this experience happened again? What can you do to develop any skills and/or knowledge you need to act in this way next time?

KEY INFORMATION

https://thoughtsmostlyaboutlearning.files.wordpress.com/2015/12/learning-by-doing-graham-gibbs.pdf

You can read Gibbs' work here. It provides more depth on the ideas discussed in this section.

SKILLS FOCUS FOR THE TWENTY-FIRST CENTURY: NECESSARY OR EMPEROR'S NEW CLOTHES?

KEY QUESTIONS

What are the current trends in education?

What research is there to support these trends?

How might these pedagogies promote learning in the classroom?

In education, there are often new fads that gain momentum and are written into policy, forcing schools and teachers to adopt them. In most cases, these fads are based on robust research, but this is not always the case.

Neuromyths: learning styles

An example of this is the myth of visual, auditory and kinaesthetic (VAK) learning styles. The theory is that students have a preferred learning style (e.g. a student performs better if material is presented in a 'visual' form rather than an 'auditory' form). However, most of the research related to learning styles has shown that there is not adequate evidence that there is a link between learning styles and performance (e.g. see Pashler et al., 2008), but people will express a preference for how they learn. It is important that with any research, you take a critical approach.

Mastery approach

'Mastery' is a term being bandied around a lot at the moment as the government tries to improve attainment in mathematics, basing its ideas on the mastery approach used in Singapore and China, among others. A mastery approach to learning requires all learners to master an idea before moving on to the next idea. There has been a lot of investment in developing a mastery approach in mathematics in recent years. However, the idea of mastery itself is not a new one. For Bloom (1968), mastery involved a student learning at their own pace, allowing them the time to do this, and breaking a course into smaller units of learning to help them achieve this. Slavin (1987) reconsidered mastery and Bloom (1987) responded to this; these papers together show how research can be open to interpretation and misinterpretation. Blair (2014) considered what mastery in mathematics might look like.

(Continued)

We could expand the argument I have started to present on mastery using the following framework:

- Describe: I would start by looking at Bloom's and Slavin's work and then presenting more modern ideas and approaches (e.g. Blair's work).

- Synthesise: I would look at the similarities and differences between the articles on mastery. In particular, I would be interested in the similarities and differences between recent research and Bloom's research.

- What does this mean for practice? I would attempt to answer the following questions:

  o Does the research show that key elements have been successful in the classroom?

  o Are these elements all based on new research, or are some of them from older research?

  o What are the implications for teachers (i.e. what should teachers be incorporating in their day-to-day practice to improve their pedagogy)?

- Conclude: Mastery is not a new idea; it has developed over time, but some of the original ideas are still important. Teachers can incorporate these into their pedagogy but should be critical about why they are including them and the effect it has on learning.

TO CONCLUDE

In this chapter, we have looked briefly at what is meant by teacher identity and how a teacher develops their identity. The identity that an individual has as a teacher will inform their pedagogical approaches in the classroom. Pedagogical approaches range from teacher-led to student-centred pedagogies and include a variety of dialogic pedagogies. Teachers are encouraged to engage with research to inform their teaching practice. However, new teaching ideas must be researched critically to ensure there is adequate evidence to justify their use and avoid any detrimental effect on student learning.

RESOURCES FOR FURTHER LEARNING

The *Times Educational Supplement* (Tes) website: **www.tes.com/new-teachers**

This website has some short articles giving advice to new teachers. These can give you an insight into the life and work of a teacher.

Jenlink, P.M. (2014) *Teacher Identity and the Struggle for Recognition: Meeting the Challenges of a Diverse Society*. R&L Education.

If you wish to read more about teacher identity, this book looks at what is meant by identity and some of the issues faced by teachers striving for recognition.

Pollard, A. (2002) *Reflective Teaching: Effective and Evidence-Informed Professional Practice*. London: Continuum.

This book looks at what it means in practice to be a reflective teacher.

The Chartered College of Teaching's journal, *Impact*, has easily digestible articles on a variety of topics, written by a mix of academics and practitioners.

REFERENCES

Bakhtin, M.M. (1981) *The Dialogic Imagination: Four Essays*, ed. M Holquist, trans. C. Emerson and M. Holquist. Austin, TX: University of Texas Press.

Blair, A. (2014) *Inquiry and Mastery*. Available at: www.inquirymaths.co.uk/posts/inquiryandmastery

Bloom, B.S. (1968) Learning for mastery: instruction and curriculum – Regional Education Laboratory for the Carolinas and Virginia, topical papers and reprints, number 1. *Evaluation Comment*, 1(2): 1–11.

Bloom, B.S. (1987) A response to Slavin's 'Mastery learning reconsidered'. *Review of Educational Research*, 57(4): 507–8.

Freire, P. (1970) *Pedagogy of the Oppressed*. New York: Continuum.

Friend, M. and Cook, L. (1997) Student-centered teams in schools: still in search of an identity. *Journal of Educational and Psychological Consultation*, 8(1): 3–20.

Gibbs, G. (1988) *Learning by Doing: A Guide to Teaching and Learning Methods*. Available at: https://thoughtsmostlyaboutlearning.files.wordpress.com/2015/12/learning-by-doing-graham-gibbs.pdf

Lewin, K. (1948) *Resolving Social Conflicts*. New York: Harper & Row.

Mason, J. (2002) *Researching Your Own Practice: The Discipline of Noticing*. London: Routledge.

Pashler, H., McDaniel, M., Rohrer, D. and Bjork, R. (2008) Learning styles: concepts and evidence. *Psychological Science in the Public Interest*, 9(3): 106–19.

Sinclair, J. and Coulthard, M. (1992) Toward an analysis of discourse. In M. Coulthard (ed.), *Advances in Spoken Discourse Analysis*. London: Routledge, pp1–34.

Slavin, R.E. (1987) Mastery learning reconsidered. *Review of Educational Research*, 57(2): 175–213.

Vygotsky, L. (1978) *Mind in Society*. Cambridge, MA: Harvard University Press.

14

WHAT IS VOCATIONAL LEARNING?

STEVE INGLE

KEY WORDS

- **VOCATIONAL**
- **TECHNICAL**
- **SKILLS**

- **APPRENTICESHIPS**
- **EMPLOYABILITY**
- **DUAL PROFESSIONALISM**

- **PEDAGOGY**
- **ANDRAGOGY**

KEY NOTES

- Vocational learning is essential for economic development and prosperity.
- Vocational learning is perceived differently in different parts of the world and in its parity with more academic learning.
- Vocational learning is often provided by colleges and employers, but schools are increasingly offering vocational options to learners from age 14 onwards.
- There are some key differences in the approaches taken by many teachers and trainers when teaching vocational subjects, as opposed to academic ones, and when teaching adults rather than children.

INTRODUCTION

Vocational learning, often referred to as technical and vocational education and training (TVET), is not easily defined or classified; it can mean different things to different people. Generally, however, vocational learning is often considered in contrast to the teaching of more traditional, academic subjects, such as English, maths and science, to the learning of knowledge and skills linked to specific occupational skills, careers or job roles.

In this chapter, we will explore what vocational learning includes, who might teach it and where, the role and purpose of vocational education, the links to adult learning, and possible considerations and implications for those teaching and assessing vocational learning programmes.

WHAT IS VOCATIONAL AND TECHNICAL EDUCATION?

It is difficult to find one formally accepted definition, but for many 'vocational learning' is a term used simply to describe courses and qualifications that are not traditional academic subjects, such as GCSEs or A levels. But what does vocational learning mean to you?

KEY QUESTIONS

Have you undertaken any vocational courses or qualifications yourself?

What made them 'vocational', and what do you feel are the similarities and differences with learning traditional 'academic' subjects?

Some people would take the view that many vocational courses are not as valuable or credible as more academic ones. Do you feel that vocational courses and academic qualifications have parity when it comes to how they are valued and viewed by universities, parents and employers?

When considering what vocational learning means to you, you may have identified a number of different key terms or concepts, such as:

* work-related learning or learning required to perform a specific job role or function;

* development of applied and technical skills;

* employability skills;

* hands-on, experiential and practical learning; and

* 'learning by doing'.

One key difference between vocational and academic learning programmes is the opportunities for learners not just to learn about theories and ideas, but also to develop and apply the specific work-related practical and technical skills required in a particular industry, vocation or job role.

Education philosopher John Dewey (1915) discussed the power and impact of 'learning by doing', not just learning by listening or watching. This 'experiential' approach provides learners with the opportunity to undertake applied learning activities and learn from an experience. Experiential learning gives learners hands-on experience by applying theoretical knowledge and understanding in a real-world setting, which could be in a specific vocational area, for example.

Experiential learning

Education theorist David Kolb (1984) proposed a four-stage model or cycle of experiential learning (see Figure 14.1). Learners carry out an experience (e.g. completing a specific task in the classroom, salon, workshop or workplace). They learn by reflecting on that experience and applying new knowledge and experience to develop a deeper or new understanding. Learners can then think about how to do something differently (e.g. more effectively, quicker, with more accuracy). Through these learning experiences, they develop – or master – their vocational skills, qualities and competencies.

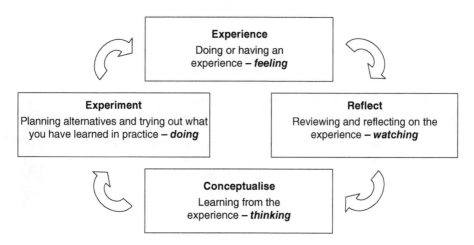

Figure 14.1   *The cycle of experiential learning*

Source: Kolb (1984)

In more recent years, and following a detailed review of vocational education in the UK carried out by Professor Alison Wolf (BIS and DfE, 2011), the UK government has focused on the development and promotion of 'technical education' rather than vocational learning more generally. In the government-commissioned *Report of the Independent Panel on Technical Education* (BIS and DfE, 2016a), Lord Sainsbury defines technical education programmes as those which focus on progression into skilled employment and require both a substantial body of technical knowledge as well as a set of practical skills valued by industry. Technical learning takes its purpose from the workplace rather than an academic discipline.

KEY INFORMATION

Review of Vocational Education: The Wolf Report (BIS and DfE, 2011)

In 2011, Professor Alison Wolf was asked to review vocational education in England and to investigate to what extent it provides for progression to higher learning and employment. The report outlined a number of key facts:

- Most English young people now take some vocational courses before they are 16, and post-16 the majority follow courses that are largely or entirely vocational.
- Many 16- and 17-year-olds move in and out of education and short-term employment.
- Between one-quarter and one-third of the post-16 cohort take low-level vocational qualifications, most of which have little to no labour market value.
- Less than 50 per cent of students have both English and maths GCSE (at grades A*-C) at the end of Key Stage 4 (age 15/16), and at age 18 the figure is still below 50 per cent. Only 4 per cent of the cohort achieve this during their 16–18 education.
- Many of England's 14-19-year-olds do not progress successfully into either secure employment or higher-level education and training, with many leaving education without the skills that will enable them to progress at a later date.

Report of the Independent Panel on Technical Education: The Sainsbury Review (BIS and DfE, 2016a)

This report set out a number of key recommendations for reforming skills-based vocational and technical education in England. All of the recommendations proposed by the independent panel, chaired by Lord Sainsbury of Turville, were adopted in principle in the government's *Post-16 Skills Plan* (BIS and DfE, 2016b). The plan sets out a common framework of 15 technical education routes, leading to T-level qualifications and apprenticeships.

This change in terminology from vocational to technical education may be helpful to address the differences in the way employers and parents perceive the value of vocational and technical courses compared with more traditional 'academic' qualifications. Vocational courses, such as BTECs, apprenticeships, National Vocational Qualifications (NVQs) and Tech Awards, have often been viewed as easier, less-demanding options for less-able learners who are likely to progress straight into work. In contrast, academic GCSEs and A levels are often seen as more demanding and suited to the more-able learners who are progressing to higher education courses. The reality is that many vocational learning programmes include significant – and demanding – academic content, along with opportunities for the development of practical and applied technical skills. Most vocational courses at level 3 also facilitate access to higher education programmes, attracting UCAS points, for example.

This lack of perceived parity is not common in many other countries. In Germany, Switzerland and the Netherlands, vocational and technical education is often regarded as high-quality and high-value and as demanding as academic qualifications, if not more so. Participation rates in vocational and technical learning programmes in these countries is high. In Switzerland, around two-thirds of people choose vocational learning routes at the age of 15 or 16, usually undertaking a three- or four-year apprenticeship programme. The apprenticeship includes three to four days of learning on and off the job at a host company (for which they get paid) and one to two days in general education. With some of the lowest levels of youth unemployment in the world, Switzerland's vocational and technical education and skills system is often seen as a key factor in the country's economic success (Shafique, 2019).

IS VOCATIONAL LEARNING SEEING A COMEBACK?

In many countries around the world, including the UK, funding and investment in vocational education and training has been on the decline. However, in recent years, various governments have been reviewing the purpose and function of vocational and technical education to try to attract more students to undertake high-quality technical courses, to develop skills to underpin productivity and a strong economy.

STUDY SKILLS

How might I think critically about this material?

You can use a variety of information sources, such as formal reports and government statistics, to critically explore the trends in vocational learning in the UK and abroad. Online information sources are a good place to start, as often you will find the most recent data here.

Take care to consider who has published the data you are using. Does it come from a reputable source? Is the data current?

What do the statistics show?

Explore data on the number of students taking vocational courses in the UK over the last five years. What are the trends in the number of learners undertaking vocational programmes? See: **www.gov. uk/government/collections/statistics-vocational-qualifications**

How do your findings compare with other countries?

To take a more critical perspective, it is helpful to compare your findings with other countries. Explore the 2018 report comparing international vocational education and training programmes from the National Center on Education and the Economy (**http://ncee.org/wp-content/uploads/2018/03/RenoldVETReport032018.pdf**).

Which countries are identified as having the most effective vocational learning programmes, and why?

In recent years, the UK government has attempted to overhaul the vocational and technical skills system to:

- address the perceived lack of parity and value with traditional academic qualifications;

- simplify the qualifications structure; and

- address the skills shortages and demand for specialist higher-level technical skills needed for a modern, competitive workforce.

An effective technical and vocational education system is needed to address the country's skills shortages, as well as the impact that this can have on productivity, performatively, employment and the economy. In the *Post-16 Skills Plan* (BIS and DfE, 2016b) and the *Review of Post-18 Education and Funding* (DfE, 2019), there is a clear recognition of the urgent need to improve and strengthen vocational and technical education to ensure that the country can compete with other developed nations.

KEY INFORMATION

Education and Employers (2018) *Joint Dialogue: How Are Schools Developing Real Employability Skills?* Available at: www.educationandemployers.org/research/joint-dialogue

This report draws together a review of the literature on the skills and behaviours that employers feel are most commonly needed in the workplace. Through an analysis of existing research studies (known as a meta-study), the report identifies eight employability skills and four competencies that young people need to find work and succeed in the workplace.

KEY QUESTIONS

Do we have the skills to meet the needs of the 'Fourth Industrial Revolution'?

To what extent does the current education system prepare learners to be successful in the modern world?

Advances in technology, communication and the internet have changed the world forever. We have new careers and job roles appearing now that just didn't exist a few years ago. We need an education and skills system that prepares young people for jobs that don't even exist yet.

In order to remain successful and prosperous in this new world, the workforce of today – and tomorrow – need a set of skills and qualities that will enable them to be successful in the modern world.

WHAT ARE THE DIFFERENT TYPES OF VOCATIONAL QUALIFICATIONS?

Part of the reforms recommended by the independent panel have been implemented and are shaping the current vocational learning landscape in England. The significant number of programmes, qualifications and providers can be confusing, so let's explore some of the different options available.

T levels

T levels are new two-year 'technical-level' qualifications, equivalent to three A levels, that have been developed with employers and businesses. They include a technical qualification, to develop learners' theoretical and specialist knowledge and understanding, alongside a substantial industry placement (of approximately 45 days), to give learners the opportunity to develop applied practical and technical skills through experience. T levels also require learners to achieve a minimum standard in English and maths, if not already achieved. T levels in 25 subject areas will be available in vocational areas such as accountancy, education, legal, health and manufacturing. The different aspects of a full T-level programme are shown in Figure 14.2.

Apprenticeships and traineeships

For those learners who would prefer to 'earn while they learn', they might be better suited to an apprenticeship learning programme. Apprentices are employed and receive a salary. They work alongside experienced staff and participate in 'on-the-job' training, to gain the skills and competencies needed by employers to carry out a specific role (e.g. a plumber, an IT technician, a team leader, a bus driver). Apprentices also attend regular off-the-job training as part of their working hours (e.g. one day a week might be spent away from their job in a college, to develop the required underpinning knowledge and understanding).

Apprenticeships can take between one and four years to complete, depending on the level of study. By the end of their programme, apprentices need to be able to demonstrate the professional standards required, which have been developed by key employers from that industry. Apprentices must successfully complete an 'end-point assessment' (EPA) in order to achieve their qualification. There are over 600 different 'apprenticeship standards' available at different levels: intermediate (level 2), advanced (level 3), higher (levels 4–7) and degree (levels 6 and 7) in a wide range of vocational subject areas, including:

- business, administration and management;
- construction, planning and engineering;
- manufacturing and logistics;
- health, public services and care;
- information and communications technology; and
- retail and enterprise.

Introduced in August 2013, Traineeships are an education and training programme, lasting up to six months, for learners who do not yet have the skills or experience needed to secure an apprenticeship

223

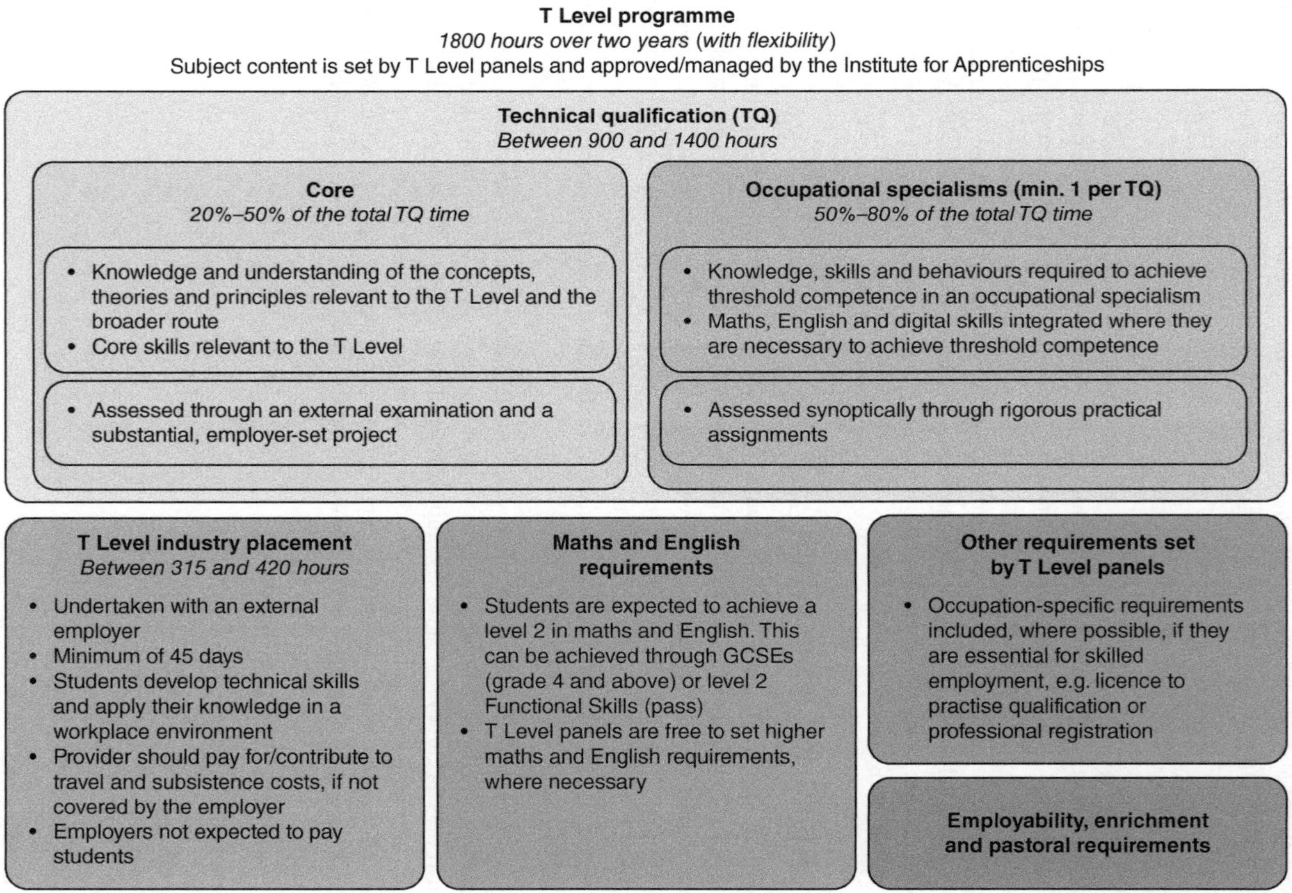

T Level programme

1800 hours over two years (with flexibility)

Subject content is set by T Level panels and approved/managed by the Institute for Apprenticeships

Technical qualification (TQ)

Between 900 and 1400 hours

Core

20%–50% of the total TQ time

- Knowledge and understanding of the concepts, theories and principles relevant to the T Level and the broader route
- Core skills relevant to the T Level

- Assessed through an external examination and a substantial, employer-set project

Occupational specialisms (min. 1 per TQ)

50%–80% of the total TQ time

- Knowledge, skills and behaviours required to achieve threshold competence in an occupational specialism
- Maths, English and digital skills integrated where they are necessary to achieve threshold competence

- Assessed synoptically through rigorous practical assignments

T Level industry placement

Between 315 and 420 hours

- Undertaken with an external employer
- Minimum of 45 days
- Students develop technical skills and apply their knowledge in a workplace environment
- Provider should pay for/contribute to travel and subsistence costs, if not covered by the employer
- Employers not expected to pay students

Maths and English requirements

- Students are expected to achieve a level 2 in maths and English. This can be achieved through GCSEs (grade 4 and above) or level 2 Functional Skills (pass)
- T Level panels are free to set higher maths and English requirements, where necessary

Other requirements set by T Level panels

- Occupation-specific requirements included, where possible, if they are essential for skilled employment, e.g. licence to practise qualification or professional registration

Employability, enrichment and pastoral requirements

Figure 14.2 T-level programme

For more information on T levels, see: **www.instituteforapprenticeships.org/t-levels**

or employment. Traineeships provide learners with work preparation training, such as developing a CV and improving their applied English and maths skills, along with a high-quality work placement and a guaranteed interview at the end of the placement, to help the trainee progress.

To find out more, see: **www.gov.uk/apprenticeships-guide or www.gov.uk/guidance/traineeships**

Work- and vocation-related qualifications

A broad range of different awarding organisations (AOs), such as Pearson, OCR, City & Guilds and NCFE, all provide a significant number of different vocational qualifications designed to develop learners' knowledge, understanding and skills in a specific employment sector (e.g. sport, public services, business and finance, health and social care).

Qualifications usually include a practical element as well as the development of underpinning knowledge and skills. Popular work-related qualifications include brands such as BTECs and OCR Nationals. Applied general qualifications are available to learners over 16, at level 3, who wish to continue their education through studying subjects that are applied to different vocational areas but are not closely linked to a very specific job role. Around 200,000 16–18-year-old students take Applied Generals or Tech Levels each year, compared to over 300,000 who take A levels (Ofqual, 2019).

Technical Awards are qualifications at levels 1 and 2 designed for learners in school between 14 and 16 years old (Key Stage 4). They are the same size as a single GCSE and aim to give learners a taste of what a specific vocational sector is like (e.g. enterprise, land-based studies, travel and tourism, performing arts). Learners can take these vocational options alongside their other GCSEs in more traditional academic subjects.

National Vocational Qualifications (NVQs)

NVQs are competency-based qualifications based on the National Occupational Standards (NOS) for a specific job role. They are usually completed in the workplace, and learners need to demonstrate their ability to carry out job-specific tasks effectively, collecting a portfolio of evidence to meet the standards required. A large range of different careers are supported by NVQs, including:

- hairdressing and barbering;

- business and administration;

- cleaning;

- customer service;

- food manufacturing; and

- warehousing and storage.

National Occupational Standards are developed by standard-setting organisations who consult with employers and other stakeholders to set the standards of performance individuals must achieve when carrying out functions in the workplace. There are over 23,000 separate NOS, covering a wide range of vocational sectors and occupations, from garden centre manager to pipe fitter, scaffolder to sous-chef. To access the NOS statements, see: **www.ukstandards.org.uk**

Higher-level qualifications

A number of higher-level qualifications, above level 3, are also available in different vocational areas. Higher National Certificates and Diplomas (HNC/D) and Foundation Degrees are often related to a specific vocation, industry or occupational area. They can provide vocational learners with a route to gaining a full undergraduate degree.

WHO PROVIDES VOCATIONAL AND TECHNICAL LEARNING PROGRAMMES?

A broad range of different providers offer learners vocational and technical education options from schools to universities. Let's take a look at some of the most popular vocational education providers in the UK (see Table 14.1).

Table 14.1

General further education (GFE) colleges	There are over 170 GFE colleges across England, providing technical and professional education and training to around 1.5 million students. GFE colleges often have an excellent range of high-quality, industry standard facilities that allow learners to apply their practical skills through learning experiences that reflect the real world of work.
Sixth form colleges	Around 57 sixth form colleges provide mainly academic qualifications to around 700,000 students. Many sixth form colleges also offer a smaller programme of vocational learning options alongside traditional A levels.
Land-based colleges	Fourteen land-based colleges provide vocational pathways to students specialising in areas such as agriculture, horticulture, animal care, arboriculture, equine studies, farriery and blacksmithing.
National specialist colleges	A number of national specialist colleges offer specific vocational and technical training programmes to meet specific skills needs, e.g. the National College for Digital Skills (**https://ada.ac.uk**), the National College for High Speed Rail (**www.nchsr.ac.uk**) and the National College Creative Industries (**https://creativeindustries.ac.uk**).
Schools	Many schools also offer their learners vocational qualifications alongside more traditional academic routes, at Key Stages 4 and 5. Schools can incorporate a number of high-quality vocational and technical qualifications in their performance measures data if they feature on lists approved by the Department for Education (DFE) (e.g. Tech Awards).

Private training providers	A large number of private organisations also offer vocational and technical education programmes (e.g. employability courses, apprenticeships and traineeships). To be eligible for UK government funding, providers must be registered with the Education and Skills Funding Agency (ESFA).
Employers	Many large employers can also register as a private training provider in their own right. In 2017, the UK government introduced the 'apprenticeship levy', which required all large employers (with an annual wage bill of over £3 million) to make a financial contribution to the funding of apprenticeship programmes. Employers can use this contribution to develop the skills of their own employees by funding apprenticeship learning programmes.
Adult community learning (ACL) providers	Often managed by local authorities or charities, ACL providers often deliver a range of short courses designed to help people get back into work (e.g. employability programmes offered in conjunction with Jobcentre Plus). ACL providers may also offer a range of professional evening classes linked to specific vocational roles (e.g. professional certificates in accountancy, computing, marketing and human resources). These part-time vocational courses play a valuable part in helping individuals gain a promotion or change career.

WHO TEACHES VOCATIONAL AND TECHNICAL LEARNING PROGRAMMES?

Teachers, lecturers, trainers and assessors working in vocational education are often described as 'dual professionals', having formal teaching qualifications but also formal vocational qualifications and years of professional experience from industry. For example, a lecturer in motor vehicles may have worked as a senior technician or engineer for a major international car manufacturer for many years, before moving into an education and training role. Learners benefit from this industrial experience and the ability of the vocational expert to bring their learning to life, helping them to make links between theoretical and technical knowledge to the application of practical skills in the workshop.

KEY INFORMATION

Education and Training Foundation (ETF) (2014) *The Dual Professional Toolkit: A Guide for Those Looking to Move Towards Dual Professionalism.* Available at: www.aoc.co.uk/sites/default/files/Dual%20Professional%20toolkit.pdf

The Education and Training Foundation (ETF) is the professional development body for the further education (FE) and training sector. The ETF's development programme, Teach Too, recognises the importance of the 'dual professional' – teachers and trainers who combine subject knowledge, specialist occupational skills and expertise, and teaching, learning and pedagogical practice.

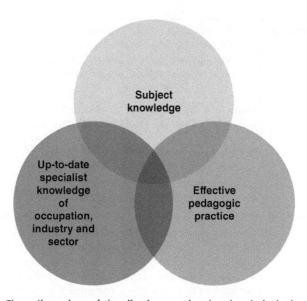

Figure 14.3 Three dimensions of the effective vocational and technical education teacher or trainer

Source: www.aoc.co.uk/sites/default/files/Dual%20Professional%20toolkit.pdf

STUDY SKILLS

The ETF publish a set of professional standards for teachers and trainers in education and training that set out the expectations of effective practice for those teaching in the post-14 education and training sector. The 20 standards outline the professional values, attributes, knowledge, understanding and skills expected by an effective dual professional educator. Teachers demonstrating these standards and working with learners age 14 and above can apply to be considered for Qualified Teacher Learning and Skills (QTLS) status.

How might I think critically about this material?

Start by exploring the 20 different standards available on the ETF website: **www.et-foundation. co.uk/supporting/support-practitioners/professional-standards**

Now think about the extent you agree that these 20 standards encompass the necessary attributes of an effective educator in the twenty-first century. Are there any standards that you do not agree with or additional standards that you feel are essential to be an effective educator, particularly when teaching vocational and technical learning programmes?

The Department for Education also publishes a set of teachers' standards that define the minimum level of practice expected of trainees and teachers working in schools, from the point of being awarded qualified teacher status (QTS). Explore the teachers' standards on the DfE website: **www.gov.uk/ government/publications/teachers-standards**

Now compare the teachers' standards with the ETF education and training standards. What are the similarities and differences? Do you feel that the standards for those teaching learners at school should be different to those teaching older learners in colleges and in the workplace? What reasons, rationale or justification would you give to support this view? Could you give any specific examples to help support your point of view?

To take a more critical perspective, you could now explore the different teacher standards expected in other developed countries (e.g. those with significant vocational and technical education systems). A good place to start could be the Federal Institute for Vocational Education and Training (**www. bibb.de**), who evaluate and observe international developments in vocational learning.

To find the very latest developments, you should make use of current academic journal articles. There are a large number of high-quality education and research journals that have been 'peer-reviewed' and provide a critical evaluation of different vocational education systems around the world. Speak to a librarian or information specialist on how to carry out a search to find the information you need.

DO VOCATIONAL EDUCATION PROGRAMMES NEED TO BE TAUGHT DIFFERENTLY?

We have explored what vocational learning is and investigated the range of different qualifications available. We have also considered the skills, standards and competencies of professional educators who are teaching and training vocational learners. Now let's consider the tools and methods of teaching, learning and assessment in vocational education and how they may differ to traditional school-based approaches.

In many traditional academic subjects, the teacher's approach to teaching and learning is often very typical: the presentation of new material in the classroom, followed by some activities, tasks or case studies, leading to a final test or exam to check that what has been taught has been remembered or learned.

We explored earlier how a key difference with vocational education is the development of practical and technical skills and learning through experience, practice and application. So, does this difference also require a different approach, or pedagogy, to be used by vocational teachers, trainers and assessors? In their report *It's All About Work*, the Commission on Adult Vocational Teaching and Learning identifies eight distinctive features of vocational teaching and learning, or a 'vocational pedagogy':

1. Through the combination of sustained practice and the understanding of theory, occupational expertise is developed.

2. Work-related attributes are central to the development of occupational expertise.

3. Practical problem-solving and critical reflection on experience, including learning from mistakes in real and simulated settings, are central to effective vocational teaching and learning.

4. Vocational teaching and learning is most effective when it is collaborative and contextualised, taking place within communities of practice that involve different types of 'teacher' and capitalise on the experience and knowledge of all learners.

5.   Technology plays a key role because keeping on top of technological advances is an essential part of the occupational expertise required in any workplace.

6.   Vocational teaching requires a range of assessment and feedback methods that involve both 'teachers' and learners, and which reflect the specific assessment cultures of different occupations and sectors.

7.   Vocational teaching and learning often benefits from operating across more than one setting, including a real or simulated workplace, as well as the classroom and workshop, to develop the capacity to learn and apply that learning in different settings, just as at work.

8.   Occupational standards are dynamic, evolving to reflect advances in work practices, and through collective learning, transformation in quality and efficiency is achieved.

(CAVTL, 2013)

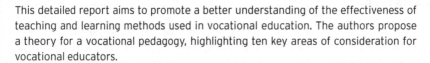

KEY INFORMATION

Lucas, B., Spencer, E. and Claxton, G. (2013) *How to Teach Vocational Education: A Theory of Vocational Pedagogy*. Available at: www.educationinnovations.org/sites/default/files/How-to-teach-vocational-education.pdf

This detailed report aims to promote a better understanding of the effectiveness of teaching and learning methods used in vocational education. The authors propose a theory for a vocational pedagogy, highlighting ten key areas of consideration for vocational educators.

KEY QUESTIONS

Do vocational learning programmes and qualifications require a specific 'pedagogy', or approach, or should educators simply use traditional tools and approaches that work across all subjects and levels?

Does teaching adult learners require a different pedagogy or approach to teaching younger learners?

What are the most important factors to consider if you had to plan teaching and learning sessions for a vocational course?

ARE THERE ANY KEY THINGS TO THINK ABOUT WHEN TEACHING ADULTS ON VOCATIONAL LEARNING PROGRAMMES?

As we have explored, many vocational and technical learning programmes are focused on the development of practical skills. Adults may participate in a vocational learning programme at some point.

But does the teaching of adult learners require a different approach, or pedagogy, to teaching children and younger learners?

Adult learners may lack confidence and study skills, having not engaged in formal learning since leaving school. Some may have had negative experiences at school or a history of poor performance. Other adult learners may well have many years of practical experience already but have no formal qualifications to support their skills, particularly when attending interviews or applying for jobs. Some academics and researchers suggest that the methods and approaches for teaching and training adult learners (andragogy) require a different approach to that of teaching younger learners (pedagogy).

Knowles (1984) identified five key characteristics of adult learners, which provide some useful considerations for those teaching adults as opposed to children and young people:

1. *Self-concept.* As a person matures, they become less dependent and more independent.

2. *Experience.* As a person matures, they gain more life experience to use in their learning.

3. *Readiness to learn.* As a person matures, they take on roles and responsibilities that require them to learn new skills and knowledge.

4. *Orientation to learning.* As a person matures, they often need to learn new knowledge and skills to solve specific problems and tasks that are needed for work or life.

5. *Motivation to learn.* As a person matures, they develop an internal desire to learn new things.

KEY QUESTIONS

If you were teaching a group of adult learners, what possible implications would the five characteristics above have for you when planning and delivering learning?

How might your approach to teaching a group of adult learners be different to teaching a group of children?

In their book *Teaching and Training Vocational Learners*, teacher educators Ingle and Duckworth (2013) highlight the different planning considerations that may need to be considered when thinking about delivering high-quality vocational education to all learners, including young people and adults. They suggest that all learners' individual needs and preferences should be considered first, along with the specific aims and objectives of the vocational course or qualification. The context and conditions of learning should also be taken into account by teachers and trainers (e.g. if training is to take place in the workplace, in a realistic working environment or in a traditional classroom setting).

Having identified learner needs and learning context, the teacher or trainer can then think about the specific approaches, tools, models, methods and resources needed. This approach is likely to include opportunities for learners to apply their developing knowledge and understanding in practical and experiential activities. It may involve employers in creating realistic scenarios, contexts or tasks. It could include visits to local businesses or expert guest speakers from industry.

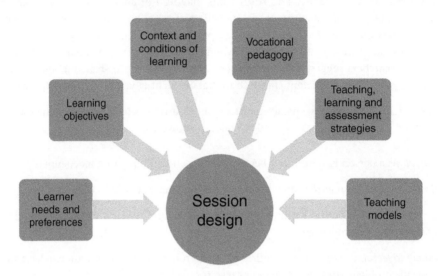

Figure 14.4 A framework for planning effective vocational sessions

Source: Ingle and Duckworth (2013)

TO CONCLUDE

In this chapter, we have explored what vocational and technical learning means to different people, and its purpose and value in developing the skills of the workforce need to be competitive in a modern world. We have reviewed the broad range of courses and qualifications available at different learning providers. We have discussed the approaches to teaching, learning and assessment of vocational education, as well as the debate around specific pedagogies and andragogies that meet the needs of all vocational learners, whether those still at school, school leavers or adults.

RESOURCES FOR FURTHER LEARNING

Centre for Real-World Learning (CRL): **www.winchester.ac.uk/research/enhancing-wellbeing-nurturing-the-individual/centre-for-real-world-learning**

Based at the University of Winchester, the Centre for Real-World Learning (CRL) carries out research on teaching and learning approaches that help learners to thrive in the real world. CRL's website includes links to a number of useful articles and research reports on vocational pedagogies.

Edge Foundation: **www.edge.co.uk**

The Edge Foundation's website includes links to a range of commissioned and published research, such as regular bulletins exploring skills shortages in the UK economy.

Institute for Apprenticeships and Technical Education (IATE): **www.instituteforapprenticeships.org**

The IATE is an employer-led, non-departmental public body responsible for technical qualifications and the development, approval and publication of apprenticeship standards.

REFERENCES

Commission on Adult Vocational Teaching and Learning (CAVTL) (2013) *It's All About Work: Excellent Adult Vocational Teaching and Learning*. Available at: cavtl.excellencegateway.org.uk/commission-news/its-about-work

Department for Business, Innovation and Skills (BIS) and Department for Education (DfE) (2011) *Review of Vocational Education: The Wolf Report*. Available at: https://assets.publishing.service.gov.uk/government/uploads/system/uploads/attachment_data/file/180504/DFE-00031-2011.pdf

Department for Business, Innovation and Skills (BIS) and Department for Education (DfE) (2016a) *Report of the Independent Panel on Technical Education: The Sainsbury Review*. Available at: https://assets.publishing.service.gov.uk/government/uploads/system/uploads/attachment_data/file/536046/Report_of_the_Independent_Panel_on_Technical_Education.pdf

Department for Business, Innovation and Skills (BIS) and Department for Education (DfE) (2016b) *Post-16 Skills Plan*. Available at: https://assets.publishing.service.gov.uk/government/uploads/system/uploads/attachment_data/file/536068/56259_Cm_9280_print.pdf

Department for Education (DfE) (2019) *Independent Panel Report to the Review of Post-18 Education and Funding*. Available at: https://assets.publishing.service.gov.uk/government/uploads/system/uploads/attachment_data/file/805127/Review_of_post_18_education_and_funding.pdf

Dewey, J. (1915) *Schools of Tomorrow*. New York: E.P. Dutton & Co.

Education and Employers (2018) *Joint Dialogue: How Are Schools Developing Real Employability Skills?* Available at: www.educationandemployers.org/research/joint-dialogue

Education and Training Foundation (ETF) (2014) *The Dual Professional Toolkit: A Guide for Those Looking to Move Towards Dual Professionalism*. Available at: www.aoc.co.uk/sites/default/files/Dual%20Professional%20toolkit.pdf

Ingle, S. and Duckworth, V. (2013) *Teaching and Training Vocational Learners*. London: Learning Matters.

Knowles, M. (1984) *Andragogy in Action*. San Francisco, CA: Jossey-Bass.

Kolb, D. (1984) *Experiential Learning: Experience as the Source of Learning and Development*. Englewood Cliffs, NJ: Prentice Hall.

Lucas, B., Spencer, E. and Claxton, G. (2013) *How to Teach Vocational Education: A Theory of Vocational Pedagogy*. Available at: www.educationinnovations.org/sites/default/files/How-to-teach-vocational-education.pdf

Ofqual (2019) *Applied Generals and Tech Levels*. Available at: https://ofqual.blog.gov.uk/2019/04/18/applied-generals-and-tech-levels-this-summer-2

Shafique, A. (2019) *If the UK Wants a Quality Vocational Education System, It Should Take Inspiration from Switzerland.* Available at: www.thersa.org/discover/publications-and-articles/rsa-blogs/2019/02/what-uk-vocational-education-can-learn-from-switzerland

The Edge Foundation (2019) *Debating the first principles of English vocational education. Vol. 2.* Available at: www.edge.co.uk/sites/default/files/documents/vocational_philosophy_2_final_-_web.pdf

PART 3

CONTEMPORARY THEMES AND ISSUES IN EDUCATION: OPINION PIECES AND COMMENTARIES

In this part of the book, the chapters comprise short opinion pieces written by experts in education. Some are practitioners, some are academics, and some are both. As you read these opinion pieces, you will see how the writing reflects and reiterates some of the themes that we have already covered in this book.

IDEAS FOR READING AND THINKING ABOUT THE OPINION PIECES

As you read the opinion pieces, it is a good idea to start thinking about them in a critical way. You could go back to Chapter 1 and look at some of the material about critical thinking that is introduced in that chapter.

Here are some ideas to get you started:

First of all, who is the person who has written this piece? What is their background? You'll find this information in the introduction to each chapter, but you can also look up people's names on the internet to get a sense of the kind of work they are doing.

Second, what might 'who the author is' mean for the piece they have written and their position on the topic?

What is the main point that the author is making about the topic?

Does the author back up their point or idea with evidence? If so, is it evidence from experience, or from academic literature, or from their own studies? How strong do you think this evidence is? For example, is it empirical evidence (i.e. it has come from direct experience, such as by doing a study) or from the author's own experiences?

It might be that the author uses more than one of these sources of evidence to back up their opinions. If that's the case, does it make it a stronger piece?

If the author doesn't use this kind of evidence, does this affect the strength of their argument? Or, as it is an opinion piece, does their standing and authority in the area give the piece the authority you think it needs?

Once you have read each piece, think about how the two pieces contrast. In what ways are they similar? In what ways are they different?

Do you feel more in sympathy with one of the pieces in particular? Can you work out why that is (e.g. is it to do with the opinions expressed or the way that the opinion piece is written)?

You may find that you disagree with some of the opinions expressed. When that is the case, it's a good time to practise developing counterarguments. You can start to think about what it is that you disagree with, and why, and about what evidence you can bring against the opinion that is expressed.

15

SOCIAL JUSTICE IN EDUCATION

VICKY DUCKWORTH AND CLARE CAMPBELL

In these two pieces, real-life issues of social justice are considered. Clare Campbell is a primary school head teacher and Vicky Duckworth is a professor of education. They write about social justice in regard to two different contexts, and you will see that their conceptualisations and discussions of social justice are very different.

Vicky focuses on further education (FE), particularly for adults, and the ways in which FE is empowering for both the adults who are involved in the learning as well as for their families and communities. She talks about the ripple effect of education. Clare's piece is about working with female pupils in a school in the Philippines and a programme in the school that focuses on developing the pupils' agency in relation to social transformation.

QUESTIONS TO THINK ABOUT

The two pieces are written in very different styles. Why do you think this is? What are the advantages of each style? Are there any disadvantages?

Consider the ideas that the authors are trying to get across. For each piece, try to distil one or two main ideas in a couple of sentences.

What ideas can you take about social justice from the two pieces? You might want to think about which words are emphasised by each of the authors – are these the same or different in the two pieces?

You could also go back to Chapter 5 and reread some of the work relating to Fraser's ideas about the dimensions of social justice. How do these dimensions relate to what you have read in these opinion pieces?

SOCIAL JUSTICE AND ADULT EDUCATION: ADULT EDUCATION, LIKE EDUCATION ACROSS THE LIFESPAN, IS NEVER NEUTRAL

VICKY DUCKWORTH

Adult education involves **ideological drivers** that shape understandings of how it is developed and enacted in and out of classrooms. Knowing our position is important and empowering. This means considering what we stand for and what we stand against. If we choose education as a flow of empowerment and liberation, it means that educators need to develop **dialogic** caring spaces where learners feel valued, are respected and can flourish to reach their potential (Duckworth and Smith, 2018b). The radical educator is driven by wanting to offer often-marginalised and left-behind communities a critical space to challenge the status quo. Radical adult education is about generating knowledge, understanding and action from the roots of communities, rather than the privileged hierarchical branches. It also requires the expectation of widespread social and political change to cement and propel the experiences of people in communities, and in doing this they expect that there is also the possibility of macro-level (large-scale) social change.

In the UK and internationally, democracy and notions of *community* are being (re)conceptualised in our public institutions through the lens of **neoliberal** ideology. Neoliberalisation is the dominant political driver of our time, bringing with it a focus on **deregulation** and economic competitiveness (both national and institutional), framed by discourses of globalisation (Davies, 2014; Duckworth and Smith, 2018a). This has led to 'free-market' competition displacing social democratic policy as a structuring force in many areas of public life. Indeed, under the premise of building a 'knowledge economy', the central duty of the nation's education system is assumed to be to provide a flexible, adaptable and skilled workforce to make the country competitive in the globalised economy. A key effect of neoliberal policy appears to be the replication of social divisions and inequalities rather than any systematic or meaningful counteraction against them. For example, learners from socio-economically deprived areas are unlikely to have the same access to opportunities as those who live in more affluent areas who are more able to attend high-achieving state schools or be privately educated (Duckworth, 2013; Duckworth and Smith, 2019).

In the face of this **instrumental** and often reductive (oversimplified) landscape, to be an agent of social change is an important and indeed urgent action. The nurturing of social and political change in the direction of greater social justice, democracy and liberation requires the construction of people and their communities' alternatives to the morally based **hegemony** of neoliberalism, which is ubiquitous and destructive of real community empowerment and collaboration.

RESEARCH AND CRITICAL ENGAGEMENT

The research project *FE in England: Transforming Lives and Communities*, sponsored by the University and Colleges Union, is a study that records and celebrates narratives about transformative teaching and learning in further education (see **http://transforminglives.web.ucu.org.uk**). FE is 'further education'; the term is used to mean any study after secondary education that is not taken as part of a degree course. Together with the exploration of learners' educational journeys, the study probes a wide range of social and economic issues, and can help to make sense of social and economic change and trends. When exploring adult education, the study illuminates how these issues relate to other factors in people's lives, such as health and well-being, work, and family and community life (Duckworth and Smith, 2019).

The research project utilised a digitally oriented research methodology to gather, explore and share project data. The data comprised a series of rich narratives from learners, teachers, employers and learners' family members. These were collected through video-recorded interviews, which were then shared via a project website. A YouTube channel (**www.youtube.com/channel/UCkDeirtGCmeBs361BgibXnA**) and a Twitter account (@FEtransforms) were further features of a multifaceted digital platform that were used to create a project audience and an interactive critical space that garnered further contributions in the form of written narratives, photographs and artefacts. The digital platform was the catalyst for what we describe as *virtually enhanced engagement*, adding to the data and extending the influence and meanings of the project in the public domain (e.g. by connecting the researchers directly with a key policymaker). The first year of the project culminated in a conference that brought together participants from across the country: students, teachers, researchers, employers and policy influencers.

The research data illustrates that despite funding cuts and heavily instrumentalised policy intervention, FE does continue to offer critical spaces that allow teachers and learners to disrupt the 'one-size-fits-all' linear model of learning that is usually found in education. This 'one-size-fits-all' model is a neoliberal one, and it assesses and sorts learners by age and qualification rather than by their individual needs, goals and abilities. Instead, further education offers organic tools for consciousness-raising (Freire, 1995) and transformation (Mezirow 2000), acting as a *hope catalyst* for significant changes in learners' lives and teachers' practice (Ade-Ojo and Duckworth, 2015). Key findings indicate that transformation involves subverting (undermining or overturning) **deficit labels** and a lack of confidence derived from negative prior educational experiences, rebuilding self-esteem and (re)constructing positive educational identities. Learners' relationships with teachers were also key in transformative journeys. FE offered a diverse learning space that embraced what learners described as their 'spoilt' identities.

The research data also provides evidence of an organic ripple effect: that the further education of individuals can benefit their families and communities, as aspiration is rekindled and agency realised. In that sense, benefits extend beyond the personal, to the social and economic.

TO THE FUTURE

Adult education needs to make real and sustained engagement with the lives of people in communities if it is going to be a resource for social action and change. It needs to demonstrate how it can be meaningful to people making history, and to do that it needs to begin where people are in relation to their hopes, fears, ideas and beliefs.

GLOSSARY

deficit labels Labels that people sometimes attach to learners – they focus on a student's perceived weaknesses rather than on their strengths and potential.

deregulation The reduction or elimination of government power in a particular area, usually to create more competition in that area (in this case, education).

dialogic Communication in the form of dialogue or conversation. Usually, in adult learning and further education, it is used to mean dialogue where the ideas that people are presenting are less related to the power that the individuals have and more to the validity of their arguments.

hegemony The dominant social group and their ideology.

ideological drivers The forces that 'drive' change and education – they are ideological because they are related to a particular set of ideas or beliefs about education.

instrumental landscape In this context, this means that the system is set up less to focus on democratic and socially just values, and more to be concerned with aims related to money and economic success.

neoliberalism An ideology and set of policies that emphasises the value of free-market competition. It is defined differently by different people, but common features in these definitions are usually neoliberalism's confidence in free markets as the most efficient allocation of resources, its emphasis on minimal governmental intervention in economic and social affairs, and its commitment to the freedom of trade.

REFERENCES

Ade-Ojo, G. and Duckworth, V. (2015) *Adult Literacy Policy and Practice: From Intrinsic Values to Instrumentalism*. London: Palgrave Macmillan.

Davies, W. (2014) *The Limits of Neoliberalism*. London: SAGE.

Duckworth, V. (2013) *Learning Trajectories, Violence and Empowerment Amongst Adult Basic Skills Learners*. London: Routledge.

Duckworth, V. and Smith, R. (2018a) Transformative learning in English further education. In C. Borg, P. Mayo and R. Sultana (eds), *Handbook of Vocational Education and Training: Developments in the Changing World of Work*. New York: Springer, pp1–16.

Duckworth, V. and Smith, R. (2018b) Breaking the triple lock: further education and transformative teaching and learning. *Education + Training*, 60(6): 529–43.

Duckworth, V. and Smith, R. (2019) *Further Education in England: Transforming Lives and Communities – Summative Report*. London: UCU.

Freire, P. (1995) *Pedagogy of Hope: Reliving Pedagogy of the Oppressed*. New York: Continuum.

Mezirow, J. (2000) Learning to think like an adult: core concepts of transformation theory. In J. Mezirow et al. (eds), *Learning as Transformation: Critical Perspectives on a Theory in Progress*. San Francisco, CA: Jossey-Bass, pp3–33.

A CASE STUDY ON TRANSFORMATIVE SOCIAL JUSTICE EDUCATION: ST SCHOLASTICA'S, MANILA, PHILIPPINES

CLARE CAMPBELL

WHERE? WHEN? ST SCHOLASTICA'S, MANILA, THE PHILIPPINES

In February 2019, I was part of a group of school leaders travelling to Manila, the Philippines, with charity EducareM to investigate transformative social justice education. We visited St Scholastica's College and learned about their social transformation programme.

St Scholastica's College is an all-girls school with 3,500 pupils on roll from pre-kindergarten to MA-level studies. Established in 1906 as an educational institution committed to women's education, it realigned its educational goals in the 1970s. It now aims to educate women for the professions and develop their awareness and critique of local and world events – that they may be agents of social change and social transformation. The realignment of the mission and vision of the college is interpreted by the mission statement:

> St Scholastica's education is committed to providing a holistic formation, anchored on academic excellence, moulding students into critically aware and socially responsible agents of change and transformation towards a just and equitable society.

Simply put, the aim is to train students to run society, but to also be agents of change if change is needed.

WHO? WHY? STUDENTS AS AGENTS OF CHANGE

The executive director and founder of the Institute of Women's Studies, Sister Mary John Mananzan, told us that the students must have 'skin-to-skin contact with poverty' in order to understand their social situation and to take action:

> For a school to be socially just and socially oriented, all the administration, faculty and students must be cognisant of the economic, political and cultural situation of the country.

For this reason, each school year starts with a 'national situationer' where all stakeholders investigate the current issues of society in the Philippines (see Table 15.1).

Table 15.1 *Mandate of challenges and St Scholastica's response*

Current challenges	St Scholastica's response
Economic justice and elite globalisation	They promote a culture of sharing and simplicity of lifestyle (e.g. students are encouraged to never wear branded clothes, no junk food, no fizzy drinks are allowed, and single-use plastics are banned from campus).
The woman question	There is a genuine sisterhood among the students and they intensify advocacy for women. All students take a mandatory three-unit women's studies course. All staff are required to complete gender sensitivity training, all policies and curricula are gender-sensitive, and gender-sensitive counselling is in place across the college.
Environmental crisis	They promote interconnectedness and earth-friendly activities (e.g. waste segregation, annual tree planting, ecological clubs, organic farming, visits to geo-farms, environmental protection plays).
Fundamentalism	The students appreciate differences and cultural diversity and have interfaith and ecumenical dialogues.
Violence, conflict and the culture of fear	They establish a culture of just peace and a promotion of a better quality of life for society by undertaking protest marches/rallies/noise barrages and supporting 'adopted' communities of rural and urban poor.

In order to respond to the challenges, a St Scholastican student must be:

- critically aware of their surroundings;
- morally and intellectually honest;
- sensitive to the plight of the poor;
- committed to academic excellence; and
- equipped to take action with regard to issues in society.

HOW? CREATING A SOCIALLY ORIENTED SCHOOL

The methodology and system of valuation at St Scholastica's consider individual differences and contribute to the development of social responsibility. The dialogical, creative and research-oriented pedagogy of the college is liberating; both student and teacher are subjects of education and they learn together. The aim is to prepare liberated and liberating citizens who are subjects of history capable of changing society; this is evidenced by the alumni, who include the first female president of the Philippines.

Figure 15.1 shows that for a school to be socially oriented, the thrusts of the school, the objectives, operations and curricula must all contribute to the development of social awareness and social responsibility.

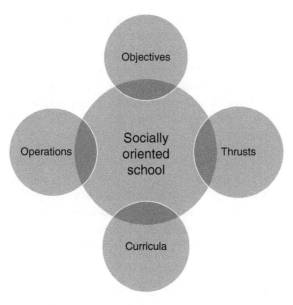

Figure 15.1 The socially oriented school

Objectives

Social justice is both a goal and a process (Adams et al., 2016). The goal of social justice is full and equitable participation of people from all social identity groups in a society that is mutually shaped to meet their needs. At St Scholastica's, the social justice objectives are for all students to be physically and psychologically safe and secure, recognised, and treated with respect. All students are to contribute to a society in which the distribution of resources is equitable and ecologically sustainable. The four core values and advocacies of St Scholastica's are outlined in Figure 15.2.

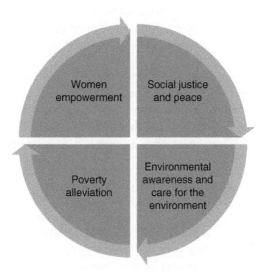

Figure 15.2 Core objectives, values and advocacies

1. *Social justice and peace.* St Scholastica's Social Action Centre (SAC) and Institutional Social Action Centre (ISAC) both have outreach centres and outreach acvitity programmes. They network with local and international non-governmental organisations (NGOs). They take a stand on issues of national concern; they support the indigenous peoples of the Philippines by 'adopting' schools in rural areas (Manobos schools), supporting medical missions, providing aid to victims of natural disasters, and educating evacuated pupils who have been forced out of their schools due to martial law. The night secondary school provides free high school education to over 150 students daily.

2. *Environmental awareness.* A Committee on Environmental Care (CEC) was established to lead the school's advocacy on Care for the Earth. The school supports environmental stewardship by supporting Earth Day and Earth Hour, as well as completing environmental audits and action plans. Each student plants a tree at the annual tree-planting ceremony. They support the ancestral land claim of the indigenous peoples and run anti-mining campaigns and forums of climate change. They set up farms and mini-forests. They have solar-powered buildings and a complete ban on styrofoam and plastics on campus.

3. *Poverty alleviation.* Supporting the ancestral land claim of indigenous peoples, adopting rural schools, supporting medical missions, providing aid to victims of natural disasters, providing free high school education to over 150 students daily.

4. *Women empowerment.* St Scholastica's pioneered women's studies in the Philippines. They established the Institute of Women's Studies and were the first school in the Philippines to mainstream women's studies. They link with women's organisations nationally and internationally.

Thrusts

The thrusts of St Scholastica's contribute to the development of social awareness, social justice and social responsibility. Sister Mary John Mananzan told us:

> The students have the choice to stand up, but they must know what they are standing up for. Fear is very infectious, but likewise – courage. If all of us are afraid, then everybody lives in fear. We need someone to stand up to be the spark; the hope is that we all pull together as a critical mass that can change society.

We witnessed this 'spark' first-hand as we attended the One Billion Rising rally in Manila with the students and staff to protest against violence to women and children. Students were well informed about the current political situation and spoke articulately about their social responsibility to give a 'voice to the voiceless'. Students were also accompanied by parents to the rally. One parent I spoke to at the rally told me, 'Scholasticans are intelligent, they are people who will not abide abuse, they are not afraid to speak out'.

Curricula

The curriculum is based on the process of see/judge/act, where social analysis and reflection are equally valued as a potent means of responding critically to situations, events and structures. The teaching strategies include plenary lectures, classroom lectures, hands-on exercises, immersion, independent work, and individual and group consultation.

Students have an immersive learning experience first, and the objectives for the students are as follows:

1. Develop a clearer understanding of the value of the dignity of the human person.

2. Understand why Scholasticans get involved with social realities and issues such as care for the marginalised and the elderly.

3. Apply the values of listening, compassion and respect for human dignity.

Examples of immersive learning experiences can be seen in Table 15.2.

Table 15.2 Immersive learning experiences and response

Immersive learning experience	Response
Tuluyan ni San Benito Orphanage	Child-friendly interior design
Baguio City	Conservation of natural environment
Santissima Trinidad	Educating the partner community
Depression treatment and research centre Manila Tytana College	Interior design projects with the community
Tondo and Baseco Compound	Film-making exploratory documentary on the phenomenon of slum tourism
Coastal areas	Coastal clean-up campaigns
Missionaries of the poor	Making eco-bricks to use as building materials in the slums
Pandacan community	Reading and sports with partner community

Operations

In operational terms, St Scholastica's follows an experiential approach to leadership development. The first step is personal leadership (to know and manage one's self). The second step is organisational leadership (to lead through influence). The third step is social change leadership, which means that the students are immersed in the community, as described above, and then take positive action with the community, respecting the wishes, needs and diversity of the community. The subject of social change leadership is the final requirement (see Figure 15.3).

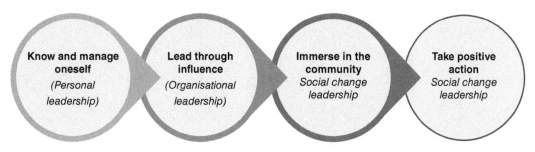

Figure 15.3 Experiential approach to leadership development

Students are expected to apply acquired skills to bring about positive social change by helping marginalised communities identify and deal with problems. The key to their success is the opportunity that every student has to interact and immerse in the school's partner communities to better understand their needs, to plan with the community on viable solutions, and to collectively take action to implement these solutions within the community.

SUMMARY: WHAT NEXT?

If we envision a world in which individuals are both self-determining and interdependent, transformative social justice involves students who have a sense of their own agency as well as a sense of social responsibility towards and with others, their society, the environment, and the broader world in which we live. These conditions we not only wish for ourselves, but for all people in our interdependent global community, and St Scholastica's gives us an inspirational example of this at its best.

REFERENCE

Adams, M., Bell, L.A., Goodman, D.J. and Joshi, K.Y. (2016) *Teaching for Diversity and Social Justice*, 3rd edn. London: Routledge.

16

LEADERSHIP AND MANAGEMENT IN EDUCATION

STEPHEN HENRY AND YVONNE MOOGAN

In these two opinion pieces, ideas about educational leadership are discussed.

Stephen Henry is an academic who has also recently been a principal of a large academy school in England. Yvonne Moogan is also an academic, and she has substantial experience in education and business education in the private sector. Stephen talks about ethical leadership and makes the point that school heads and principals cannot be responsible for the problems of the education system, nor can they put right many of the issues that arise as a result of deprivation and disadvantage. Yvonne's approach is different – she talks about management and leadership, and considers how models of leadership can be applied to education.

QUESTIONS TO THINK ABOUT

The two pieces are written in very different ways and focus on different aspects of leadership and management. Why do you think this is?

Consider the ideas that the authors are trying to get across. For each piece, try to distil one or two main ideas in a couple of sentences. You might want to think about which words are emphasised by each of the authors – are these the same or different in the two pieces?

What ideas can you take about leadership and management from the two pieces? How do you think leadership and management are different?

What do you think about Stephen's Spider-Head/Super-Head ideas? Do these ideas resonate with you? What do you think about Yvonne's idea that communication and culture are key to leadership?

You could also go back to earlier chapters in the book (e.g. Chapters 3 and 9) and think again about the purposes and functions of schools and the ways that schools work in the light of these two opinion pieces. How can you relate what you have read in these opinion pieces about leadership to what you already know from your own experience and what you have learned about education from this book?

ETHICAL VERSUS PASSIONATE LEADERSHIP: 'SPIDER-HEAD', NOT 'SUPER-HEAD'

STEPHEN HENRY

The creation and proliferation of academies, free schools and multi-academy trusts (MATs) has gone hand in hand with the growing interest school leaders have shown in what is known as 'passionate leadership' (Davies and Brighouse, 2008). This model of leadership centres on the belief that the drive and commitment of school leaders is the key to bridging the achievement gap in schools across the UK. Indeed, with the support of organisations such as Ambition Institute and the New Schools Network, there is a strong message coming from many system leaders and politicians that disadvantage can be challenged and overcome if there is enough will and skill 'at the top'. In many schools, particularly those in challenging circumstances, you will see this approach splashed across halls and walls, with slogans such as 'Whatever it takes' and 'No excuses'. While this may seem laudable and needed to overcome low aspirations and expectations, there are hidden but growing consequences of such an approach. While much store is placed in the successes of the London Challenge and individual schools such as Mossbourne and, more recently, the Michaela Community School, less attention is paid to the price paid by those who fall victim to what I would call 'the cost of passionate leadership'.

PASSION VERSUS ETHICS

Passionate leadership can be defined as being 'about energy, commitment, a belief that every child can learn and will learn, a concern with social justice and the optimism that we can make a difference' (Davies and Brighouse, 2010, p4). How this is often interpreted at school level is that success or failure of a school can be attributed to the levels of energy and drive of the school leaders. Here, then, we have the latest incarnation of the concept of the 'Super-Head'. This is not a new concept, but the high stakes of accountability and the 'privatisation' (Ball, 2012) of education have created a new universe ripe for mission-driven superheroes. Indeed, many of the attributes of these school leaders follow in the style of the DC Comics character Superman. Typically, DC heroes are godlike or possess godlike powers (e.g. Wonder Woman, Aquaman). Similarly, Superman is depicted as one who has abilities above those of mere mortals, as well as a flawless moral character. The imperative to help those less-fortunate souls knows no limits, and in his own words Superman's drive is 'Up, up and away'. With the freedoms granted to free schools, academies and on a larger scale MATs and the 'super-accountability' culture, school leaders are now being given the 'superpowers' to tackle the educational villain of underachievement.

However, I believe that in reality, education more closely resembles the Marvel Universe than that of DC. Marvel characters are typically flawed humans whose powers often come at a heavy personal price (Lee and Conway, 2001). They are often plucked from obscurity with an ordinary backstory, and after a brush with science gone wrong end up with powers that they struggle to cope with and can sometimes end in tragedy. Spider-Man is one such Marvel character that experiences such a journey. While DC sells its readers the line that there are superheroes who will always intervene and save the day with their endless energy and moral, Marvel cautions the reader that their characters will strive for what is right but will sometimes fail, and that there is sometimes collateral damage (see Table 16.1).

Table 16.1 Are school leaders living in a DC world or a Spider-Verse?

	Super-Head	Spider-Head
Leadership model	Passionate	Ethical
Leadership style	Lead from the heart	Lead from the head
Superpower	Strength	Invisibility
Arch-enemy	Doubters	Self-doubt
Most likely to say	'No excuses'	'Ends do not justify the means'
Least likely to say	'I do not know'	'I do not care'
Would like to be	Remembered	Understood

THE MYTH OF THE 'SUPER-HEAD'

My difficulty with the concept of passionate leadership is that it implies anything is possible with the right will and drive from the school leaders. This ignores the complex and layered issues that impact on pupil underachievement. It assumes that the only factors at play holding pupils back are in the control of school leaders. Setting high expectations, having a zero-tolerance behaviour policy and ensuring teachers work harder are seen as the essential ingredients in closing the achievement gap. Where the gap does not close, as measured by an ever-changing metric, the blame must lie with a lack of will or drive from the top. Furthermore, the myth of the 'Super-Head' leaves schools open to exploitation in the worst cases by ego-driven leaders promising to deliver the earth. On a broader level, one only has to look at the rise in salaries of MAT and school leaders to understand that the gap between what is expected of these leaders and what is possible is growing. The unrealistic expectations combined with the willingness of leaders to accept the challenge is ultimately self-defeating and has contributed to the increasing turnover of school leaders.

This is not to say there have not been schools where improvements have been made. However, how many of these schools serve a largely working-class white British population? In just one region of the UK, the North West, areas such as Blackpool, Knowsley and Salford have consistently failed to meet the expectations of Ofsted, regional schools commissioners or the Department for Education (for details about education opportunity areas, see **www.gov.uk/government/publications/social-mobility-and-opportunity-areas**). Indeed, the high expectations placed on school leaders, and more recently the MATs running schools in these areas, have contributed to what is rapidly becoming a recruitment and retention crisis.

In their efforts to improve schools in these areas, many school leaders find themselves grappling with their conscience and occasionally falling foul of ethical practice and even the law. There have been numerous examples of school leaders abusing their powers in relation to finance, pupil admissions and examination rules. While such practices are to be condemned, it is easy to see why they are becoming more commonplace, as leaders have been given greater powers at the same time as being asked to take on the near-impossible task of cancelling out the disadvantage suffered by their pupils.

Head teachers and principals are mere mortals that have been given specific powers to try to improve the life chances of those pupils in their charge. What they are not are superhumans gifted with the ability to wipe out the twin evils of poverty and disadvantage.

WHAT MODEL OF LEADERSHIP, THEN, IF NOT PASSIONATE?

Ethical leadership is rooted in the motto, 'Do whatever is right'. School leaders faced with an expanding range of accountabilities across not only pupil outcomes, but also increasingly those of running a large business, should strive to do what they believe to be the right thing. Be transparent, inclusive and, yes, passionate, but acknowledge their own failings and draw on the support of others. It is possibly acceptance by the education system that no one person can, or should, lead a modern school that will see a shift from the DC-model 'Super-Head' to a more Marvel character of a 'Spider-Head'. Where instead of the kryptonite of accountability draining the strength of one leader, we see leaders drawing on the strength of other 'Avengers' in the eternal battle with the supervillain of underachievement.

RESOURCES FOR FURTHER LEARNING

Ball, S.J. (2017) *The Education Debate*, 3rd edn. Bristol: Policy Press.

This book looks at key education policy debates. It looks in detail at trends in policy and presents a passionate case for what our priorities should be for the future of education in our schools. This would be useful if you are completing an assignment on policy and politics or the sociology of education.

Benn, M. (2012) *School Wars*. London: Verso.

This book looks at the evolution of schools under successive governments, including the development of free schools and academies. It presents the case for comprehensive schooling and a new kind of progressive education. This would be useful if you are completing an assignment on education policy or leadership.

Davies, B. and Brighouse, T. (2008) *Passionate Leadership in Education*. London: SAGE.

This book looks at taking a passionate approach to school leadership in driving change. It puts the vision and drive of leaders at the centre of the debate on improving the education system. This would be useful if you are completing an assignment on leadership.

REFERENCES

Ball, S.J. (2012) Performativity, privatisation, professionals and the state. In B. Cunningham (ed.), *Exploring Professionalism*. London: Institute of Education Press, University of London, pp50–72.

Ball, S.J. (2017) *The Education Debate*, 3rd edn. Bristol: Policy Press.

Benn, M. (2012) *School Wars*. London: Verso.

Davies, B. and Brighouse, T. (2008) *Passionate Leadership in Education*. London: SAGE.

Davies, B. and Brighouse, T. (2010) Passionate leadership. *Management in Education*, 24(1): 4–6.

Lee, S. and Conway, J. (2001) *Spider-Man: Death of Gwen Stacy*. New York: Marvel Comics.

LEADERSHIP STRATEGIES

YVONNE MOOGAN

INTRODUCTION

Today, head teachers and their deputies are not really teachers in the classroom. They are managers, accountants, businesspeople, strategists and HR leaders trying to juggle endless roles while working within the constraints of demanding stakeholders (parents, pupils, employees, governors, government and the local authority). Many head teachers are responsible for other schools, whether this is due to gaining academy status or not, but they are chief executives of multiple parties trying to balance the various budgets while providing as strong an educational service as they possibly can. This is frequently not something they 'signed up' for while starting their teaching career many years previously. In addition, the administrative duties with reporting responsibilities are increasing year on year, making the role of head teacher an increasingly strategic one whereby they have to plan long term, as well as in the short period, and all with limited resources. Hence, they are more like business leaders than ever before.

This piece will document those leadership strategies that senior managers in the education sector may use. It will help you to understand the theories and practices with which leaders engage in when supporting and moving their school(s) forward. We will discuss the models that may be used by leaders in education so that you can develop your own viewpoint of what an effective leader may look like. You will therefore gain an understanding of what constitutes a senior leadership role and the challenges these head teachers face.

LEADERSHIP

To understand leadership, one can differentiate between leadership and management. For example, the leader will use the functions of management to plan, organise and control, but with their interpersonal skills of inspiring and motivating people, which is what makes them a leader (DuBrin, 2016). Basically, the head teacher must influence and inspire their colleagues so that they do have an impact, but the management tasks are often administrative roles that are also the responsibility of the head teacher. Strategic leadership is about anticipating the future with the motivation to adapt to the environment, and head teachers may not necessarily make similar decisions even when faced with the same issues. The problem could be pupil underachievement caused by numerous reasons, but head teachers in two schools may respond very differently. Hence, we should start with some basic questions, such as 'What are we doing well in our school, and how do we continue to achieve this?' (execution), followed by 'How do we get to a different and better place?' (strategy) and 'Who are we and who do we want to be?' (mission) with 'What do we want for our school's future, and how can we add value?' (vision).

According to Hayes (2018), looking after a school would be called management (consistency of day-to-day operations) while changing it is called leadership (creating a new direction). Hayes (2018) continues to say that leadership is about communicating ideas that will achieve the vision. Hence, motivating and encouraging teachers to address the difficulties of the school and provide possible solutions to reach that vision requires patience and diplomacy. This means that head teachers must constantly review the educational environment for threats (declining pupil numbers or government interference or local authority budget cuts or Ofsted ratings), identifying what is required to move the school forward into the future and maximise any opportunities along the way. In order to do this, a shared sense of purpose must be created, as well as a team approach, with teachers, teaching assistants, administrators and senior management being adopted. For example, empowering staff so that all are willing to implement change and share the vision collectively is perhaps the most important role of the head teacher and their senior management team.

Leadership styles may be classified as transactional or transformational. So, what does this all mean? If the teachers perform their job roles day in, day out, they may ask for recognition for their performance as demanded by the head teacher, whereby there is a focus on targets rather than on the vision of the school (transactional leadership). In contrast, the head teacher may inspire their staff to be team players so that the staff perform better and work for the best interests of the school (transformational leadership). As De Smet et al. (2018) note, a transformational style of leader creates a greater culture of entrepreneurship so that delivery is more effective and success is achieved. Adopting this style of leadership could be the way forward as schools today have to be innovative due to the constraints they work within. For example, how schools attract funding and generate additional income streams can be challenging. De Smet et al. (2018) talk of leading agile transformation, which strengthens the fact that leadership style is critical in developing an innovative side and being forward-thinking.

COMMUNICATION

Communication is the most important part of any leadership role. Timely and relevant communication can reduce confusion in the school so that every employee knows exactly what is expected of them and what they must undertake. For example, everyone must be working towards a common set of strategic goals, which Mintzberg (2009) notes as the key in developing a strategy whereby all the team are rowing in the same direction as one unit. But trust is just as important when communicating new strategies (Thompson et al., 2017). This is because staff can regularly have competing aims and objectives, even within the same school. This means that it is the responsibility of the senior management team of the school to set the school's objectives in order to achieve their strategic vision.

So, how does the head teacher communicate this strategic vision? The vision is often determined by senior management with the governors' approval and a strategy will then be agreed. However, the head teacher has to communicate clearly and informatively, involving everyone so that all staff understand and 'sign in' to it. Hence, agreement has to be within the whole school.

So, how can a head teacher implement a vision and develop this strategy? There are several models that support strategic implementation, and one of those is the McKinsey 7S Framework, which concentrates on the seven interconnecting elements around a shared value centre point that all other elements feed into (De Smet et al., 2018).

CULTURE

There can, however, be barriers within schools when developing a new strategy, and one barrier is that of cultural factors. For example, culture is made up of the values and social codes that are developed from shared beliefs, whereby the teachers realise there is a line of authority. Understanding the stakeholders of the school is equally important. This is because multiple stakeholders may have different roles, responsibilities and interests that need to be managed by the head teacher. For example, if the head teacher wishes to transform the school from one structure to another, it will demand cultural change to go with it, which in turn may require a look inwards first at the school and the senior management team at the onset. Hence, the leader needs to transform themselves and then the teams, followed by the rest of the school in this process. There could also be further issues, especially where schools are in a group academy status. For example, there may be different styles and attitudes with varying degrees of emotions, even in the same school.

Understanding culture in retaining teachers and enhancing motivation of employees within the organisation is crucial when becoming a leader (Bartlett and Ghoshal, 1990; Rashid et al., 2003; Katzenbach et al., 2012). This is because deeply entrenched cultures in a school will interfere with the overall programme, making the development of a strategy difficult. For example, schools with similar cultures and backgrounds may be easier to manage as cultural conflict is less likely, although there could be surface layers at the top that are not noticed, whereas at the bottom inexplicit assumptions with beliefs may exist.

CONCLUSION

In this piece, I have discussed the fact that leadership and management are two very different concepts. We have seen that different cultures and communication styles can facilitate or constrain leadership in different ways, depending on the situation. As we have seen throughout this book, education comprises a complex set of interactions that have to be understood in context if they are to be understood at all.

RESOURCES FOR FURTHER LEARNING

Hayes, J. (2018) *The Theory of Practice of Change Management*, 5th edn. London: Palgrave Macmillan.

Chapter 9 of this text is an academic source with current theories and models focusing on the service sector. It also has a management focus.

Kotter, J.P. (2007) Leading change: why transformation efforts fail. *Harvard Business Review*, 85(1): 96–103.

This article is a good practical alternative to Hayes.

REFERENCES

Bartlett, C. and Ghoshal, S. (1990) Matrix management: not a structure, more a frame of mind. *Harvard Business Review*, 68(4): 138–45.

De Smet, A., Lurie, M. and St. George, A. (2018) *Leading Agile Transformation: The New Capabilities Leaders Need to Build 21st-Century Organizations*. Available at: www.mckinsey.com/business-functions/organization/our-insights/leading-agile-transformation-the-new-capabilities-leaders-need-to-build-21st-century-organizations

DuBrin, A.J. (2016) *Leadership: Research Findings, Practice and Skills*, 8th edn. Boston, MA: Cengage Learning.

Hayes, J. (2018) *The Theory of Practice of Change Management*, 5th edn. London: Palgrave Macmillan.

Katzenbach, J.R., Steffen, I. and Kronley, C. (2012) Cultural change that sticks. *Harvard Business Review*, 90(7/8): 110–17.

Kotter, J.P. (2007) Leading change: why transformation efforts fail. *Harvard Business Review*, 85(1): 96–103.

Mintzberg, H. (2009) Management: PwC's Strategy &. 2014. *What is a capability*.

Rashid, M.A., Sambasivan, M. and Johari, J. (2003) The influence of corporate culture and organisational commitment on performance. *Journal of Management Development*, 22(8): 708–28.

Thompson, A., Peteraf, M., Gamble, J. and Strickland, A. (2017) *What Is Organisational Culture? Crafting and Executing Strategy: The Quest for Competitive Advantage – Concepts and Cases*. London: McGraw-Hill.

17

EARLY YEARS EDUCATION AND PLAY

ELEANOR HOSKINS AND LIZ GREGORY

In these two opinion pieces, you will read about the value of play in early years. The pieces are written by two specialists in early years. Elly Hoskins is an academic and an expert in early years with a good deal of experience working in the early years sector. Liz Gregory is an academic from a different background in English teaching and is also very experienced in early years.

In Elly's opinion piece, she makes a strong argument for the value of play in early years. Liz frames the argument rather differently, as you will see, while still emphasising the value of play.

QUESTIONS TO THINK ABOUT

Consider the ideas that the authors are trying to get across. For each piece, try to distil the main idea that the author is communicating in a couple of sentences of your own.

How is Liz's piece different from Elly's? Do you think that Liz's piece opposes what Elly is saying, detracts from the strength of Elly's argument, or adds to its strength?

What ideas can you take about play in the early years from the two pieces? Do you think that play is a foundation for academic learning? Or do you think that play *is* learning? Think about times when you have seen preschool children playing. Is play just 'for its own sake' or do you think that there are additional benefits to play?

You could also go back to earlier chapters in the book (e.g. Chapters 9 and 10) and think again about the purposes and functions of education and of schools. Another aspect that you could consider is the physical places where education does (or should) take place. Does education have to take place in formal settings? Or might it be better, especially in the early years, that it doesn't?

How can you relate what you have read in these opinion pieces about play in the early years to what you already know from your own experience and what you have learned from this book?

EARLY YEARS EDUCATION AND PLAY

ELEANOR HOSKINS

If I had a pound for every time I heard the comment 'How do children learn in early years when all they do is play all day?' then I would be a wealthy person by now!

Early years education often causes confusion as the approach, organisation and core principles within this phase differ from primary, and the flexible, often less-structured approach unsettles many. What do the children in early years do all day? Is early years education really that important when young children's attention spans are so limited? Are play and learning really related? This writing aims to unravel misconceptions about early years education while clarifying the core principles and practice that underpin this critical first stage.

WHAT IS THE IMPORTANCE OF EARLY YEARS EDUCATION?

Imagine building a house without any foundations. The house would be unable to stand without the deep footings and base keeping it upright and steady. The strength of any building lies in the quality foundations created at the first crucial stage of construction.

Early years education is essentially the same as it lays down the firm foundations for any future formal teaching and learning. Without these first foundation footings, there would be no steady educational ground to build upon and develop further. Throughout the early 'foundation' years, children develop their thinking, actions and emotions while beginning to make sense of the world around them via an exploratory, expressive, creative approach. During the early years of education, the young brain is still developing its connections, which is reliant upon stimulation (Katz, 2010). For this essential stimulation, young children's brains need engaging, open-ended and inspiring activities that will spark their interest and begin to formulate ideas for children to recall during future formal learning.

The pieces are easy to connect; consider writing a creative story without ever having experiences of exploring expressive, creative role play that encourages the imagination to run wild, or understanding the physics of buoyancy without observing floating and sinking objects at the water tray. Consider tackling mathematical equations without playing many games with numbers, or learning and following the rules of rugby or tennis without numerous occasions to explore open-ended throwing, catching or bat-and-ball play. It is crystal-clear that open-ended, unstructured, trial-and-error experiences within early years education lay the foundations for future life learning and formal education, where vital early experiences will help the learner join the dots.

WHAT IS PLAY?

When we think about our own memories of play, we will often remember playing with favourite toys and games alongside siblings, other family or friends, often for hours on end. We will almost certainly have memories of warm summer holidays or other family celebrations where we played with open freedom. Although these memories and thoughts are accurate and based upon our own experiences, they also often lead us to associate 'play' as the opposite to work (Andrews, 2012). This, in turn, can influence us to categorise play as unimportant, lacking in purpose and something children will grow out of as they mature into adults, but such a view is often mistaken (Whitebread, 2012). Play is the open door to a whole world of complete discovery. It can happen in many ways and will lead a child to discover, explore, problem-solve, investigate and develop through simultaneous experiences. Play underpins the Early Years Foundation Stage (EYFS), but do our own perceptions of play lead us to categorise this crucial element as unimportant?

WHAT ARE THE BENEFITS OF PLAY?

Children are born ready, able and eager to learn. They actively reach out to interact with other people, and in the world around them. Development is not an automatic process, however. It depends on each unique child having opportunities to interact in positive relationships and enabling environments.

(Early Education and DfE, 2012, p2)

Considering 'development is not an automatic process' in order for children to have the 'opportunities to interact in positive relationships and enabling environments', they need the freedom to explore, tinker, discover, observe, share and try without too much structure, but with lots of stimulation. While children play alongside each other, they will learn to share, take turns, work as a team and understand how to manage conflict. These essential social and emotional interactions begin to shape the young mind for a future of communications within education and general life. Alongside this, the experiences gained through exploration, problem-solving or unlimited imaginative re-enactment changes the structure of the developing young brain in important ways.

So, does all of this outline the benefits of play? Consider the impact upon children's language and social development if they existed in isolation without opportunity to freely chatter with other children or observe another's actions. Imagine the implications upon future friendships and relationships if children do not have the open opportunities to explore cooperation or the changing feelings of others. Envisage the restrictions upon children's problem-solving and intellectual development without the tinkering opportunities where they will discover through a trial, error and repeat cycle, or the limitations of a creative mind without the freedom to explore hours of role play and re-enactment. Yes, this does outline the benefits of play; in fact, 'children suffering from play deprivation suffer abnormalities in neurological development' (Whitebread, 2012, p6), which spells out the implications if the benefits of play are not recognised.

SUMMARY

So, is there any importance in early years education? Yes. If you consider importance in the development of intellectual, creative, social, emotional, physical and language skills within every child.

Early years and the free-flowing, flexible approach provides fertile soil for little seedlings to grow. It offers the platform for learning through play, which we have already established has clear and concise benefits. Early years is the only educational stage where children can learn and discover through play without limitations, as once children progress into primary, the formality of timetable restrictions and strict objectives reduces opportunities for open-ended discovery. Learning through play needs time and space for those engaged to reap the full fruit of benefits, and within early years education this can happen. So, 'How do children learn in early years when all they do is play all day?' I think the answer to this is: very well indeed!

REFERENCES

Andrews, M. (2012) *Exploring Play for Early Childhood Studies*. London: SAGE.

Early Education and Department for Education (DfE) (2012) *Development Matters in the Early Years Foundation Stage*. Available at: www.foundationyears.org.uk/files/2012/03/Development-Matters-FINAL-PRINT-AMENDED.pdf

Katz, L.G. (2010) How young children learn: a developmental approach to the curriculum in the early years. In S. Schmidt (ed.), *Key Issues in Early Years Education*. London: Routledge, pp9–18.

Whitebread D. (2012) *The Importance of Play: A Report on the Value of Children's Play with a Series of Policy Recommendations*. Available at: www.importanceofplay.eu/IMG/pdf/dr_david_whitebread_-_the_importance_of_play.pdf

WRITING BACK: COMPARING PRESCHOOL PHILOSOPHIES – PLAY OR ACADEMIC LEARNING?

LIZ GREGORY

Kids should be kids, right? Well, not necessarily. Debate continues to rage about what exactly our preschoolers (i.e. children aged between 3 and 5) should be learning before they enter the more formal schooling system. According to some, play-based is the way to go – a child-centred, free play environment in which children can just enjoy being, well, children. On the other side of the fence are those who see preschool as a chance to establish the more structured, teacher-directed routines that await children during the rest of their academic careers. As usual, there are two sides to every story.

PLAY-BASED LEARNING

There's far more weight behind play-based learning than the natural urge to let children just enjoy being children. For one thing, preschoolers are often simply not ready cognitively or socially to cope with the rigours of more structured instruction, and exposing them to this kind of failure is potentially setting them up for a lifetime of antagonism in the education system. Many of the foundations of academic study – such as seriation (the ability to organise items in size order, and therefore the basis of all number studies) or conservation (the understanding that objects which change their physical appearance can retain some or all of their original properties) – are not acquired cognitively until school age, and learning cannot take place until these key concepts have been obtained.

In any case, play doesn't have to be just play. Research has identified at least 16 different types of play (Hughes, 2002), each of which can provide vital learning opportunities; indeed, studies such as the Researching Effective Pedagogy in the Early Years (REPEY) project have shown that children offered a play-based curriculum with learning opportunities based around social and communication skills made the most progress (Siraj-Blatchford et al., 2002). The early years are the perfect time to learn key life skills such as independence, creativity, and working cooperatively and collaboratively with their peers. Some of these activities provide a natural opportunity to begin learning about the organisational structures children will encounter at school (such as carpet or circle time activities, where children learn to sit quietly together in a large group). This kind of preparation is far more valuable than a curriculum-based focus, for which some children will not yet be ready.

The REPEY project also highlighted the difficulty faced by practitioners working in a range of diverse settings with children from different backgrounds and with differing abilities in trying to adhere to a fixed notion of what a child might need as preparation for school, with one participant pointing out:

> *There isn't a list of ten skills that we would like children to reach here and then feel on that basis that they will do really well in reception.*

(Siraj-Blatchford et al., 2002, p77)

Indeed, such a list doesn't even exist, with no clear definition of school readiness available, despite the topic being so widely discussed. The EYFS refers to 'the broad range of knowledge and skills that provide the right foundation for good future progress through school and life' (DfE, 2017) – guidance that is open to a wide range of interpretations.

In any case, what parent would want their child's individuality and personal qualities to potentially be neglected in pursuit of a set of standards that not all children will be able to meet?

ACADEMIC LEARNING

Whether we like it or not, these days academic success is measured in terms of academic grades and qualifications. A recent report on school readiness suggests that children are falling behind in the early years, with the majority of schools expressing concerns about the school readiness of the children joining them (NAHT and Family and Childcare Trust, 2017). Of particular concern was children's lack of speech, language and communication skills, with the social, emotional and physical development of some children also a worry for schools – schools who carry the significant responsibility of ensuring their new intake can start learning from day one. Nobody wants a child to feel left out or left behind because they lack the essential skills to survive and thrive in this challenging new environment.

Teachers are required to assess children at the end of the school year in which they turn 5, and while this is observation-based rather than requiring children to sit an exam, it marks the beginning of a cycle of continuous testing and assessment throughout their academic career. A new baseline assessment for children in reception is due to come in from 2020, and standard attainment tests (SATs) to measure pupil progress against the national curriculum await children at the end of Key Stages 1 and 2. The EYFS states that in the early years, children will be taught mostly through games and play (DfE, 2017), but does this really prepare our children for what is to come?

Research such as the NAHT and Family and Childcare Trust (2017) report indicates that preschool provision is most certainly not setting our children up to succeed later in life. High-quality early years education is one of the best ways of giving a child a good start in life, and is particularly important in helping close the gap that children from disadvantaged backgrounds face in the education system (e.g. see House of Commons Education Committee, 2019). If left unaddressed, this gap widens as children progress through their schooling, with recent data suggesting that 21.7 per cent of children on free school meals achieved good GCSE passes in maths and English compared to 45.8 per cent of their less-disadvantaged peers (DfE, 2018). Nobody is saying that children shouldn't be allowed to play and enjoy themselves in their early years, but if we do not equip them with the skills they need at school, we are surely doing them a grave disservice.

THE VERDICT

This particular debate isn't going to go away any time soon, but do the two sides of the argument need to be so diametrically opposed? Must different philosophies of learning constantly be portrayed as competing with one another in a vicious fight to the death, encouraged by a media whose sole aim is to divide opinion and promote controversy? The recent focus in the press on school readiness suggests that there *is* an issue with preschool provision and its ability to prepare youngsters for the demands of the education system. However, such narrow coverage ignores the idea that preschool education can provide far more than academic preparation for school – a nurturing environment in which children can discover what they love, develop their creativity and interests, and enjoy the social benefits that peer-based cooperation can bring. With so much at stake, perhaps now is the time to blur the lines between pedagogies for the benefit of children, parents and teachers alike.

FURTHER READING

Whatever your thoughts on the issue of early years curricula, the Early Years Foundation Stage (EYFS) is essential reading for anyone involved in the education or care of young children. The EYFS is a government publication setting out the statutory framework which all schools and Ofsted-registered providers of early years education, such as childminders and nurseries, must follow. It sets the standard for the learning, development and care of children aged between 0 and 5 years old. You can find it via the link in the References (DfE, 2017).

The REPEY project discussed in the article also makes for interesting reading, drawing on case studies conducted in a range of early years settings.

REFERENCES

Department for Education (DfE) (2017) *Statutory Framework for the Early Years Foundation Stage.* Available at: https://assets.publishing.service.gov.uk/government/uploads/system/uploads/attachment_data/file/596629/EYFS_STATUTORY_FRAMEWORK_2017.pdf

Department for Education (DfE) (2018) *Revised GCSE and Equivalent Results in England, 2016 to 2017.* Available at: https://assets.publishing.service.gov.uk/government/uploads/system/uploads/attachment_data/file/676596/SFR01_2018.pdf

House of Commons Education Committee (2019) *Tackling Disadvantage in the Early Years.* Available at: https://publications.parliament.uk/pa/cm201719/cmselect/cmeduc/1006/1006.pdf

Hughes, B. (2002) *A Playworker's Taxonomy of Play Types*, 2nd edn. London: Routledge.

NAHT and Family and Childcare Trust (2017) *School Ready? A Survey of School Leaders by NAHT and Family and Childcare Trust.* Available at: www.familyandchildcaretrust.org/school-ready-survey-school-leaders

Siraj-Blatchford, I., Sylva, K., Muttock, S., Gidlen, R. and Bell, D. (2002) *Researching Effective Pedagogy in the Early Years.* London: DfES.

18

MENTAL HEALTH AND WELL-BEING

GEMMA STEPHENS, JONATHAN GLAZZARD AND SAMUEL STONES

For these two pieces, mental health and well-being is the topic. This is a current issue – as you will read, the government, schools and colleges, and people in general are thinking more and more about mental health and well-being.

The two pieces are written by very different people. Gemma Stephens is a very experienced psychology teacher who has worked for many years with young people, particularly those aged 16–19. She has a lot of experience in working with young people who have mental health issues, and her training in psychology as well as in teaching means that she can bring an in-depth professional understanding to her work with young people. Jonathan Glazzard is Professor of Inclusive Education in the Carnegie School of Education at Leeds Beckett University. He is an experienced teacher educator and committed to ensuring that mental health difficulties at school do not stand in the way of young people's future success. His co-author, Samuel Stones, is also a teacher educator, and is an associate researcher in the Carnegie School of Education at Leeds Beckett University.

QUESTIONS TO THINK ABOUT

In what ways do these pieces frame the issue of mental health and well-being differently? Why do you think that is?

How do the two pieces describe and explain how mental health problems might affect young people?

Are the issues that are identified as key in the two pieces the same? What kinds of evidence do the authors use for the points they make? Do they talk about empirical studies, or their own experience, or do they take what might seem to be a more common-sense 'woman or man in the street' point of view? Or a mixture of these? Does the evidence used add to the strength of the arguments that are being made?

Do the authors suggest different or similar solutions to the issues?

Consider your own view of mental health and well-being. Do you think that this is the big problem it is presented as? Why or why not? Are there any solutions that you can think of that these opinion pieces haven't covered?

MENTAL HEALTH AND WELL-BEING

GEMMA STEPHENS

Mental illness is on the rise, so as teachers we need to be aware of what mental fitness means and how to spot the signs even if we are told those immortal words, 'I'm fine'. If we consider the statistics, around one in ten young people experience a mental health issue at any one time. For adults, this is one in four. Mental health refers to our psychological and emotional well-being. This can change depending on the stresses and strains of life. We often associate mental illness with adults, but this simply is not the case. More and more children are being diagnosed with mental health conditions, so it's important that we educate them on how to keep fit mentally, not only physically. One of the biggest challenges for many people is admitting that they have a mental health condition. There is a stigma surrounding mental illness that makes individuals worried about how they will be labelled and stereotyped, discounted and discriminated against. This stigma is decreasing, but there is still an enormous amount of it in existence, which – coupled with the desire to 'fit in' during our school years – could lead to disastrous consequences.

SOCIAL AND EMOTIONAL WELL-BEING IN SCHOOLS

Social well-being in a school environment suggests that young people are able to have positive relationships with others and do not show any behavioural concerns such as disruption or bullying. Emotional well-being suggests that young people are happy and confident in their own abilities. Teachers may become concerned about individuals showing poor social and emotional well-being in school if a child becomes anxious, disruptive, inattentive or shows changes in their behaviour. Some children will be more vulnerable than others, such as those with parents who have drug/alcohol problems, those whose parents have mental health problems, those who experience family relationship problems such as domestic violence, those who have physical disabilities or communication difficulties, and those who have very young parents or parents with low academic attainment. Of course, there are young people who will not experience any of these but will have poor social and emotional well-being for other reasons.

So, why is it important for us as teachers to nurture positive social and emotional well-being in schools rather than simply focusing on the academic side of school? First, it helps provide the foundations for young people to achieve academically. If a child is unhappy, anxious and unsettled, they are unlikely to be in a state of mind to learn. Second, it helps to prevent mental illness and behavioural problems in younger years, but also long term, including substance abuse and other antisocial behaviours.

SOCIAL AND EMOTIONAL WELL-BEING IN SCHOOLS: A HOLISTIC APPROACH

A holistic approach means a whole-school approach. If all staff in the school are working as a team to promote positive social and emotional well-being among young people, it promotes a positive and productive atmosphere that is conducive to learning, and therefore achievement. In addition, it will help to reduce any anxiety/depressive symptoms among young people and help them to improve their self-control, understanding and recognition of their own and others' emotions. This can be achieved in many ways through curriculum planning, by giving young people a voice, through teaching and learning, ensuring that all young people feel safe to learn, ensuring there is appropriate support services and provision for children who are at risk of showing poor mental health/social/emotional well-being, and encouraging a culture/environment within the school where young people are encouraged to accept, understand and celebrate each other's differences.

MENTAL HEALTH INITIATIVES

World Mental Health Day is on 10 October every year. Schools have a crucial part to play in this to educate young people about the signs and symptoms of mental illness, as well as teaching them coping strategies and resilience techniques. Education helps to rid the stigma of mental illness and empowers young people to be open about their feelings. Coping strategies and resilience techniques enable young people to thrive throughout their life. Therefore, mental illness should be a priority in schools, not something showcased once a year. In order for this to happen, there will need to be a social and political change in education where mental health, social and emotional well-being are as important as other core curriculum subjects. However, that doesn't mean we need to wait for this to happen. As teachers, we can embed these healthy behaviours in all lessons and one-to-ones we have with young people.

If we educate the child, we save the adult! A small part of life is what happens to us; a large part of life is how we respond to it. We cannot always control our life issues and events, nor can we change our worries. However, we are able to manage how we respond to them. Keeping responses to a minimum and shortening the length of them brings the mood and destabilisation down to acceptable levels. Once this has occurred, we can utilise the tools effectively to help us manage the issues as they arise. Without this, we are at risk of managing issues ineffectively, which could potentially lead to poor mental health and well-being. However, with education, we are able to prevent the peaks and troughs of life getting out of hand.

Mental Health First Aid training teaches adults involved in a young person's life how to have the confidence and skills to step in if they suspect a young person is struggling and in need of support. The sooner any issues are recognised, it can prevent the issue turning into a crisis as they can get the help that they need, in which case Mental Health First Aid training can ultimately save lives. In addition to the support adults can provide for young people, training can also help us to provide a supportive environment within our schools where young people feel safe to open up and have the conversations necessary to get them the support they need. It is crucial that we create an environment where, just like physical illnesses, mental illnesses are also just part of everyday life.

In our college, we encourage students to take responsibility for their own mental health so that they feel empowered to help themselves. We facilitate this by creating a space for them to solve their own problems and we encourage resilience through tutorial sessions and subject lessons. If students are unable to overcome barriers themselves, we encourage them to seek help through external agencies and provide advice on how to do this. Some mental health issues are flagged by subject/personal tutors who refer our young people to our programme management team. On occasions, young people refer themselves, or in other circumstances they may be picked up by the team due to attendance or progress issues, which is when their difficulties become apparent. We have a team in place consisting of safeguarding and well-being officers, who are all trained externally by the local authority in how to guide and advise our young people who may be facing some poor mental health issues. In addition, staff are trained internally and update their qualifications every three years to ensure they have up-to-date knowledge on how best to support our young people. Sometimes our students come to us from school with already-diagnosed mental health issues; in some cases, our staff meet with staff from school to ensure a smooth transition for those individuals. We also do transition meetings for all students with our partner high schools. We have a data-sharing agreement with them that complies with the General Data Protection Regulation (GDPR), which means that we know about all of our students, not just the ones that present with difficulties.

When students come to us to enrol, we collect information and complete any relevant concern sheets, encouraging students to inform us of their needs. We are then able to disseminate this information to key staff within the college to ensure all young people are appropriately supported emotionally as well as academically. After enrolment, we have an induction phase where we introduce a 'pass it on' campaign. Posters are put up around college and sessions are delivered during tutorials by members of the programme management team as a way of introducing key members of staff to students and encouraging students to speak to relevant staff if they experience any issues or know somebody experiencing issues. This ensures early intervention strategies can be put into place before things get worse. Throughout the academic year, we have a coordinator who organises events in the college foyer where students pass at busy times such as lunchtimes. We have many different professional bodies come into college to talk to students about different matters, including mental health awareness. Ensuring our young people are aware of how to seek help for any issues they may face is important to us and allows us to create a happy and healthy learning environment.

RESOURCES FOR FURTHER LEARNING

Cantopher, T. (2015) *Overcoming Depression: The Curse of the Strong*. Louisville, KY: Westminster John Knox Press.

Peters, S. (2012) *The Chimp Paradox: The Mind Management Programme for Confidence, Success and Happiness*. London: Random House.

Tolle, E. (2010) *The Power of Now*. Novato, CA: New World Library.

MENTAL HEALTH AND WELL-BEING

JONATHAN GLAZZARD AND SAMUEL STONES

INTRODUCTION

Barely a week has gone by during the last two years when mental health in children and young people has not been discussed in the media. It is certainly a 'hot topic', and commercial organisations have been quick to jump on to this in a desperate bid to sell their products to schools. In 2017, the government in England published its long-awaited Green Paper, *Transforming Children and Young People's Mental Health Provision* (DoH and DfE, 2017), which set out its priorities for the next five years. The then Prime Minister, Theresa May, referred to mental health as one of the 'burning injustices' of our time, and the Green Paper was an attempt to rectify this. Mental health disorders cost individuals and societies dearly. If left untreated, they can be long-lasting, resulting in devastating consequences on individuals, families and the economy. This opinion piece challenges some of the assumptions in the Green Paper and outlines some possible solutions to addressing children and young people's mental health.

WHAT IS MENTAL HEALTH?

The World Health Organization defines mental health in the following way:

> *Mental health is defined as a state of well-being in which every individual realizes his or her own potential, can cope with the normal stresses of life, can work productively and fruitfully, and is able to make a contribution to her or his community.*

> (WHO, 2019)

This is a useful definition of mental health because it emphasises being mentally healthy rather than mental illness. A quick search through the Green Paper reveals that the word 'disorder' is used 75 times, illustrating a focus on mental illness, which is the extreme of the mental health continuum. A focus on the role of schools in enabling children and young people to maintain mentally healthy lives, rather than an emphasis on mental disorders, would have presented a more positive perspective on mental health.

IS THERE A CRISIS?

Media reports that emphasise the mental health 'crisis' generate hysteria. While the evidence in the Green Paper indicates that one in ten has some form of clinically diagnosable mental health disorder, equating to 850,000 children and young people, it is important to consider reasons for this other than simply to suggest that the numbers are escalating. There is currently greater public and professional awareness of mental health than was previously the case. This means that people are in a better, more informed position to recognise mental ill health, and therefore for mental ill health to be diagnosed clinically. In addition, in recent years, and particularly in the UK, the stigma associated with mental illness is gradually being eradicated, resulting in more people talking about mental health. This is a significant step in the right direction, but it does not necessarily mean that there is a greater prevalence of mental ill health, despite the statistics suggesting that this is the case. It is possible that cases of mental ill health were previously undiagnosed or 'swept under the carpet'. It is still the case that in some countries, and even within some cultural groups within the UK, a stigma still exists in relation to mental illness. The increased visibility given to mental illness in the media and the reduction of the stigma associated with mental ill health could have resulted in greater numbers of people coming forward seeking a medical diagnosis. Previously, the same people may have been less willing to seek a diagnosis due to fear that an official diagnosis would have a detrimental impact on their lives. While an increase in the prevalence of mental ill health cannot be disputed statistically, it is important to recognise that the figures may suggest a worsening situation, which may not necessarily be the case.

SHOULD SCHOOLS INVEST IN MENTAL HEALTH?

The Green Paper states:

> There is clear evidence that schools and colleges can, and do, play a vital role in identifying mental health needs at an early stage.

> (DoH and DfE, 2017, p4)

It emphasises the role of schools in addressing mental health, but at the same time it is important to remember that educators are not health professionals. Their primary role is to educate young people, not to treat mental health conditions.

Schools cannot solve all the problems in society. The responsibilities on teachers to address children's holistic needs have increased substantially over the last two decades, to the extent that teachers are now expected to identify and protect children from extremism, child abuse, online abuse and mental illness. At the same time, they are expected to raise children and young people's academic attainment and enable them to access further and higher education and employment. Where do the responsibilities of teachers end and what are the responsibilities of parents within this? We cannot keep adding more and more responsibilities to the duties of teachers while at the same time holding them accountable for young people's academic outcomes. It seems that teachers are now expected to function as parents, social workers, parental advisers (particularly for parents with mental illnesses) and health professionals all in one. Surely, a better solution is to ensure that children and young people's mental health needs can be met by adequately public-funded health and social care services so that teachers are in a better position to focus on educating them rather than fixing all the other problems.

WHAT ARE THE SOLUTIONS?

The Green Paper presents some simplistic solutions to support the mental health of children and young people in schools. These include the introduction of designated leaders of mental health in schools, mental health support teams, and shorter waiting times to access external health services. While these ambitions are laudable, they will only reach between one-fifth to one-quarter of schools by 2022/23. Access to support is therefore a postcode lottery, resulting in at least 75 per cent of young people not getting the support they need. These solutions are not adequate, and schools are simply placing a sticking plaster over the real causes of mental ill health.

To address the issues of mental ill health in children and young people, it is necessary for the government to address the causes, rather than diverting the problem on to schools. Adverse childhood experiences, including poor attachment, trauma, parental alcohol and drug abuse, domestic violence, and poverty, contribute significantly to mental ill health in children and young people (House of Commons Select Committee, 2018). In addition, high-stakes testing, exam pressure and the narrowing of the curriculum are significant school factors that can contribute to mental illness (House of Commons Select Committee, 2018). All of these require a political response, rather than simply passing the problem of mental ill health on to schools.

SUMMARY

This opinion piece has questioned the claims about the increased prevalence of mental ill health in children and young people. It has argued that schools and teachers cannot be expected to be accountable for an increasing range of societal issues, and that the government should ensure health and social care services are properly funded so that schools can focus on their core educational responsibilities. This opinion piece has argued that the government needs to address the underlying causes of mental ill health, including poverty, adverse childhood experiences, exam pressure and curriculum restriction, in order to solve the mental health crisis in children and young people. Therefore, a political response is required, rather than asking schools to place a sticking plaster over the issues.

RESOURCES FOR FURTHER LEARNING

Glazzard, J. and Bancroft, K. (2018) *Meeting the Mental Health Needs of Learners 11–18 Years*. St Albans: Critical Publishing.

This book is useful for trainee teachers and qualified teachers in the secondary phase. It will be useful for writing an assignment on mental health in adolescence.

Glazzard, J. and Bligh, C. (2018) *Meeting the Mental Health Needs of Children 4–11 Years*. St Albans: Critical Publishing.

This book is useful for trainee teachers and qualified teachers in the primary phase. It will be useful for writing an assignment on mental health in primary schools.

Glazzard, J. and Bostwick, R. (2018) *Positive Mental Health: A Whole School Approach*. St Albans: Critical Publishing.

This book outlines the elements of the whole-school approach to mental health. It is relevant for senior leaders in schools.

Glazzard, J. and Mitchell, C. (2018) *Social Media and Mental Health in Schools*. St Albans: Critical Publishing.

This book outlines the positive and negative effects of social media on children and young people's lives. It will be useful if you are writing an assignment on the impact of social media on young people's mental health.

REFERENCES

Department of Health (DoH) and Department for Education (DfE) (2017) *Transforming Children and Young People's Mental Health Provision: A Green Paper*. London: DoH/DfE.

House of Commons Select Committee (2018) *Child and Adolescent Mental Health Green Paper: Government Response to Committee Report*. Available at: www.parliament.uk

World Health Organization (WHO) (2019) *Mental Health*. Available at: www.who.int/features/factfiles/mental_health/en

19

TECHNOLOGY IN THE CLASSROOM

PETE ATHERTON AND STEVE INGLE

In this chapter, we consider two different views on educational technology in a digital world. They are written by two experienced educators: Steve Ingle and Pete Atherton.

Pete Atherton is a teacher educator and the author of *50 Ways to Use Technology Enhanced Learning in the Classroom*. His research interests include social media as a pedagogic tool, emerging literacies, and edtech and autoethnography. Steve Ingle is an experienced consultant, inspector, teacher educator and author with many years' experience. A specialist in teacher education, vocational pedagogy and technology-enhanced learning, Steve has worked with over 3,000 teachers, tutors and trainers throughout the UK and overseas to enhance the quality of education and its impact on learners and their lives.

QUESTIONS TO THINK ABOUT

The two pieces focus on very different issues in relation to edtech. Do you think that they ask equally important questions? What assumptions do each of the pieces make?

What do you think about Steve's point of view? Do people need to be digitally literate? What kind of skills do you think are necessary to live in our digital world? Is it up to schools and colleges to teach those skills?

This is what Pete has said about opinion pieces:

As a highly experienced educator with knowledge of a variety of settings and an author on edtech, I feel that I am well placed to offer an opinion piece on this issue. Though opinions are naturally subjective, they are in this case informed by extensive reflections on teaching and learning. In this respect, an opinion piece can make a valuable contribution to wider debates, as the personal can help illuminate the broader issues.

What do you think about this?

Do the two opinion pieces you have just read make a contribution to wider debates, with the personal informing the broader issues?

WHY DO TEACHERS NEED TO EMBRACE TECHNOLOGY IN THE CLASSROOM?

PETE ATHERTON

INTRODUCTION

In this piece, we will endeavour to identify the issues surrounding teachers using technology in the classroom. In doing so, we will examine, critique and contextualise the role of educational technologies in contemporary education. We will also discuss the importance of opinion pieces in contributing to wider debates. The piece will also look ahead to the ways in which edtech (or educational technology) could make a valuable contribution to children's education.

THE BROADER CONTEXT

You may already be aware that the world outside of education is technologically advanced. You may see highly skilled employees deploying state-of-the-art technology. You will certainly see a proliferation of young people using their phones to perform increasingly diverse and sophisticated tasks.

The employees of many high-tech firms will have developed their skills somehow, but did they acquire the knowledge, skills and behaviours at school? When I visit schools and colleges, which I do frequently, I am struck by how they can be indifferent to or fearful of new and emerging digital technologies. To put it bluntly, mobile phones are regarded as a nuisance. There may be an interactive whiteboard in many classes, but it is not very interactive. There may be educational technology (or edtech) tools used in lessons, but the extent to which they speed up or enrich the learning experience is often very small. All too often, edtech tools are being used in a 'command style' (Mosston and Ashworth, 1990), where the teacher stands at the front and addresses a passive classroom. It stands to reason, then, that children are therefore being denied the opportunities to develop the skills of problem-solving, adaptability and creativity that are necessary for the post-industrial landscape. In many cases, they are also being denied a basic education in everything else, but that's a moot point.

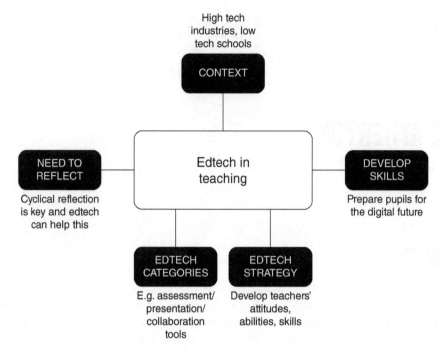

Figure 19.1 Why edtech in the classroom?

WHY TECHNOLOGY?

After nearly a decade of austerity, it is no surprise that the education sector has failed to keep up with new and emerging technologies. To address this, in 2019, Education Secretary Damian Hinds announced a much-trumpeted £10 million worth of investment in educational technologies. You may be surprised that this initiative took this long. In a document entitled *Realising the Potential of Technology in Education*, the Department for Education called for edtech to help create a more efficient and inclusive learning culture while making a contribution to a vibrant economy (DfE, 2019).

Underpinning the strategy will be a commitment to 'empower' teachers to use technology to help learning. This will be supported by an effective infrastructure and a responsibility for safety, security and privacy (DfE, 2019). At the time of writing, it is too early to assess the impact of any of this. Successive governments have arguably neglected edtech, but what is clear is that the DfE are making the connection between the technology that we use to teach, how people learn, and what makes it all work. The thinking behind the strategy is, thankfully, backed up by research evidence. Indeed, the DfE have been working and will continue to work with leading academics in the field of edtech (e.g. Professor Rose Luckin from University College London).

WHICH TECHNOLOGIES MIGHT YOU USE?

The tools and apps that teachers might be likely to try in the classroom fall into the following overlapping categories:

- Assessment or assignment tools that help teachers create and assess work. Examples of these are Spiral, GoFormative, Learnium and Socrative. These platforms will increasingly incorporate artificial intelligence (AI). An example of an AI assessment platform is CENTURY Tech.

- Social media that can be part of the learning process. Effective social platforms for learning are Facebook, Twitter, Snapchat, Instagram and Pinterest. Because of safeguarding risks, if teachers want to use these, their use always needs to be cleared by the senior leadership team, thoroughly risk-assessed and evaluated.

- Video and audio tools are increasingly important if used appropriately. Teachers often consider YouTube for sourcing videos, EDpuzzle for using video to create and assess work, and govidigo for screen capture. The popularity of podcasts has opened up many ways for using audio for learning. Useful apps are Audacity and GarageBand for audio-recording and editing.

- Collaborative working in real time can be aided and assessed via apps such as Google Docs, Padlet and Pearltrees, as well as the aforementioned assessment tools.

- Presentation tools can help make lessons more interactive and resources more professional. Google Slides is a good tool for collaborative presentations in real time, as well as Emaze or Padlet for multimedia online presentations that can double as revision resources or collaborative research tools.

- Games such as Kahoot! and other learner response systems (e.g. online polls) are excellent ways to capture diagnostic assessment.

- Management information systems such as SIMS or ProMonitor. Trainee teachers and others working in classrooms can't always get permission to use these – they tend to be used by permanent staff at schools and colleges – but it's a good idea to try to find out a bit about them.

(Atherton, 2018a)

NEXT STEPS

In terms of using edtech, how might teachers and others working in education proceed in their development? It would be churlish to prescribe a specific course of action here. There is no single edtech platform that will be a golden ticket to outstanding and fulfilling teaching. Instead, teachers often focus on mindset, not skill set (Dweck, 2012). The best teachers and educators are adaptable to change and open to experimentation.

Once educators are able to reflect on when technology can sometimes obstruct learning, they can start to pinpoint how we could deploy edtech as a series of tools, as someone might use a spanner or a screwdriver. Tools are there to help us reach our goals more quickly. If teachers' use of edtech is aligned to their pupils' learning goals, they will be moving in the right direction. What's more, teachers can use edtech tools to help assess better or develop students' thinking skills (Atherton, 2018b).

With that in mind, as you think about how teachers teach, or – if you are working in an education setting – how you work with pupils, you may wish to consider a small supported experiment with a single edtech tool or platform. For example, you could work with a colleague to trial a collaborative presentation using

Google Slides. You could reflect in a cyclical manner to ensure that your evaluation of the experiment is objective, thorough and ongoing.

There is a disconnect between the use of digital technologies in schools and the outside world. The Department for Education have declared that they intend to address the issue of how education uses technology. An awareness of the different categories of edtech might be a useful starting point.

RESOURCES FOR FURTHER LEARNING

Atherton, P. (2018) *50 Ways to Use Technology Enhanced Learning in the Classroom.* London: SAGE.

My book is a practical guide for teachers on how to use a range of edtech platforms for teaching and learning.

Dweck, C. (2012) *Mindset.* London: Robinson.

One good place to start would be Dweck's Ted Talk on growth mindset that you can find on YouTube.

USEFUL WEBSITES

www.edtechimpact.com

You could impress your placement by using Edtech Impact to help them find the most useful technologies for their school.

https://impact.chartered.college/issue/special-issue-january-2019-education-technology

This special edition of the *Chartered College* magazine provides an insight into how useful it is to place greater emphasis on the impact of edtech.

www.teachertoolkit.co.uk

Teacher Toolkit is not specifically about edtech, but still contains a wealth of tips for and debates about teaching and learning.

REFERENCES

Atherton, P. (2018a) *50 Ways to Use Technology Enhanced Learning in the Classroom.* London: SAGE.

Atherton, P. (2018b) More than just a quiz: how Kahoot! can help trainee teachers understand the learning process. *TEAN Journal*, 10(2): 29–39.

Department for Education (DfE) (2019) *Realising the Potential of Technology in Education.* Available at: https://assets.publishing.service.gov.uk/government/uploads/system/uploads/attachment_data/file/791931/DfE-Education_Technology_Strategy.pdf

Dweck, C. (2012) *Mindset.* London: Robinson.

Mosston, M. and Ashworth, S. (1990) *The Spectrum of Teaching Styles.* New York: Longman.

TECHNOLOGY IN THE CLASSROOM

STEVE INGLE

Education has always made use of technology, from simple chalk and slate, to pen and paper, audio recordings and video tapes, and now to tablets, virtual reality headsets and interactive whiteboards. But how well is our education system preparing students to be the innovative, creative entrepreneurs and leaders of tomorrow, in today's fast-paced, dynamic and connected world? Do our schools, colleges and universities develop the real-world skills that learners will need to be successful in jobs that may not even exist yet? Do today's educators have the skills necessary to prepare students to develop the digital literacies and wisdom needed to be safe and successful in a modern, technological era?

DOES EDUCATION TODAY MEET THE NEEDS OF THE 'NET GEN'?

Many different educational thinkers and commentators have contributed to the debate on the needs, qualities, skills and behaviours of today's learners. From labels such as 'digital natives and immigrants' (Prensky, 2001, 2009, 2011) to the 'net generation' (Net Gen) (Tapscott, 1998) and 'new millennium learners' (Pedro, 2006), academics and researchers have proposed that the learners of today learn differently from learners of the past: they have a natural affinity for all things digital and technological, they're socially connected, they access resources and information in different, non-linear ways, and they are fluent in different types of multimedia. But what if being truly 'digitally literate' was much more than being able to add a filter to an Instagram photo, send a Snapchat or post a retweet?

The importance of developing students' 'digital literacies' has been highlighted by the UK government-funded organisation for the use of technologies in further and higher education, previously known as the Joint Information Systems Committee, or just JISC. JISC (2014) defines digital literacies as the capabilities that fit someone for living, learning and working in a digital society. They argue that in order to be successful in today's modern world, educators and educational institutions have a role to play in developing and supporting learners to have a basic level of ICT proficiency, to be able to use information and data effectively, to communicate and participate digitally, and to be aware of their digital identity. If learners are not able to function effectively in a digital world, they are likely to be less successful in both work and society. There is a compelling case to ensure that all learners develop the digital skills and know-how to solve problems, overcome challenges, be creative and demonstrate innovation to really thrive in today's global, dynamic, connected and unpredictable world.

Given the importance of this new 'functional life skill', as technology becomes ever-more pervasive and ubiquitous in our living and learning lives, is the role of educators also changing? In the past, the role of the teacher 'expert' was to give students access to knowledge, to unlock the key concepts, theories and history of a particular subject, discipline, vocation or profession. In today's 'information age', learners are now empowered and enabled to access the world's knowledge bank themselves with a few simple clicks in the search engine. They can ask Alexa for facts and figures, fill in the Google bar to get the latest theories, and connect with people around the world – in a forum, chat room or WhatsApp group – to instantly seek answers to the important questions. They don't really need the traditional teacher to get 'knowledge', but who will teach learners to use all of this information effectively?

Sharpe et al. (2010) identify that creative production, critical reading and collaborative knowledge building are digital practices that are required for successful lifelong learning. So, rather than the traditional role of 'knowledge expert', perhaps the crucial role of the twenty-first-century teacher, tutor or trainer is that of a 'digital guide', an information expert who develops the digital wisdom of their learners. With so much information instantly accessible at our fingertips, who is it that teaches learners to discriminate the most useful information from the tens, thousands or even millions of results returned at the click of a key? Whose role is it prepare learners to question the reliability and validity of the data returned on their screens? How can we best ensure that learners are able to work safely, with integrity, protecting their identity and the indelible 'digital footprints' they leave behind? Who will help learners to develop the creativity, ingenuity, independence and resilience to be able to meet the needs of their future employers in jobs and roles that don't yet exist? Perhaps the development of these digital skills, literacies and wisdom has now become the most valuable role for the modern educator.

Institutions are beginning to consider these key questions and are adapting to meet this twenty-first-century literacy and skills agenda. For example, many schools, colleges and universities are introducing 'flipped learning' opportunities, where learners engage with the knowledge content independently online before using the lesson, lecture or seminar time with the tutor to check, clarify and challenge their understanding. More educators than ever are exploring the myriad of software and hardware options to be used within the classroom, as well as wholly online options or 'blended learning' approaches (a mix of face-to-face lessons and online, distance learning experiences). Virtual learning environments (known as VLEs) are common in almost every educational institution, from nursery level to PHD, providing learners with access to resources, assessments and feedback any time, any place, anywhere. Soon the traditional qualification certificate and CV could be replaced with the online accreditation badge posted on a student's LinkedIn profile, demonstrating instantly to would-be employers their skills, competencies and credentials. These are just a few of the many ways that education providers are beginning to harness the power of technology-enhanced learning.

As well as the many benefits that technology can offer both learners and tutors, institutions and educators should also proceed with some caution when adapting to this digital revolution. In the pursuit of strategies, teaching approaches and resources to prepare learners to be digitally literate and wise, it should be noted that even today, there is a significant 'digital divide' between the technology 'haves' and the 'have-nots'. Up to as many as 1 million children in the UK have little or no access to a device or cannot get online at home (E-Learning Foundation, 2018), and therefore as practitioners we also 'need to be alert to the disparity in technology access and associated skills development and consider ways that our use of learning technologies can be inclusive and empowering' (Ingle and Duckworth, 2013, p16).

TO CONCLUDE

We have considered the key role of educators in a modern, connected information age and the needs of its twenty-first-century learners and employers; we have considered the most important skills and qualities needed for the workforce of tomorrow to prepare learners to be successful and resourceful in a dynamic and unpredictable world; and we have touched on the ways that educational institutions are adapting to meet the needs of the so-called 'network generation'.

USEFUL WEBSITES

JISC: **www.jisc.ac.uk/guides/developing-students-digital-literacy**

Previously the Joint Information Systems Committee, the JISC website provides a broad range of resources and articles that promote the use of learning technologies, including the need to develop learners' digital literacies.

Flipped Learning Network: **www.flippedlearning.org**

A non-profit online community for educators utilising – or interested in learning more about – the flipped classroom and flipped learning practices.

Association for Learning Technologies (ALT): **www.alt.org.uk**

A charitable organisation that represents individual and organisational members from all education sectors. ALT provides a wealth of resources, publications, professional accreditation and the open-access journal *Research in Learning Technology*. This journal aims to raise the profile of research and share good practice in different areas of learning technology (e.g. online learning, distance learning, mobile learning, wearable technologies, simulation, social media).

REFERENCES

E-Learning Foundation (2018) *About Us*. Available at: https://learningfoundation.org.uk/about/our-vision-and-beliefs/

Ingle, S. and Duckworth, V. (2013) *Enhancing Learning Through Technology in Lifelong Learning: Fresh Ideas, Innovative Strategies*. Maidenhead: Open University Press.

JISC (2014) *Developing Digital Literacies*. Available at: www.jisc.ac.uk/guides/developing-digital-literacies

Pedro, F. (2006) *The New Millennium Learners: Challenging Our Views on ICT and Learning*. Available at: www.oecd.org/dataoecd/1/1/38358359.pdf

Prensky, M. (2001) *Digital Natives, Digital Immigrants*. Available at: www.marcprensky.com

Prensky, M. (2009) *H. Sapiens Digital: From Digital Immigrants and Digital Natives to Digital Wisdom*. Available at: https://nsuworks.nova.edu/cgi/viewcontent.cgi?article=1020&context=innovate

Prensky, M. (2011) 'Is the digital native a myth? No'. Learning and leading with technology. *International Society for Technology in Education*, 39(3): 6–7.

Sharpe, R., Beetham, H., De Freitas, S. and Conole, G. (2010) An introduction to rethinking learning for a digital age. In R. Sharpe and H. Beetham (eds), *Rethinking Learning for a Digital Age*. London: RoutledgeFalmer, pp1–12.

Tapscott, D. (1998) *Growing Up Digital: The Rise of the Net Generation*. New York: McGraw-Hill.

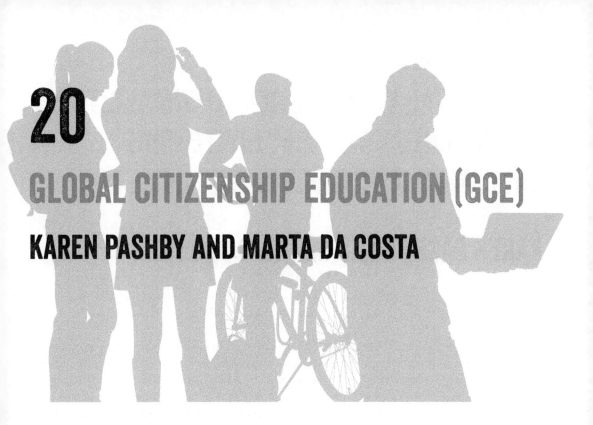

20

GLOBAL CITIZENSHIP EDUCATION (GCE)

KAREN PASHBY AND MARTA DA COSTA

In this final chapter, we consider the opinions of Marta da Costa and Karen Pashby on the topical issue of global citizenship education.

Karen is a reader in education with a background as a teacher. Her international experience gives her an expertise and unique perspective in the area of global citizenship education. She works with teachers and other educators all over the world. Marta is an experienced tutor in education who has worked in the area of global citizenship education in recent years. Together, they bring a dynamic set of opinions on global citizenship education together in this chapter.

QUESTIONS TO THINK ABOUT

This chapter starts off by focusing on neoliberal and liberal-humanist approaches to global citizenship education. What assumptions do each of these approaches make? How are they similar and how are they different? What do Karen and Marta mean when they suggest that there is a 'false dichotomy' between these approaches?

Towards the end of this chapter, Marta and Karen talk about colonialism and how a postcolonial approach to GCE might be considered desirable. Do you agree with de Sousa Santos' strong opinion that colonialism could be described as 'epistemicide'?

What do you think about the postcolonial approach to global citizenship education, where we are described as being both part of the problems and part of the solutions to current global issues? Do you agree?

How important do you think global citizenship education is? Should it be part of the curriculum in all schools and educational institutions?

NEOLIBERAL VERSUS LIBERAL-HUMANIST APPROACHES TO GLOBAL CITIZENSHIP EDUCATION: TWO SIDES OF THE SAME COIN?

KAREN PASHBY AND MARTA DA COSTA

The field of global citizenship education (GCE) has a high profile within formal, informal and non-formal education settings. The turn of the twenty-first century saw a rise in its popularity, having emerged in response to what was considered an increasingly globalised world. Particularly evident in English-speaking countries such as the UK, Canada and New Zealand, students were seen to need to learn about global/international issues alongside developing their citizenship skills in order to interact in an increasingly interdependent world (Pashby, 2011). The prevalence of GCE was further established by its inclusion in the UN Sustainable Development Goals (Target 4.7).

However, GCE is also a complex and contested field. There is much disagreement around its conceptual definition, with many different and contradictory practices carried out under its banner. Consequently, some authors argue that GCE has become a 'floating signifier' (Mannion et al., 2011, p444) – a term that different scholars, practitioners and policymakers make use of to fulfil different agendas. It would therefore be overly simplistic to endorse one definition of GCE. Instead, in this opinion piece, we cover two approaches to GCE. The first is the neoliberal approach to GCE and the second is the liberal-humanist approach. In this piece, we aim to map the different approaches, as well as the relations and tensions between them, as a way to look at the key debates.

This chapter demonstrates that GCE and its complex and different approaches reflect wider issues in education that you have been reading about in this book. Specifically, we will explore what appear to be two distinct mainstream approaches and consider to what extent they are fundamentally different. Finally, we will suggest an alternative approach: *a post/decolonial approach to global citizenship education.*

NEOLIBERAL APPROACHES TO GCE

Neoliberalism – broadly based around principles of a global free market, privatisation of public property and services, and growth through competition – is the extension of a market rationale from economics to all other spheres of society, including education. At the individual level, neoliberalism manifests itself in the concept of human capital, whereby each individual is responsible for enhancing their competitive position in the global market (Brown, 2015).

Under neoliberal ideology, education settings aim to achieve a better place in the national and global knowledge economy. In this competitive setting, GCE can be an effective way for institutions to rebrand and/or place themselves as internationally active producers of global human capital. GCE presents a set of skills to be learned and put to work in the global market. Critics of this approach suggest that the studying of global issues in so-called 'developing countries' is approached superficially, reducing global concerns to a lack of resources in countries who have the issue (usually those perceived as 'developing' countries). The solutions explored generally prioritise economic investment by 'developed' countries into so-called 'developing' countries, allowing poorer countries to 'catch up' (Shultz, 2007; Stein, 2015). Extracurricular GCE activities in this approach often involve learning a language or studying abroad, and students are able to earn certificates or use their experiences in order to improve their CVs (Schattle, 2008).

Neoliberal approaches are evident in policy and practice. For example, a UK Department for Education policy document suggests that graduates must have 'the knowledge, skills and understanding they need to fulfil themselves, to live in and contribute effectively to a global society and to live in a competitive, global economy' (DfE, 2004, p3). Extracurricular experiences also often reflect a neoliberal approach. For example, Global Vision International – an organisation that designs and delivers international volunteering programmes – lists ways that young people can become global citizens. These are based on individual development and CV building, and include buying maps and books, taking leadership and business courses, and eating at different ethnic restaurants. The organisation also promotes gaining practical experience, developing skills, and advancing one's career through engaging with global issues (Clark, n.d.). Such approaches highlight economic gain and individual development over deep engagement in global issues and may not actually transform the current systems of inequality (Diprose, 2012).

LIBERAL-HUMANIST APPROACH

A liberal-humanist approach shares with neoliberal approaches a basis in liberalism whereby individual development leads to progress and growth. As neoliberal approaches have gained ground, liberal-humanist approaches have presented a strong voice for reasserting the moral quality of GCE. Neoliberal approaches are criticised for focusing on transactional relations and reducing global citizenship to economic participation (e.g. Stein, 2015). In contrast, liberal-humanist approaches present global citizenship as a cosmopolitan virtue whereby all humans are responsible to take action to better the lives of all. Providing an overarching narrative of universal values and common humanity, these approaches also acknowledge the relationship between different local and global communities. For example, Martha Nussbaum (2002) refers to the need for citizenship to reach out from our local to national to global communities.

In education, liberal-humanist approaches to GCE are often initiated by non-governmental organisations (NGOs). For example, Oxfam, a global charity that aims to eradicate poverty, designs resources and supports global learning in schools. They define a global citizen as 'someone who is aware of and understands the wider world – and their place in it' (Oxfam, n.d.). GCE is understood as an educational framework that allows students to

> *build their own understanding of world events; think about their values and what's important to them; take learning into the real world, challenge ignorance and intolerance; get involved in their local, national and global communities; develop an argument and voice their opinions; see that they have power to act and influence the world around them.*

> (Oxfam, n.d.)

Liberal-humanist approaches can range from a charity-based approach to one focusing more on issues of equality and social justice. They decentre the neoliberal rationale away from a narrow economic focus and highlight the importance of social justice, acknowledging the relations (and potentially tensions) between local communities and global issues. However, some argue that both neoliberal and liberal-humanist approaches coexist in complementary ways because they fundamentally share an instrumental, competency-based approach focused on individuals. Action often comprises of giving to charity or raising awareness of the issues. Such individual initiatives may skip over the role of wider social, economic, cultural and political structures (Stein, 2015), leaving little room for students to explore the limits of their individual perspectives, or even their and their own nation's complicity in global issues (Andreotti, 2006). When liberal-humanist approaches acknowledge and attempt to challenge power structures, institutions of so-called 'developing countries' are often the sources of the answers. In this way, students may overlook how these institutions are implicated in the very social injustices in question.

In summary, although liberal-humanist approaches to GCE emphasise the importance of social justice, moving beyond the economic focus of neoliberal approaches, they may not encourage students to deeply and critically reflect and engage with systems and structures at the root of global issues. We argue that these opportunities are required for students to understand the complexities, interdependencies and inequalities in interacting global and local contexts, and to grapple with their own complicity and positionality in global power structures. Only then can students start to consider ways to think and act otherwise, challenging and transforming the current global establishment.

A POST/DECOLONIAL APPROACH TO GLOBAL CITIZENSHIP EDUCATION

> *Global futures need to be imagined and constructed through de-colonial options; that is, working globally and collectively to de-colonise the colonial matrix of power; to stop the sand castles built by modernity and its derivatives.*

> (Mignolo, 2009, p49)

Sometimes, when focusing on our common humanity, we can avoid discussing humans' difficult histories. This section of the chapter roots discussions of GCE in the history and present of colonialism and argues for a critically reflexive approach.

Modernity is both a historical era and a set of norms and practices. Ushered in through the Renaissance period of the seventeenth century, developed more fully through the Enlightenment period in the eighteenth century, and normalised in the nineteenth and twentieth centuries through industrialisation and cultural, social, and political movements, modernity was founded in principles of rational thinking and science. Whereas the Church had been the main source of knowledge and power, at this time of great change, technological, theoretical and cultural advancement occurred alongside the development of democratic practices of political organisation and establishments of nation states. Reality was thought to be objective and discoverable through scientific methods while knowledge was considered universal and applicable to all contexts. The narrative of modernity included the belief that scientific innovations and social engineering would lead European society and the rest of the world towards more health, wealth and continuous progress.

The rise of modernity in Europe also spurred a civilising mission, spreading (although some might say imposing) the European ways of being and knowing to all societies through processes of colonisation. These included forcefully moving people from, for example, what is now known as Africa, to be enslaved in new colonies in order to produce raw materials that could then be made into products and sold back in Europe. It also involved claiming land abroad, ruling over and in some cases forcefully removing inhabitants who had been living there for thousands of years through both violence and cultural imposition. In Canada, this process has been referred to as cultural genocide. Although countries that were former colonies may be 'independent' today, many of the same systems of exploitation of resources and people remain, and the legacy of imperialism continues. Importantly, indigenous communities around the world remain vital and are active in responses to today's global issues.

Postcolonialism is a school of thought that puts colonialism at the root of current global issues. According to Andreotti (2010), the 'post' in postcolonialism means 'interrogation of, not after' (p240), allowing us to deconstruct taken-for-granted assumptions that enable colonialism. Postcolonial theory questions the predominant ways of being (ontology) and knowing (epistemology) produced and established by modernity. Mignolo (2009) argues that modernity has a light side which includes the advancement of society through technological advancements and the building of an international system of nation states based on democratic principles. However, he argues that modernity also has a darker side, coloniality, on which the benefits of the light side are built and depend – slavery, genocide, racism and capitalism. De Sousa Santos (2014, p149) adds that colonialism is a form of *epistemicide* – the wiping out of an entire culture's knowledge system by discrediting, devaluing or appropriating it. Education has played a role through the enforcement of European formal school systems in the countries that were colonised (e.g. Willinsky, 1998). By establishing European knowledge as the norm, modernity established a hegemonic ontology and epistemology, and defined a single, universal view of development and progress. Through this process, 'the West' (Europe and so-called 'developed countries') was able to define and maintain a global hierarchy which places countries that are 'developed' above the ones that are not (Mignolo, 2009).

Although postcolonial scholars have related colonialism to current global unequal power structures, colonialism is rarely evident in conversations about global issues within mainstream neoliberal and liberal-humanist GCE approaches. Drawing on Spivak, Andreotti (2006) calls this denial of colonialism in Western societies *sanctioned ignorance*. Overlooking colonialism or placing it strictly in the past allows for the continuation of modernity's project, including its dark side. While working within a liberal paradigm can help to ensure all humans have access to their fundamental rights, without an educational approach that provides a space for students to reflect on how they are implicated and complicit with current global social inequalities, certain 'global citizens' are able to position themselves as the saviours of the poor, uncivilised developing countries. This approach can perpetuate rather than challenge the power relations at the heart of many of today's inequalities.

Andreotti (2006) distinguishes between soft and critical approaches to GCE. A *soft* approach aligns with neoliberalism and liberal-humanism, focusing on helping those who suffer from a lack of development and aiming at universality. She promotes a *critical* approach, applying a postcolonial critique of modernity by explicitly engaging with the systems, cultures and structures that perpetuate global inequalities. Critical GCE acknowledges a complicity on the part of 'developing' countries in the 'Global North' in what are being constructed as global problems but are being understood as 'Third World' problems. Criticality in this context is not about making decisions about right and wrong or true or false, but about engaging with the origins of assumptions and implications of actions. Pushing beyond modernity's narrative, critical literacy understands knowledge as context-bound, partial and incomplete. Students are encouraged to engage with their and others' perspectives, in order to learn 'to think otherwise' from the modern narratives they are socialised into (Andreotti, 2006, p49). According to Andreotti (2006), action is a choice that students make after deeply considering the context of intervention, as well as the short- and long-term consequences of their action. In this way, Andreotti (2010, p242) argues that in order to develop a critical approach to GCE, one must unlearn, learn to listen, learn to learn, and learn to reach out.

In order to support students to identify and challenge normalised assumptions and representations about global issues, particularly in the 'Global North', Andreotti (2012) produced a critical analysis tool: HEADSUP (see Table 20.1, column 1). This approach can be used in formal and non-formal settings. Based on participatory work with teachers in England, Finland and Sweden, Pashby and Sund (2020) created a teaching resource that includes an adaptation of HEADSUP into a reflection tool for teachers (see Table 20.1, column 2).

Table 20.1 Andreotti's HEADSUP checklist and Pashby and Sund's teacher reflection tool

Historical patterns of oppression often reproduced in global learning materials	Teacher reflection questions
Hegemony (justifying superiority and supporting domination)	In my teaching, how can I raise inherited and taken-for-granted power relations? Do I identify mainstream discourses and marginalised perspectives/norms and trends?
Ethnocentrism (projecting one view as universal)	In my teaching, can lessons address that there are other logical ways of looking at the same issue framed by different understandings of reality/experiences of the world?
Ahistoricism (forgetting historical legacies and complicities)	In my teaching, how can I avoid treating an issue out of context as if it just happened now? How are today's issues tied to ongoing local and global trends/patterns/narratives?
Depoliticisation (disregarding power inequalities and ideological roots of analyses and proposals)	In my teaching, how can I ensure issues are not treated as if they are politically neutral? Who is framing the issue and who is responsible for addressing it? Who are the agents of change and what mechanisms for change are available?

Salvationism (framing help as the burden of the fittest)	In my teaching, how can we take up good intentions to want to help others through generosity and altruism without reinforcing an us/them, saviour/ victim relationship?
Uncomplicated solutions (offering easy and simple solutions that do not require systemic change)	In my teaching, how can we address people's tendency to want a quick fix? How can we grapple with the complexities, root causes and lack of easy solutions?
Paternalism (seeking affirmation of authority/superiority through the provision of help and the infantilisation of recipients)	In my teaching, how can we put aside our egos and self-interest? Are we open to being wrong, to not being the ones who know best?

Source: Andreotti (2012, p2) and Pashby and Sund (2020, p318)

In this chapter, we have pushed beyond what we argue is a somewhat false dichotomy between neo-liberal and liberal-humanist approaches to GCE. Whereas those mainstream approaches focus on economic progress and individuals helping those in need, we argue for an approach that takes up postcolonial theory. In this chapter, we have offered some pedagogical tools that can assist in this educational imperative. Only by tracing current global issues to our colonial pasts and presents can we understand the deeply embedded systems of inequality that mean we are all both part of the problems and part of the solutions, albeit differently depending on our contexts. A post/decolonial approach to GCE is committed to critical literacy, fostering thinking, knowing and being *otherwise* from modern approaches entrenched in progress for some, but also oppression and exclusion for others. This approach allows students not only to identify and challenge global unequal structures of power, but also to start deeply considering how to relate ethically with others in our shared world and enact systemic change.

RESOURCES FOR FURTHER LEARNING

Andreotti, V. (2006) Soft versus critical global citizenship education. *Policy and Practice: A Development Education Review*, 3: 40–5. Available at: www.developmenteducationreview.com/issue/issue-3/soft-versus-critical-global-citizenship-education

Andreotti, V., Stein, S., Sutherland, A., Pashby, K., Suša, R., Amsler, S. and the Gesturing Decolonial Futures Collective (2018) Mobilising different conversations about global justice in education: toward alternative futures in uncertain times. *Policy and Practice: A Development Education Review*, 26: 9–41. Available at: www.developmenteducationreview.com/issue/issue-26/mobilising-different-conversations-about-global-justice-education-toward-alternative

Centre for Global Education/Taking it Global (2017) *International Youth White Paper on Global Citizenship (IYWPGC)*. Available at: www.epageflip.net/i/796911-international-youth-white-paper-on-global-citizenship

Pashby, K. and Sund, L. (2019) *Teaching for Sustainable Development Through Ethical Global Issues Pedagogy: A Resource for Secondary Teachers*. Available at: www2.mmu.ac.uk/esri/teacher-resource/

REFERENCES

Andreotti, V. (2006) Soft versus critical global citizenship education. *Policy and Practice: A Development Education Review*, 3: 40–5.

Andreotti, V. (2010) Postcolonial and post-critical 'global citizenship education'. In E. Geoffrey, C. Fourali and S. Issler (eds), *Education and Social Change: Connecting Local and Global Perspectives*. London: Continuum, pp238–50.

Andreotti, V. (2012) Editors preface: HEADS UP. *Critical Literacy: Theories and Practices*, 6(1): 1–3.

Brown, W. (2015) *Undoing the Demos: Neoliberalism's Stealth Revolution*. New York: Zone Books.

Clark, J. (n.d.) *Seven Steps to Become a Global Citizen*. Available at: www.gvi.co.uk/blog/7-steps-to-become-a-global-citizen/

Department for Education (DfE) (2004) *Putting the World into World-Class Education: An International Strategy for Education, Skills and Children's Services*. Available at: https://dera.ioe.ac.uk/5201/7/Putting%20The%20World%20Into%20World-Class%20Education_Redacted.pdf

de Sousa Santos, B. (2014) *Epistemologies of the South: Justice Against Epistemicide*. London: Paradigm Publishers.

Diprose, K. (2012) Critical distance: doing development education through international volunteering. *Area*, 44(2): 186–92.

Mannion, G., Biesta, G., Priestley, M. and Ross, H. (2011) The global dimension in education and education for global citizenship: genealogy and critique. *Globalisation, Societies and Education*, 9(3/4): 443–56.

Mignolo, W. (2009) Coloniality: the darker side of modernity. In C. Klinger and B. Marí (eds), *Modernologies: Contemporary Artists Researching Modernity and Modernism*. Barcelona: Macba, pp39–49.

Nussbaum, M. (2002) Education for citizenship in an era of global connection. *Studies in Philosophy and Education*, 21: 289–303.

Oxfam (n.d.) *Education for Global Citizenship: A Guide for Schools*. Available at: www.oxfam.org.uk/education/resources/education-for-global-citizenship-a-guide-for-schools

Pashby, K. (2011) Cultivating global citizens: planting new seeds or pruning the perennials? Looking for the citizen-subject in global citizenship education theory. *Globalisation, Societies and Education*, 9(3/4): 427–42.

Pashby, K. and Sund, L. (2020) Critical GCE in the era of SDG 4.7: discussing HEADSUP with secondary teachers in England, Finland, and Sweden. In D. Bourn (ed.), *International Perspectives on Global Learning*. London: Bloomsbury, pp314–26.

Schattle, H. (2008) Education for global citizenship: illustrations of ideological pluralism and adaptation. *Journal of Political Ideologies*, 13(1): 73–94.

Shultz, L. (2007) Educating for global citizenship: conflicting agendas and understandings. *Alberta Journal of Educational Research*, 53(3): 248–58.

Stein, S. (2015) Mapping global citizenship. *Journal of College and Character*, 16(4): 242–52.

Willinsky, J. (1998) *Learning to Divide the World: Education at Empire's End*. Minneapolis, MN: University of Minnesota Press.

AFTERWORD

JANET LORD

At the start of this book, I introduced some questions about the nature and functions of education, and about the ways in which you might want to start thinking about education in a critical way. As you have read chapters and opinions in the book, you will have been stimulated, challenged and interested in a variety of aspects of education. You will have started to think critically and to ask questions of the material that you have read, and you will have developed various skills and ways of thinking about education that will be useful as you think, read and work in the field. You will have seen the complexity of the field, and how various ideas and subjects interplay in complex ways.

To finish, I'd like to remind you of the Nelson Mandela quote from the start of the book:

Education is the most powerful weapon which you can use to change the world.

You will have seen how true this is as you have read the chapters and thought about the ideas that we have introduced in this book. If you have had experience in schools or other education settings, you will have seen just how powerful education can be. It changes individuals' lives, and because of that it can change the world too.

If you work in education, you will sometimes be frustrated and challenged, but I guarantee that you will never be bored. You'll be involved in one of the best professional arenas there is – and one of the most worthwhile. As you move on with your studies and your work in education, I hope that you feel encouraged to use education to help others to empower themselves. That's how you will be starting to change the world.

INDEX